26.2 MILES TO BOSTON

26.2 MILES TO BOSTON

A Journey into the Heart of the Boston Marathon

MICHAEL CONNELLY

LYONS PRESS
Guilford, Connecticut
An imprint of Globe Pequot Press

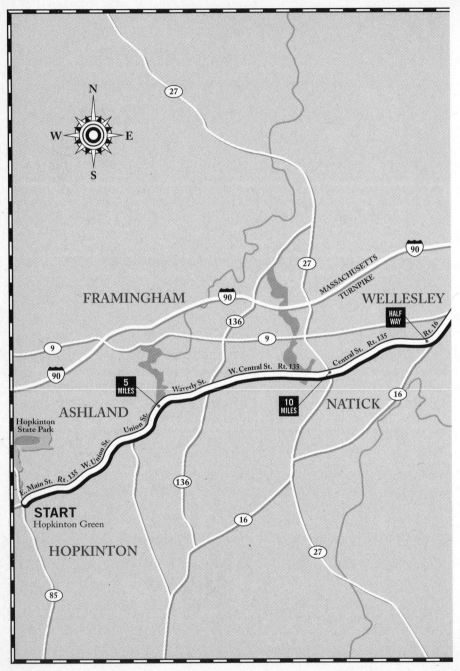

COURTESY OF THE BOSTON ATHLETIC ASSOCIATION

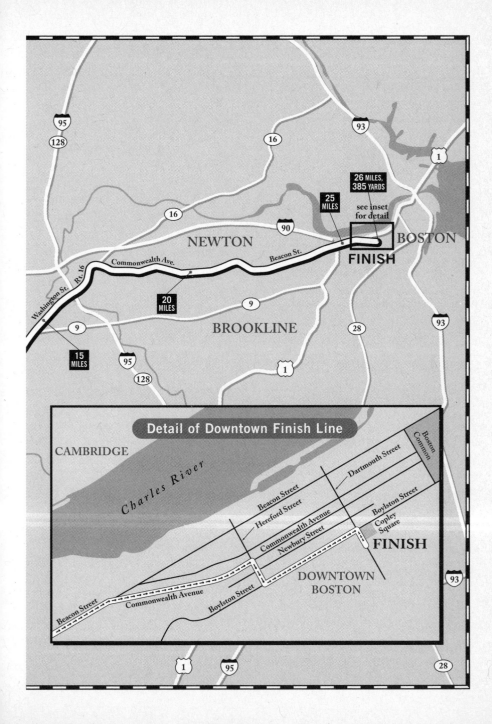

To buy books in quantity for corporate use
or incentives, call **(800) 962-0973**
or e-mail **premiums@GlobePequot.com**.

Lyons Press is an imprint of Globe Pequot Press.

Text design: Sheryl Kober
Layout artist: Sue Murray
Project editor: Ellen Urban

Library of Congress Cataloging-in-Publication Data is available on file.

ISBN 978-0-7627-9635-9

Printed in the United States of America

10 9 8 7 6 5 4 3 2 1

This account of the world's greatest race is dedicated to Martin Richard and his smile that makes you smile; Krystle Campbell and her spirit that will always shine bright; Lu Lingzi, who traveled to Boston to share her life with us; and Sean Collier, whose dream to protect and serve will always remain a shining example. I would also like to honor all the victims—both of spirit and body—and the great city of Boston.

As a lifelong resident of Boston, I love this city. I love its quaintness and vastness; I love to walk it and sit in it; I love its people and their uniqueness; I love the North End and the South End and everywhere in between. As a fan, runner, and author with Boston Marathon ties, I love the race. I love the day. I love what it stands for and what it is. I love that we have tangible evidence at least once a year that people are good at their core. I love that people go home from the Boston Marathon to their cities around the world and love Boston like I do.

To—
Nana Kenny, who inspired me to write
Nana Connelly, whose perpetual smile made a Sunday lunch more than lunch
My father-in-law, Tom Concannon, who showed me courage through a simple walk
My siblings, who aren't just my brothers and sisters, but also my friends
My parents, for their love and guidance
My wife Noreen and my son Ryan, for filling my life with love and purpose

Contents

CONTENTS

FOREWORD

WHEN MICHAEL CONNELLY CONTACTED ME TO WRITE A BIT ABOUT HIS book, *26.2 Miles to Boston*, I wasn't overly enthusiastic. It seemed to me that the race had received enough attention as it was. Was I wrong! Connelly writes about the race from many new and interesting angles. You can't help but be seduced by this book. The stories flow one after another, like a marathon runner's footsteps. Each story adds to the razzle-dazzle of the race's long and colorful history.

Of course, that's exactly what the Boston Marathon has to offer—lots of colorful history over the 117 years of the race. But no one has told the stories of the race beyond those of the top runners. Connelly gives other perspectives and thoughts, and I salute him for doing so, as it is only in recent days (as you'll see from reading the book) that the top runners have received respect as world-class athletes. As recently as my win in 1975, a well-known Boston sports commentator indicated that the runners at the Boston Marathon weren't athletes at all.

Because of my own background as a competitive runner, I've always been interested in reading about the top runners at the Boston Marathon, and enjoyed the accounts of the race. People like Clarence DeMar, Johnny Kelley, and Joan Benoit Samuelson have told of their exploits as champions at Boston. Today's top racers have been of interest, too, but what I truly enjoyed reading in *26.2 Miles to Boston* were the stories that are never told—accounts of volunteers, police officers, medical personnel, merchants in stores along the route, spectators, officials, and, of course, the so-called "average runner." The athlete's challenge is what the Boston Marathon is all about. The athlete's heart beats inside all of us.

Having run the race thirteen times, won four, and dropped out of the race twice, I know what it feels like to take on the challenge of running the Boston Marathon. Michael Connelly does, too, but he goes on to explore why a simple foot race has the impact it has on runners and non-runners alike. An overly intellectual, sedentary fellow once observed that runners never seem to smile as they run; surely he was never at the Boston Marathon. Had he been, he would have seen the real smiles, the ones with really deep satisfaction behind them.

To run the Boston Marathon is not an easy thing. To write well about it and explain its charisma is even harder. Michael Connelly's *26.2 Miles to Boston* succeeds in this regard. Not many sports books have the capacity to make you feel as though the event was happening only ten feet away. This one does that. Connelly has exposed the special qualities of the Boston Marathon foot race and why it is more than an ordinary sporting event.

The Boston Marathon endures; it continues on, just as its athletes have done, despite the violent attack in 2013. Maybe the Boston Marathon's ultimate strength is that it is a great equalizer of humanity—that it brings people together in peace and friendship. Anyone who has been to Boston knows that.

Maybe it's too narrow to say that the Boston Marathon is a road race. Maybe it's more accurate to say that it's a celebration of life itself.

BILL RODGERS

PREFACE

Life shrinks or expands in proportion to one's courage.

—ANAÏS NIN

THE BOSTON MARATHON IS A LIVING MICROCOSM OF THE WORLD THAT orbits around it. From start to finish, the course serves as a real-life stage on which Shakespearean dramas are played out by thespians in sneakers, with the glory of the finish line in their hearts. Since 1897, when co-leader Dick Grant of Harvard collapsed and John McDermott was carried on the shoulders of admiring fans to victory at the finish line, the race has been a canvas that has held—simultaneously—glory and anguish, exultation and exasperation, triumph and, sadly, even treachery.

This was never more apparent than at 2:49 p.m. on April 15, 2013, during the running of the 117th Boston Marathon. At that time in the race many people running on behalf of charities were reaching Boylston Street, only to have the beating heart of the beloved race stopped by the malicious hands of terrorists. Not a single person near the finish line at the moment of impact, or the millions who watched the coverage of it later, could comprehend the purpose of such a senseless and hateful act.

The wonder of the Boston Marathon is that it is a purveyor of competition at its most sincere level, allowing runners to travel in the footsteps of those who have run before. It has gone on—and continues to go on—no matter what (weather, war, malevolence) swirls around it. This is the story of the 26.2 miles of the Boston Marathon—a race, and the people who love it, who prove every year that the pure heart of good conquers the blighted spirit of evil. Always.

In the end, despite the horrific loss that day, especially of Martin, Krystle, Sean, and Lu, and the pain that continues for many others, something special happened. That's the paradox of April 15, 2013. On a day filled with sadness and pain, the people of Boston showed their finest selves. On that day the city's essence shone at its brightest, and its spirit—somehow—was strong enough to overcome.

Michael Connelly
Boston, Massachusetts
December 2013

ACKNOWLEDGMENTS

26.2 Miles to Boston is not a prescriptive running book. It does not lecture you about carbohydrates, oxygen consumption, glycogen, and the nuances of form running. This book was written so that the reader can appreciate the multiple perspectives of the world's greatest race, including its history, the strategy of the greats, and the experiences of those who ran before.

My passion for writing is equaled by my passion for research. It is within the pages of history that I can transport myself in time and start to connect the puzzle of the Boston Marathon, linking common threads in order to share a story. It's in those archives that the Boston Marathon comes to life. This research was greatly aided by the *Boston Globe* archives, an amazing resource. I thank the authors of those thousands of *Globe* articles—mostly Lawrence Sweeney and Jerry Nason, who were the custodians of the race for over seventy years—and their generational coworkers from the *Globe*, including writers Tom Fitzgerald, Joe Concannon, John Powers, Shira Springer, John Vellente, Jack Thomas, Ray Fitzgerald, Victor Jones, Leigh Montville, Mike Madden, Marvin Pave, and countless others (my sincere apologies for any omissions). Others who are referenced in the book include Wellesley historian Beth Hinchliffe and Bob Brown.

I would also like to thank Jon Sternfeld of Lyons Press, who ran the extra mile for this project; Jack Fleming and Gloria Ratti of the Boston Athletic Association; and champions that represent over fifty laurel wreaths, especially John "The Elder" Kelley, Uta Pippig, Bill Rodgers, Geoff Smith, Jean Driscoll, and Jim Knaub, along with other runners, such as soccer great Kristine Lilly, Olympic gold medalist Summer Sanders, musical personality and son of Boston Joey McIntyre, Rick and

Dick Hoyt, Mayor Ray Flynn, NBA executive Pat Williams, and Henry Staines, for sharing their stories.

Also, I would like to give special thanks to those from the 2013 race, including Thomas Ralston, Dr. David King, David Fortier, Lee Ann Yanni, Carlos Arredondo, and two-decade race official of the Boston Marathon, Tom Meagher, my former Government teacher at Catholic Memorial.

Prologue

April 1996

WHY RUN NOW? I STOOD AT THE STARTING LINE OF THE 100TH BOSTON Marathon and asked myself this most basic of all questions.

Why, after spending the previous thirty-one Patriots' Days on the sidewalks of Newton, had I now decided to run Boston? Sure, I admit I had always been curious. Year after year, I had stood in awe of the competitors passing in front of me. But I was also confused; they all seemed to look conflicted, existing in some state of contradiction. It was almost as if they were trapped in a trance of joy *and* discomfort, satisfaction and apprehension, fulfillment and emptiness. But, if this were truly the case, why would they return? Why travel here each and every April to do it all over again?

Ultimately, I guess I stood in Hopkinton in some warped quest to unwrap this riddle. I had to run to find out why they run.

I can tell you this: I didn't run Boston because, as George Mallory said of Mount Everest, "It was there." It is closer to the truth to say that, by the age of thirty-two, I was starting a process of review. I had entered a stage of life where things were no longer taken for granted. I was beginning to grapple with mortality. Now, the lessons that bored me in philosophy class years ago had started to have relevance. Now, Socrates' famous warning that "The unexamined life is not worth living" had taken on palpable meaning.

Into my thirties, my impulses to venture outside of my perceived abilities had always been quashed by an instinct that told me sedentary was safe. Just stand still and avoid challenges, and I would never be exposed to

1

disappointment and failure. That was until my thirty-second year, when the magnetic pull of the Boston Marathon was able to penetrate my insecurity, compelling me and exploiting my primal need to discover.

What I didn't know when I began was that during this journey, my life would change. I didn't realize that the magic of Boston was so much more than placing one foot in front of the other. Instead, Boston was about taking an inventory of my life. It wasn't just about running; it was about *living*.

Until that year, I had lived a life devoid of exploration. Now my heart was telling me to endeavor outside of my element and test my limitations, because if I didn't do it now, I would always wonder. I would always ask the questions, but I would never have the answers. So I went to Hopkinton that year to explore while I still could climb.

I ran to write a new chapter in my life.

~•~

As part of this quest to run Boston, I would have to do more than just log miles and stretch my quads—I would have to risk something quite serious. Thirteen years earlier, I had been diagnosed with a cardiac arrhythmia known as Wolff-Parkinson-White syndrome. Its faulty wiring held me hostage; the electronics of my heart would trigger manically spiked heart rates that could exceed 200-plus beats a minute—only to then plummet to perilous lows.

Since its detection in my late teens, I had aged, receded, and gained a wife and child. The medical field had been busy developing a procedure, called radiofrequency catheter ablation, which offered the potential to rid me of my disease. A catheter would be guided into my heart and used to destroy the tissue that interfered with its normal electrical function.

In late October 1995, my wife, playing nurse, gave me two options: surgery or the sidewalk. Determined to get off the sidelines, I traveled to New England Medical Center, where I was placed on an operating table and into the able hands of my cardiologists. One hour later, my wife joined me in the recovery room; she was pleased with the results.

Then the heart monitor read flat-line. *Code Blue.*

My life was passed into the hands of a greater Being who would determine the outcome. While I lay in a state of unconsciousness, my wife watched as medical personnel hustled to my side. They inserted an intubation tube while a doctor leapt onto my table, straddling my chest with a knee on each side, prepared to light up my chest with the paddles of life while breaking my ribs with compressions.

My life didn't pass before my eyes, nor did my soul travel on some impromptu out-of-body experience where I was called home by some beautiful light. (I hope that's not a bad sign.) Instead I lay still, on the precipice of life, sliding—maybe—toward death. Thankfully, it wasn't my time. I regained consciousness. When I woke, I knew I had to take advantage of this gift.

The following dawn was clear and bright—a beautiful Indian summer day. My wife took me by the arm and we moved slowly around our block at home. I couldn't help but think what a great day it would be to run, although I was thankful to just be walking. Ten days later, I ran two miles, and I was back. My running continued, and I was more motivated than ever. Already, my mission to run Boston had paid dividends: As a result of my decision to compete, I no longer had heart disease. Two miles became four miles, then six.

There was no more ambivalence. Boston was my opportunity to put all my fears and concerns to rest. I would train and succeed to prove to everyone, but mostly to myself, that my heart was my greatest asset.

❧

I ran Boston—along with my friends Rich Twombly, Mike Radley, and Jack Radley—because my heart told me to. I bring to this book the perspective of a writer and a runner (albeit, not a sanctioned one) with four decades of Boston Marathon history in my blood. To me, the Boston Marathon is a singular event fueled by a unique purpose and legacy. The only tangible thread that connects one runner with another is that each runs east with the hope of realizing a dream. The fact that I had not run a qualifying time didn't minimize my personal journey one bit. My goal was to fulfill a lifetime dream, and that's what I set out to do.

It should be noted that running Boston without qualification has been a part of the Boston Marathon from the moment the gun was sounded in 1897. For over a century, part of the allure of Boston was that the "open" race allowed individuals to toe the line in hopes that on the day, the marathon gods would look down upon them and deem them worthy. Prior to the race in 1914, *Globe* writer Lawrence Sweeney wrote, "It is not beyond the realm of possibility that some slip of lad heretofore unknown as a star in the athletic world will burst forth like a meteor tomorrow afternoon and bring unexpected glory to Boston."

Over the history of the great race, seven champions of Boston had never run a marathon before the day they improbably won it. The greatest of all of these was Johnny Miles, a Nova Scotia harrier (cross-country runner) and the author of the most unlikely upset in the race's history. Prior to the gun being sounded that day in 1926, the *Boston Globe* wrote that it was Miles's "first attempt in the Boston race, [but] he feels certain of being close up with the leaders, if not the winner." In the end, his pre-race bravado was prophetic, compelling the following day's *Boston Post* headline to read UNKNOWN KID WINS THE GREATEST OF ALL MARATHONS!

In victory, he ran in front of an unprecedented crowd of one million onlookers who lined the streets to witness the much-anticipated duel between local favorite, and record holder, Clarence DeMar and Olympic champion Oskar Stenroos. As the spotlight shone on the favorites, the Canadian Miles traversed the streets of the course, gradually capturing the hearts of the city. Three years later he would win Boston again and become one of the most popular runners ever to run the race. If there were qualification standards in 1926, Miles would not have been allowed to run.

The first female runner, Roberta Gibb Bingay, in 1966; the first wheelchair-bound competitor, Eugene Roberts, in 1971; and Rick and Dick Hoyt were all "bandits" (runners without an official number). In running without a qualifying time, they changed the history of Boston for good. In response to the restrictions that mandatory qualifying times place upon the field, runner Steven Lester aptly noted, "The Boston Marathon represents the perseverance of the human spirit. There are no qualifying times for that."

I sincerely appreciate the quest so many undertake in order to qualify. In fact, I am in awe of them. Their efforts were never more personified than in 1978, when Dennis Rainear was so focused on his goal to run an eligible time in the Grand Valley Marathon that at Mile 10, he ignored a feeling of discomfort in his head and finished the race. When he crossed the finish line, it was discovered that he had been shot, and that a .22 caliber bullet was lodged in his head.

What makes Boston special is that the race is inclusive; runners arrive from every corner of the world. Elite runners are there to win; others are there to run against time, others, to run for charities, while many run simply to finish. It is the responsibility of each runner to not interfere with the journey of others.

I have had the opportunity to witness the race from almost every angle possible. In the early years, I would spend Patriots' Day watching the race from my father's shoulders; in college, I watched from a keg party in an apartment overlooking Cleveland Circle; after college, I cautiously stood on a rooftop just past Kenmore Square; years later, I took the baton from my father, and provided shoulders for my own son; and finally, for the 100th running of the Boston Marathon in 1996, I celebrated the event by witnessing the race from the inside out as a competitor—fulfilling my annual pledge that someday I would run Boston.

Did I feel that my accomplishment was less because I didn't run a time that considered me worthy? Not in the slightest. I was forced to undergo corrective heart surgery in order to run this event. I took a cortisone shot in my left knee and struggled through months of physical therapy. I trained through the worst winter in the history of Boston—running through fifteen-inch snowstorms and 8-degree mornings. I ran that day with thousands of runners who had a number but didn't qualify either (many of whom finished behind me). Why was some other back-of-the-pack runner more welcome than I was, just because he or she had a political connection, or was part of a foreign tour group, or had enough money to make a large contribution to the right charity, or was lucky enough to have their name pulled out of a hat?

For thirty years I had stood in the rain or under the beating sun with cheek-pinching aunts in Newton, or inebriated college friends at Cleveland Circle, or at the twenty-mile mark with my wife and newborn son, to cheer on some ten-minute miler just because he or she had dared to try. When I ran Boston in 1996, I did not have a number on my chest, but I did have the storied history of the Boston Marathon in my blood.

I know that was more than enough.

The First Step

The difference between a successful person and others is not a lack of strength, not a lack of knowledge, but rather a lack of will.
—VINCE LOMBARDI

ON RACE DAY, THE AVERAGE MARATHONER WILL TAKE OVER 30,000 steps—with none more important than that very first one. During the simple act of raising one's foot for the first time, the soul takes control over the body; the irrational seems rational, and mind decides to take on matter.

Running Boston isn't physics, but rather metaphysics. It is one of those rare opportunities to transcend human boundaries, defeating one's perceived limitations, the hindrances of the innate, the ticking of time, acts of God, and an unforgiving racecourse. It is the first step, and every step that follows, that introduces the runner to the breathing and vengeful leviathan that is the Boston Marathon racecourse. On that third Monday in April, the road that comprises the 26.2 miles from suburban Hopkinton to downtown Boston is more than hot top and pavement. It becomes the creation of a mad scientist, born in test tubes; it's pavement and potholes and manhole covers, surrounded by teeth-baring dogs and over-zealous fans. On that day, the world's greatest racecourse imposes its will upon those who dare to pass.

Prior to the Boston Marathon in 1941, the Boston Athletic Association (BAA) made the following recommendation to all competitors: "[It is] inadvisable for anybody to attempt the race without proper preparation."

Although this warning is seemingly self-evident, the process of run-ning twenty-six miles is so foreign to the ordinary mortal that the gov-erning body of the world's greatest race felt compelled to remind people that the journey they had agreed to undertake was so awesome that the BAA would be *irresponsible* not to provide forewarning. The BAA was operating under the premise that the decision to run Boston in the first place proved someone's reckless nature.

Running Boston is a passion reserved for the possessed. For the honor of traversing the eight towns of Boston, one must prepare accordingly. Marathon fan and sometime race official Governor Curtis Guild advised prior to the 1905 race, "[The runner] has first to deprive himself of the luxuries of life and learn what real hardship is. And by this I mean he should dispense with all tempting viands. No matter how nice the good things appear that Mother makes, if they come under the head of pastry, they must be put on the 'excluded' list."

One must make serious sacrifices to even get to the starting line in Hopkinton: Show restraint at the dining-room table, show obedi-ence to that alarm clock for the morning run, show resilience to get up and do the late-night speed work, and show the discipline to do cardio work on the weekend. From frontal lobe to temporal lobe, the challenge dominates every waking thought. It's everything one has to do rolled into one: the thesis paper to write, the leaves to remove from the gutters, the report at work, the teenager to pick up. The restrictions placed upon a runner's conscience are immense. "I sacrificed many opportunities to be here," men's wheelchair champion Jim Knaub said after one of his five conquests.

Running Boston requires an all-out commitment to preparation. Lawrence Sweeney of the *Boston Globe* wrote prior to the 1920 race, "To endure hardships of such a grueling grind, a competitor must be well knit, have a full development of chest power, and a muscular and nervous sys-tem that come only of maturity."

To be "well knit," one must not just log miles, but log miles relevant to—and reminiscent of—the Boston course. The angulating course is

Non-qualifying applicants for the Boston Marathon tried to influence the Boston Athletic Association by sending letters, pictures, and even a metal rod that was removed from a runner's leg during surgery. PHOTO COURTESY OF THE *BOSTON HERALD*

so topographically unique that it is almost impossible to simulate not only the uphills of the race but the critical downhills as well. It is this rolling topography that inevitably impacts the runners, causing them to spend the final hours of daylight on Patriots' Day lamenting their lack of plan and preparation, promising that it will be different next year. Next time, they will train on a route that incorporates downhills; or spend less time on a track and more time on uphills, or at least a pushing incline on a treadmill; or commit to running corners on tangents. This is what makes Boston unique: Its subtle nuances just can't be duplicated, although they're plenty feared.

The runner needs to know that the Boston Marathon isn't run in April, but instead in the winter months prior, when there are no cheering fans, cameras, or medals—only self-discipline. Champions understand this, and endeavor year after year to develop a system that best prepares them for the coming April.

John "The Younger" Kelley finished second at Boston five times—despite having the lead—and was determined never to be caught from behind again. He amended his training to include a twenty-pound pack to wear, to help build stamina. It must've worked; he would go on to win the 1957 Boston Marathon, setting a course record. Marathon winner Uta Pippig left Germany to run in the high altitude of Colorado. Clarence DeMar, who never missed a day of work, even the day after the Marathon, ran the eight miles back and forth to work every day. Finnish runner Heikki Olavi Suomalainen ran in two feet of snow to strengthen his hips, while four-time winner Gérard Côté from Canada did his speed work in off-season snowshoe competitions.

In John "The Elder" Kelley's opinion, for every marathon mile he ran, he trained five miles. He knew that to run three hours, he must run *thousands* of hours.

❦

Ultimately the quest for Boston takes on a life of its own. The mission becomes a living, breathing entity that has to be fed, nurtured, and cared for. It transcends a simple run and can evolve into an obsession, compelling the participants to feed the monster before the monster feeds on them.

They will find that one of the by-products of running—beyond the physical benefits—is that it also flexes one's spiritual being. The simple act of separating from the distractions of the daily grind gives the runner a release. The runner double-knots the laces on his or her sneakers, picks up the water bottle in his or her hand, and takes to the road, gaining respite in a now-solitary world. Ironically, on race day, such solitude can turn into loneliness—despite the size of the crowds.

In the book *Born to Run: A Hidden Tribe, Superathletes, and the Greatest Race the World Has Never Seen,* writer and amateur runner Christopher McDougall talks to an ultramarathon runner, Ann Trason, who discusses the concept of "breaking through" in her runs. McDougall writes about the simple joy and Zen-like state Ann achieves in running: "Relax enough and your body becomes so familiar with the cradle-rocking rhythm that you almost forget you're moving." Trason even finds "that soft, half-levitating flow" a romantic thing.

Olympic swimmer and 2013 Boston Marathon competitor Summer Sanders spoke to me of the altered state that occurs out on her runs, in which her breathing calms and she undergoes a transformation in her mind. She said: "I don't know if it's the endorphins or the power of reflection, but at some point in my run, I have this amazing creative release where there is great clarity on life or work, allowing me to run in a state of both happiness and excitement. It's at this moment that I could run forever."

It is in this state that a runner can get lost in the run. With blood flowing to the muscles and breathing settled, one is provided a unique opportunity to reflect in peace. The running becomes effortless; the machine-of-the-stride is almost self-propelling, allowing one to separate physical and mental. The runner's feet move as if he or she were suspended in a sleepwalk: no conscious steps, no thoughts, no intentional focus. It is out on the road that the runner comes to realize more about him- or herself. Running can be lonely and at the same time cathartic, cleansing, and thought-provoking. Questions that stymie the runner before a run—as an employee, a parent, a spouse—always seem clearer from the perspective gained on the road. The very process of removing oneself from the stressors in life allows for regeneration. The runner wakes from slumber or stretches after a run somewhere between refreshed and reborn.

While moving, runners are provided the opportunity for honest discourse. They can ask themselves questions and then answer such queries without risk of judgment. It is in the midst of the run that runners have the chance to recognize their personal limitations, both as athletes and as people. This, in turn, allows them to assess how to improve and remedy what has caused life's constraints.

There are no boundaries within these private conversations. For some, they can be personal; others may extend the dialogue beyond their earthly confines to include a higher being. In the form of prayer or meditation, they can give thanks, seek guidance, or ask for inspiration well beyond the run itself. Afterwards, when they stretch or ice down following a run, they can begin to resolve issues that had troubled them beforehand. Work, family, and finances—it all can be placed in order after some time alone on the road.

These moments can also include interaction with loved ones who have passed and may offer perspective. After all, no person has greater perspective than those who were enlightened in their final moments. As life faded, they lived anew; through the lens of true understanding they saw the miracle of life in every snowflake, raindrop, sunrise, and breath. Runners can draw upon this strength when their quads tighten and their breath shortens. This is the power of running. It's not miles and hills and oxygen intake— it's exploiting the run in a way that allows you to become reacquainted with your blessings.

In 2001, Korean runner Lee Bong-Ju ran with a heavy heart. In the months leading up to the race, he had lost his father. How could he run Boston without him? Finally, he relented and arrived in Hopkinton. Suffocated by the memory of his earnest dad who had worked the rice farm up to his dying day, he took the first step to Boston. As he ran, he sensed his father there. He said, "I felt him when I needed encouragement and confidence." When Lee crossed the finish line as champion, he would later say in profound reflection, "I felt that my father was with me today."

Seven-time winner Clarence DeMar knew success in Boston meant more than running. He said that there are "three sides to winning a marathon— physical, mental, and moral. On the physical side, one must have plenty of sleep and also clean habits, while freedom—which will make training a pleasure rather than a bore—and confidence . . . make up the mental side of the victory, and prayer constitutes the moral side."

For many, running is sanctuary. Local Boston newscaster Jack Hynes, son of longtime Boston mayor John Hynes, found refuge in running. "The marathon is a crucible for the soul as well as the body," he said, "and the end is absolution and peace. It is an escape from the frustration, the triviality, the anger, the pettiness . . . a single physical act without encumbrance, without expense, without reason or regard, and I can do it alone."

Running and preparing for a marathon provides the competitor the opportunity for physical and spiritual fulfillment, but there is peril and risk in such a crazed mission. In 1929, veteran Boston Marathoner Albert "Whitey" Michelson was hit by a car while preparing for Boston. Cut, bruised, and battered, Michelson picked himself up and refused a ride home from the driver so that he could run the remaining five miles home. Thirty-one years later, champion John "The Younger" Kelley was running through a blizzard in Connecticut when he stopped to help push a car out of a snowbank. In the process he tore ligaments in his ankle and was never the same.

So much is sacrificed on the quest. The runners are vulnerable, as are their families, friends, jobs—the world that they touch. Morning commutes are delayed, lunch hours extended, events missed. The runner prefers the microwave and a lonely dinner rather than having to skip miles. *Globe* writer Michael Madden wrote of the impact of such a singular venture: "Marriages hit the wall too often with marathoners . . . the cause is rarely the other wife, but usually the other life of training, preparing, and dedicating a year."

This sacrifice was exemplified four days before the 1936 Boston Marathon, when the wife of John Semple was granted a divorce from her husband. In court papers, she stated as the reason for the fractured relationship, "spending too much time training for marathon races." John (later known as Jock) traded in his wife for his mistress—the Boston Marathon—which he would administer for over six decades. Years after his divorce, in one of the Marathon's most infamous incidents, Jock's inability to allow a woman to coexist with the Boston Marathon would confront him on the streets of Ashland.

For the runner's loved ones, there is no distinction between being a supporter and being an enabler. The significant other serves as trainer, motivator, psychiatrist, and coach.

On the morning of the 1942 Boston Marathon, in Melrose, milkman Joe Smith refused to get out of bed. He had suffered through a winter of disjointed running and was more than content to pass on the day's events. Joe's wife had a different idea. She stormed into the bedroom and told him, "You're grouching and bellyaching around here just like you did before the national marathon last year, and what happened? You won. It's a good sign, so stop grumbling about how bad you feel. I'll be at the finish, and I won't be surprised to see you come in first."

Joe "The Milkman" Smith runs to a victory that only his wife believed was possible in 1942. The statue of Leif Eriksson is in the background. ©RUNNING PAST

Joe got out of bed and won Boston. When he crossed the finish line, his wife was there waiting. He ran to her and kissed her. He was then led away by officials to be examined, only to break away to come back and kiss her again, and then a third time. At the post-race press conference he said, "The only person who knew I could win was my wife. She knew I was going to win."

It is also the responsibility of loved ones to recognize the difference between being passionate and being foolhardy. How far can someone let a loved one swim out into a riptide? The demands of training and running any marathon can be overwhelming. But the very thought of not running can drive some would-be participants to desperation.

In 1914, the *Globe* reported that a Lynn, Massachusetts, man was so distraught over the progress of his training that the beast of Boston got the better of him: "Continuous training to keep in shape for the Marathon caused [Emil] Clem to break down several months ago, and his mental condition finally became such that his wife feared he would carry out alleged threats to do her bodily harm. She appealed to police to apprehend him." A true long-distance runner, Clem was eventually caught in a sprint against the local constabulary, was arrested, and admitted to Westborough State Hospital. As the race approached, his dream of running Boston did not fade. Prior to the race, while walking the grounds, he again put his legs to use and escaped from incarceration. He never made it to Hopkinton, but his compulsion to run Boston was something to behold.

The will to accomplish something that 99 percent of the world is incapable of is powerful. The very thought of fulfilling one's dream is prone to cloud one's better judgment. Occasionally, this will compel a spouse to offer an ultimatum, such as the one Tom Nealon received in 2013. In the prior year's race, 90-degree temperatures wore him down over the course, causing him to flat-line at the finish. After recovery at a nearby hospital, he announced that he was determined to run Boston the following year. That is, until his wife offered a simple threat: "If you run again, I'll divorce you."

In many ways, the process of training for Boston is harder than the race itself. But to have the privilege to run in the world's greatest race, you must train accordingly. You must bow to its history and show it proper respect. Your mind, your legs, and, most of all, your heart, must be worthy of running in the footprints of DeMar, Côté, and Benoit Samuelson. You can't take your mark as a dabbler, only as a disciple. The Boston Marathon can break a runner down to their most vulnerable state and spit them out onto the wayward sidewalk. For over a century, runners have sat on curbs of the race's eight towns, lamenting the deficiencies of their training, begging forgiveness from the course, in hopes of someday coming back next time prepared, fit, and ready.

Marathon Weekend

Day and night I was dreaming of winning the Boston Marathon.
And I did what I was dreaming of.
—HAILU NEGUSSIE, 2005 BOSTON MARATHON CHAMPION

LIKE CHRISTMAS MORNING IN DR. SEUSS'S *HOW THE GRINCH STOLE Christmas!*, it's in April that Boston turns into Whoville. From all over the world, runners begin to descend upon the city. Logan Airport greets well-conditioned athletes—water bottles in hand and sneakers in suitcases—throughout the weekend. Runners travel thousands of miles to run a mere twenty-six. From Japan to Kenya, and from every treadmill, trail, and personal course in between, athletes journey to Boston to seek the Holy Grail of running. It is a pilgrimage of the faithful. They travel to run, pay homage, and, God willing, to conquer.

Prior to the days of corporate sponsorship, Boston Marathon runners were left to their own means to get from their homes to the starting line. In 1943, four-time champion Gérard Côté of Canada was fighting in World War II for the Allies in North Africa when he was granted permission to run the race that he would win four times. After securing seats on transport planes, Côté traveled halfway across the world in the midst of the most treacherous time known to man to run the Boston Marathon. He arrived in Hopkinton fifteen minutes prior to the start and ran on to victory. Even back when victory only meant a wreath and beef stew, competitors would travel by any means possible to be able to compete.

Similar to Côté, popular Chicago runner William "The Bricklayer" Kennedy had to be resourceful to run in Boston in 1913. Desperate to run the race, but with no financial means, Kennedy hoboed his way from train to train, hitched rides, and walked when necessary—despite having just recovered from typhoid fever. When he arrived at Huntington Station in Boston, he leapt off the roof of the baggage car before conductors could catch him. Without a cent to his name, he walked the streets of Boston, finally taking up residence in a billiards hall, where he spent the night sleeping on a pool table. Four years later he would win Boston in one of the greatest triumphs of the race's history.

After negotiating for months to secure an exit visa in 1998, Russian marathoner Andrey Kuznetsov was finally granted one, but he was only allowed to travel with the sweat suit on his back and the sneakers on his feet. His journey to Boston started on the prior Wednesday, from his home in the central Russian village of Khabarovsk. To travel just from his village to Moscow took the elite Masters competitor (age forty and over) eight hours. From there he hopped on a flight to Helsinki, where he connected to New York and then bused to Boston.

He arrived in Boston on Sunday night to find no vacancies, and had to resort to napping in a chair in the lobby of the Fairmont Copley Plaza. On Monday morning he made the whole odyssey worthwhile, winning the Masters race with a time of 2:15:27. He would win it again the next year, shaving a minute off his time.

To maximize their chances to fulfill their potential on Monday, race day, it is critical that runners settle into the city. That means arriving in Boston as early as possible and acclimating to the city, its time zone, climate, and topography. Of course, the athlete needs to prepare and be organized. Running Boston is not for the impulsive. Miles must be logged, official numbers secured, flights booked, and lodging reserved. On calendars in kitchens or offices or on iPhones across the running universe, athletes have circled the third Monday in April.

A famous exception to this rule was Irish runner John Treacy, who rolled over in his bed the Thursday night before the race, 3,000 miles from the starting line, and told his wife that he had decided to run the 1988 Boston. Three days later he was leading the race in Mile 21, only to finish

Members of the Korean contingent (left to right: Manager Sohn Kee Chung, Song Kil Yoon, Hann Kil Yong, and Choi Yan Chil) arrive at Logan Airport for the 1950 Boston Marathon. PHOTO COURTESY OF THE *BOSTON HERALD*

third with a time of 2:09:15. "I was convinced I could win the Boston Marathon," he recalled. "I had a great week of running, and felt I was as prepared as I could be. I knew I'd run well; sometimes that's enough."

Over the last century plus, the Marathon has blossomed from a half-day event into an entire week of Marathon Madness. Sometimes the weekend prior to the race is a marathon of another kind. Bars and restaurants busy themselves with Marathon-related activities, while the Boston Athletic Association (BAA) prepares the course and ties up loose ends. The city must get ready.

In 1630, Massachusetts governor John Winthrop's vision for the new city of Boston was that it would be a "city upon the hill." Winthrop meant

that its inhabitants would be burdened with the responsibility of uphold-
ing the core values on which the city was founded, because the world
was watching. For four hundred years, the city has accepted such responsibility. Boston would become known as "The Cradle of Liberty" for its
role in the Revolutionary War; as the hub of the antislavery abolitionist
movement; as a leader in medical care and education. It was in Boston
that the country's first public school was formed, Boston Latin; the first
university of higher education, across the Charles River in Cambridge,
Harvard University; the first public park, the Boston Common; and the
first subway, the Tremont Street Subway.

Boston is known as a walking city for its cozy confines. Stretching
forty-eight miles wide from boundary to boundary, the city is comprised
of a patchwork of twenty-one distinct neighborhoods and 600,000 residents. Its most famous landmark is the home of the beloved Red Sox,
Fenway Park. And its tallest building is the John Hancock Tower, stretch-
ing 790 feet into the sky and the headquarters of the primary sponsor of
the Boston Marathon.

Throughout the weekend, the city and its surrounding towns play
host to an enormous influx of visitors. In 2013, around 12,000 hotel
rooms were booked; 500,000 spectators showed up to watch 26,800 runners (and 2014's estimates are even higher).

Hotels hang NO VACANCY signs out front, while North End restaurants draw long waits, and tickets to Red Sox games are sold at a premium.
In all, the Boston area reaped an estimated $123 million in revenue from
the Marathon in 2013. Business owners, desperate for a capital injection
after a long winter, push to sell their products to marathoners and spectators alike—all of whom are too distracted by the race to notice, or mind,
that their wallets are being emptied.

On Saturday and Sunday, the John B. Hynes Convention Center,
aptly named after the longtime mayor of the 1940s and '50s, and great fan
of the Boston Marathon, hosts the John Hancock Sports & Fitness Expo.
For convenience purposes, runners are required to pick up their numbers
at the convention center, a detour that provides the Expo a captive, and
mandatory, audience.

Like the Marrakesh marketplace in Morocco, the Expo is bursting with a smorgasbord of booths where "goat traders" attempt to sell their product, or get you to sign up for their marathon, or test-drive their new sneaker. The event attracts 100,000 people and is reminiscent of the suffocating chaos of a Fifth Avenue sidewalk in Manhattan during Christmas week. Along with the myriad products available for purchase, the runners can also get acclimated to the mayhem that will greet them in Hopkinton on Monday morning.

Those who somehow survive the bumping, pulling, and elbowing take their bags filled with long-sleeved T-shirts, gels, and free posters and go to seek peace as only a runner knows how—by running. Coaches and veteran marathoners will universally advise that by this point, you've either logged sufficient miles in your training runs or not. The true value of a pre-race jog is twofold: to loosen muscles, and to burn off nervous energy.

Many runners will lace up, stretch out, and head over to scenic paths along the Charles River for a light jog. Named after King Charles I of England, the river separates Boston and Cambridge, and is the site of Boston's famous Fourth of July celebration. The mouth of the Charles meets the Atlantic Ocean just miles from the finish line, while the source of the river is—ironically—just miles from the race's start in Hopkinton. Those who prefer to do their practice running on the actual course must beware; the temperamental roads that connect Hopkinton to Boston are not to be toyed with. Impulsive running can spike a marathoner's adrenaline and confidence, but the course itself will show no mercy; after all, it doesn't know it's not race day.

Such was the case in 1949, when Swedish runner Karl Gosta Leandersson decided to run the entire course just days before the race. After traversing the 26-plus miles, he realized that he had run what would have been a course record. In the midst of his personal marathon, however, Leandersson injured his Achilles tendon. On race day, the Swede was compelled to ignore the pain, winning the race by more than three minutes.

Preparation like Leandersson's—so close to Monday's race— is not recommended for the average runner. Runners are wise to sign up for one of the many tours that chauffeur runners—on wheels—over the course, providing insights on strategy and history.

This form of pre-race homework is helpful for some, intimidating for others. Prior to his first run at Boston, four-time champion Robert Kipkoech Cheruiyot found it helpful to see the course beforehand, though the hills gave him pause: "It's tough to go uphill—it's tough to go downhill." His attitude wasn't shared by Nova Scotia runner and grocery store clerk Johnny Miles, who when asked if he would be scouting the course prior to the 1929 race smugly shook his head and said, "Why? I'll see enough of it tomorrow."

By the eve of Marathon Day, the jog is completed and Expo bags are packed away. Many men and women partake in the traditional Sunday-night pasta dinner. The original carbo-load once took place a mile from the finish line at the now-closed Eliot Lounge. It was there that runners assembled to get a beer, eat pasta, and partake in ad hoc running symposiums. In the kitchen, Steve Gentile cooked a thousand pounds of pasta while Boston Marathon poet laureate and bartender Tommy Leonard would hold court. All year Tommy lived for the Boston Marathon, hanging the flags of all the countries represented in that year's race. Now the runners' dinner is held at City Hall Plaza, with just as many noodles but not the same charm. At the Eliot in the 1980s, you could always find the top runners in the world seated at the bar, talking running and suds.

With fuel in the tank for the next day's race, runners return to their hotels or rented rooms or parked cars to seek sleep. With millions in town to run or watch the race, lodging is always a challenge. Since the race's origin, houses along the route have taken in runners, while the BAA has always done its best to find a roof and a bed for all—including in 1961, when German great Fritz Gruber ended up sleeping on a Ping-Pong table in the Boston Garden.

No matter where the runners lay their head, the mission is slumber—although the next day's event makes it tough. Even two-time champion John "The Elder" Kelley struggled to relax and log sufficient sleep. Prior to his 1939 run, Kelley noted, "The hours before the race instead of the race itself are the most trying. You run the race many times each night the week of the big race."

In the months leading up to the Marathon, runners find that even in their sleep they can't hide from the magnitude of the coming race. In some of these visions, they dream of running the last yards of the race in jubilation, like Clarence DeMar, who won all seven times when he actually dreamt of Marathon glory in the nights preceding the race. As for his twenty-six other attempts, he claims he wasn't visited then by the specter of the wreath in his dreams.

Some runners arrive in Boston in a state of denial, but are likely visited in their sleep by anxiety or fear, perhaps even nightmares. Some might have visions of lost sneakers, while others arrive at the starting line too late. (Two-time champion Joan Benoit Samuelson admitted that she dreamt of missing the start because she was window-shopping in Hopkinton boutiques.)

There is no lying to one's subconscious. It knows when one is nervous, tentative, and insecure. The subconscious seems to revel in its ability to produce visions of failure, knowing that the runner is trapped in the theater of REM sleep.

In 1971, Irish runner Pat McMahon found himself overwhelmed by a recurring dream in which he was winning the Boston Marathon, the finish line in sight. Sadly, his vision would always end with him being caught from behind, victory eluding him. He'd sit straight up in bed in a cold sweat. On the actual race day, McMahon was running in the lead with 150 yards to the finish line when Alvaro Mejia of Mexico ran up next to him, elbowed him out of the way, and ran on to victory. McMahon was left to watch him from the side of the road—the best seat in the house—as the Mexican runner broke the tape. His nightmare had literally come to life.

❦

Meeting the challenge of Boston is the pinnacle of pressure for marathoners; they must take on the course, the conditions, and other competitors—and sometimes, even more. Prior to the 1913 race, one runner was confronted with a whole other level of pressure. Before traveling from Maine to run Boston, Penobscot Indian Andrew Sockalexis, who had placed second the previous year, proposed to his girlfriend, Pauline Shay. Expecting a yes, he was instead given an ultimatum. As the *Globe* reported the morning of Patriots' Day, 1913: "She will only accept his offer of marriage if he wins. She is the only Squaw in all the wide, wide, world that he would have grace his wigwam . . . her suitor must dangle the scalps of the finest athletic warriors in America at his belt, or she will have none of him."

Once again, he placed second. His girlfriend said yes anyway, but he never ran Boston—or any other athletic event—again.

Marathon Morning

I suppose our capacity for self-delusion is boundless.
—JOHN STEINBECK, *TRAVELS WITH CHARLEY*

ON THE MORNING OF THE 1972 BOSTON MARATHON, OLAVI SUOMA-lainen of Finland looked out the window of his hotel room and saw the overcast skies and smiled. He then turned back to his wife, who was still in bed, and said, "This is a good day to win a marathon race." Later that day, he would.

For most, their mission is not of conquest, but instead, a contest. Will they use that day's race as a metaphor to run all of life's races? A catalyst to venture farther, higher, and faster? A fulcrum to open all of life's possibilities? Because isn't that why they come to Hopkinton—to live, and learn how to live?

It is an exercise of self-discovery. When the sun seems hottest, the hill seems highest, the next water table farthest away, they bare their very being. Can the heart push forward when every other muscle pleads with them to stop? From Hopkinton to Boylston Street, every runner confronts these questions. Ultimately, their success is a function of a single thing: will.

❧

The anticipation of the race causes many runners to rise that Monday morning before the sun. As they prepare, they stare at themselves in the bathroom mirror and wonder if the person in the reflection is capable of finishing. Or will that person fade away in the fog of the shower's steam?

Prior to the first Boston Marathon on April 19, 1897, the runners gathered at the Boston & Albany Station and traveled by train to Ashland, where they were dropped along with their personal attendants. The *Boston Globe* reported that they proceeded to the Central House Hotel for a pre-race dinner, where the banquet hall was divided between two groups: the New York contingent on one side, and the Boston and Cambridge runners on the other. The reporter noted, after getting a look at the field, "Some of the runners are cracks from New York . . . these men are a fast set."

Of course, the race has evolved over time. Where a single car on a westbound train was sufficient to transport the fifteen competitors to the first Boston Marathon, now hundreds of yellow buses are needed. It's from the torn, upholstered seats of these vehicles that runners stare out the window on the ride to Hopkinton and are left to wonder. In reality, the mode of transportation could not be more apropos. It's in these very seats where vulnerability lives every weekday. It's where spitballs fly and bus drivers yell; where the self-conscious wonder if their clothes are cool enough, or if the girl will say yes. Vulnerable, insecure, on the path toward self-discovery—these are all the same feelings that the runner also experiences in that yellow bus.

———

The Boston Marathon is run each year on the Massachusetts holiday of Patriots' Day, the day the state commemorates the famous ride of Paul Revere ("The British are coming!") and the battles of Lexington and Concord, which ignited the American Revolution. Patriots' Day is widely celebrated throughout the state with many events, including reenactments of battles, replays of Paul Revere's ride, a rare eleven a.m. Boston Red Sox game at Fenway Park, and, of course, the Marathon itself.

For 364 days of the year, the sleepy colonial town of Hopkinton slowly rises to welcome each new morning. But on the 365th, no matter if Hopkinton tries to hide her head under the pillow, she cannot escape. On that morning, the sound of chirping birds perched on the budding maple trees around the town common are drowned out by a parade of shuttle buses; the smell of fresh coffee is overpowered by the aroma of muscle-soothing liniment; the sound of a thrown newspaper hitting the front door is replaced by the knock of a total stranger with a bursting bladder, requesting the use of a bathroom.

The town of Hopkinton was founded in 1715, when money donated to the town from John Hopkins was used to buy land from the Natick Indians. The town is rural yet bucolic, quiet yet robust. It has a long history of devotion to its country. In the American Revolutionary War, 115 of its men fought for freedom, including warrior Danny Shays, whose brave stands at the battles of Lexington, Bunker Hill, and Saratoga were legendary. In honor of Shays's many acts of heroism, General Lafayette presented him with an ornamental sword.

When Shays arrived home, he discovered that his service to the cause had left him penniless and in debt. (In 1786, Shays would lead a rebellion against unfair debt and tax collection, especially against veterans, that came to be known as Shays's Rebellion.) Desperate to avoid jail, he sold his cherished sword. Shays was summoned to court at the behest of Governor John Hancock and ruled to be insolvent. (Ironically, Hancock's image would be the face of the insurance company that would later save the Boston Marathon as the race's main sponsor.)

Two generations later, the Union Army would call upon Hopkinton's young and bold residents. Reportedly the town committed more men to the war than any other town in the nation. In all, 330 men answered the call, many never to return home. No family suffered greater loss than the Bixbys. When President Lincoln was informed that Lydia Bixby had lost all five of her boys in battle, he felt compelled to pen the following note to the bereaved mother:

Executive Mansion,
Washington, Nov. 21, 1864.

Dear Madam—

I have been shown in the files of the War Department a statement of the Adjutant General of Massachusetts that you are the mother of five sons who have died gloriously on the field of battle.

I feel how weak and fruitless must be any word of mine which should attempt to beguile you from the grief of a loss so overwhelming. But I cannot refrain from tendering you the consolation that may be found in the thanks of the Republic they died to save.

I pray that our Heavenly Father may assuage the anguish of your bereavement, and leave you only the cherished memory of the loved and lost, and the solemn pride that must be yours to have laid so costly a sacrifice upon the altar of freedom.

Yours, very sincerely and respectfully,
A. Lincoln

It turned out that three, not five, of Lydia's sons perished. The two that were mistaken for Lydia's children were actually her nephews. Yet her sacrifice was still enormous.

The history of Hopkinton's commitment was further supported in World War I, when a hundred members of the town fought in the "war to end all wars," including George V. Brown. Brown would return home to fire the gun at the start of the Boston Marathon for more than three decades. His name is inscribed on the doughboy statue at the starting line.

Along with its commitment to its nation, Hopkinton is also known for being home to the family of Brigham Young; the fact that George Washington and General Lafayette would stay in the village when traveling from the south up to Boston; and the fact that the mills and factories that comprised the Davenport Block in the mid to late 1800s were some of the top producers of shoes in the country.

Because of the risk that twenty-six miles presents to athletes, the Boston Athletic Association demanded in the earlier days of the race that each runner undergo a physical examination to determine whether the runner's constitution was deemed sturdy enough to withstand the undertaking. A check of the heart, a cough, and logging of their weight was the extent of the probe.

Prior to the 1903 race, John Lorden approached the BAA doctors at the starting line and informed them that he received a physical, and that he'd been approved to run. The officials didn't know that there was a doctor's letter in Lorden's pocket advising *against* participation. It read: "This is to certify that I have advised Mr. John Lorden not to participate in the race to be held on Monday, April 20, owing to the trouble with his bowels." Doctors never asked to see the letter, and Lorden would go on to win the race that day.

For years, Dr. Blake was responsible for the oversight of the runners. His experience in the Civil War at the Battle of Bull Run prepared him for the mayhem and excitement before the Marathon gun. Dr. Blake knew about marathons, as his son ran in the first ever marathon in Athens at the original Olympics, in 1896.

Like Dr. Blake, BAA officials' responsibilities often extended beyond the job description. It is their intention to allow runners the best chance to run the race on that day. Occasionally this will even include providing personal funds to the runner. It was prior to the 1939 race that pre-race favorite and eccentric Tarzan Brown approached officials and informed them that he couldn't afford the one-dollar entry fee. Quietly, a member of race official George Brown's family slipped him a dollar, and he went on to win the race.

These days, the operation and oversight of the race falls under the realm of Dave McGillivray, the race director. His preparations for the race start the moment the last runner crosses the finish line in the previous year's event. As custodian of the world's greatest running event, he has the awesome burden of not only ensuring the integrity of the course, but also protecting every runner and spectator. The Boston Marathon is truly one of the state's most valuable possessions. His job was made significantly more difficult after the 9/11 attacks, and the subsequent fear became a terrifying reality in 2013, when two terrorists detonated two bombs—thirteen seconds apart—near the finish line on Boylston Street, killing 3 people and injuring 264 others.

In the formative years, officials like George Brown, Will Cloney, and Jock Semple administered every task from starting gun to winner's wreath and everything in between. Back then, as long as competition was fair (and there were no women on the course), it was deemed a success. Now, race coordination includes bomb-sniffing dogs, 1,500 police, 400 National Guard members, helicopters providing life feeds, bag checks at the start and finish, and radar to detect for bomb elements.

If the disasters at the Munich and Atlanta Olympics proved anything, it was that those bent on mayhem will always see sporting venues as an ideal stage upon which to act. Twelve years after the World Trade Center tragedy, events at the 2013 Boston Marathon would unfortunately affirm the need for such a presence.

<hr/>

As the clock ticks toward the start, runners from the Athletes' Village at Hopkinton High School work their way toward their assigned corral, while the elite, who find sanctuary in a nearby church, march through the neighboring cemetery in order to gain unmolested access to the starting line.

This strange and rapid change in scenery has always created a wide range of emotions for three-time champion Uta Pippig:

One moment I'm sitting in a church, where you are supposed to be quiet and respectful. Before you know it, you're walking through a cemetery over graves and by tombstones. In a different way, I feel a quiet connection with the people who might lie beneath my feet. Then, after quickly reflecting upon the lives of people who are no longer with us, I walk out on the street, and there stand thousands of people who are waiting to start the most alive competition in the world. In the span of five minutes, I passed through every facet of life.

Standing guard at the starting line is a statue of a World War I dough-boy, which was sculpted to honor the Hopkinton residents who fought in Europe. On the base of the statue are the names of those from the town who fought in the Great War, including longtime starter of the Boston Marathon, George V. Brown. For some, the depiction of the infantry sol-ider is unnerving. For decades he has presided over the start with a gun on his shoulder and a concerned look on his bronze face—seeming to march in the opposite direction of the race.

Despite the fact that the inanimate statue is trying to walk away, the minute hand climbs toward the promised hour. The starter's gun is loaded. By this point the runners have made peace with the Lord or Yahweh or Mohammed or the Golden Sneaker god. Minutes slowly tick by on the digital watches of the runners just as surely as they dripped off the time-pieces of derby-clad gentlemen in years gone by. The last-minute stretch-ing, the faraway stares, the nervous babble—all of these final rituals seem to speed the clock forward.

Runners spend the last minutes before the race in one of two ways—either they banter nervously, or they slip into a cocoon. Winner of the 1957 race, John "The Younger" Kelley—not to be confused with the John "The Elder" Kelley, who won in 1935 and 1945—used to concentrate on anything other than the race: "It was important to put the race in per-spective. If you didn't, you would go crazy. I remember trying to focus on the fields and woods of Hopkinton while at the same time ignoring all the talk around me. I often thought that my friends and peers must have thought I was a jerk, but that's just the way I was on race day."

By contrast, 1976 winner Jack Fultz preferred to talk with the run-ners around him before the race: "It's important to have relaxed concen-tration. It's not like being a sprinter, who needs to be hyper-focused. A marathoner who is obsessed with concentration will not be able to relax sufficiently enough to run to his or her potential."

There is plenty to keep your attention. Helicopters hover overhead, officials bark into two-way radios, trucks capped with satellite dishes fight for parking spaces, and members of the National Guard take position. As the clock approaches the moment of reckoning, thousands of athletes toe the line, more than a century after the original starting line was drawn in the dirt, just down the road in Ashland. It is in this moment that four-time champion Catherine "The Great" Ndereba of Kenya actually finds reconciliation through her relationship with the Almighty. "I think I've done everything I'm supposed to do," she says. "And the rest I leave to God."

On the bandstand, to the right of the elite, the band baptizes the largest one-day sporting event in the world with a Rockwellian rendition of "The Star-Spangled Banner." Following the anthem in 2002, a quartet of F-15 fighter jets performed a flyover in Hopkinton and then followed the race route into Boston. It took them four minutes to complete the race.

In 2013, Summer Sanders stood in her corral, debating when to start her watch. It was essential that she run at the proper pace in order to achieve the desired time. She looked around and suddenly realized something: She didn't have to run a particular time. In past marathons she'd been obsessed with time because *she had to qualify for Boston*. But now, she was here; she was *at* Boston, the starting line of which she had dreamt. She turned from her watch and decided to run, pure joy in her heart. She would appreciate every aspect of Boston: high-five every kid, smile at every well-wisher, share with every running neighbor. She ran to pay homage, because it was Boston, and that's what you do there.

＊＊＊

With Francis Scott Key's notes still echoing off the maple trees of the Hopkinton Common, race officials hold their breath while the runners contemplate their mission and try to control their emotions. Over the last year, these competitors have logged thousands of miles in an effort to reach their respective goals. Whether the goal is to win, to break a time barrier, or simply to finish, it's all of equal importance. It doesn't matter in these last seconds before the gun.

All of those long runs—in the dark of night, through the slippery back roads of a New England winter, on a monotonous treadmill in Oslo, in the early morning on streets of Tokyo before work, or sneaking back to their desks before their boss realizes their split time has exceeded their lunch hour. All they have endured—the sore muscles and knees, the blisters, the dog bites, that game of chicken with the pickup truck. All those nightmares of forgetting their sneakers. All of these sacrifices they have made and trials they have faced in order to stand on this line.

It could be argued that some of the runners have no right to stand on the starting line of the world's greatest race. But there they stand, and the fear starts the journey from the subconscious to the conscious. When it arrives, some realize that they have swum out too far and are now caught in the riptide. Maybe they should have stayed home. Maybe they had bitten off more than they could chew. But the tide takes them, and they let it.

In 2013, Joey McIntyre, music star with the New Kids on the Block, stood at the starting line, looked around at his surroundings, and took it all in. The special layout of Hopkinton allows the runner to take in the moment. He saw the opportunity of standing on the starting line in Boston as a privilege—not just to run the race, but also to train, as his wife and children had sacrificed so much so that he could pursue his goal. For years he had hung out at parties at Cleveland Circle during the race. But on this day, he stood in the woods of the suburbs that he'd never experienced growing up as a city kid. "There is a crispness in the air out in Hopkinton," he told me. "You stand in this suburb with trees all around you. You're in the best shape of your life, and you know that you're part of something really special. Not only are you part of the Boston Marathon, but also you are a citizen of this running community, which is so inclusive."

While he looked from tree to common, he was overtaken by concern: *What if he was the one runner out of thousands whose timing chip didn't work?* The Boston boy had always dreamt of running his hometown marathon. He had trained for months in the hills of Los Angeles for this very moment. He looked at his watch, down at his chip, and then at his neighbors' chips, hoping to God that his worked. Either way he was going. He decided to have faith in the technology and focus on his coach's advice for the early tempting miles: "Put on your smoking jacket and chill."

<hr>

The racers fall into place as they await the sound of the gun; with stern faces and elbows extended, they strike the same pose that runners have struck for the past century. Whether mill workers with scally caps on their heads and leather shoes on their feet or Kenyans with speed pulsating through every muscle of their being, in the moments before the crucible, they are all one, linked from era to era, country to country. They are all now brothers and sisters of the Boston Marathon, sharing a collective gasp, frozen in time, while the starter cocks the gun.

Mile 1

You can never cross the ocean until you have the courage to lose sight of the shore.

—CHRISTOPHER COLUMBUS

FOR MORE THAN A CENTURY, ANYWHERE FROM FIFTEEN TO FORTY thousand runners have stood ready, waiting for the opportunity to run to Boston. For months, they have prepared for this moment.

Sometimes it can be so overwhelming that runners can't contain themselves.

In 1953, one runner was so concerned with the importance of a fast start that he brought sprinter's starting blocks to Hopkinton. In 1900, Canadian runner John Barnard was considered a favorite by Canadian gamblers, who waged heavily on their countryman to win the race. The added pressure to win caused Barnard to jump the gun, leading officials to order the only restart in the Boston Marathon's history.

These incidents speak to the urgency of the moment. BAA officials like George Victory Brown, who signaled the start of the race for thirty-three years, are obliged to rein in the runners. After runners got feisty prior to the 1905 race, Brown declaimed, "Don't crowd here; you've got twenty-six miles ahead of you! Now kneel down and get ready."

For almost a century, a member of the Brown clan has fired an anti-quated colonial pistol into the air to christen the race and send the runners down Route 135 toward Boston. The sounding of the gun triggers not only a prerecorded howitzer, but also electronically starts all the clocks along the route. The Browns are not only one of the most prominent Hopkinton families, but also one of the most influential forces in Boston

Just minutes before the 1906 start, runners pose for a picture at the starting line on the High Street railroad bridge in Ashland. PHOTO COURTESY OF THE BOSTON ATHLETIC ASSOCIATION

sports. Along with their contribution to the Boston Marathon, the family owned the Boston Celtics and, at one point, the Boston Bruins. For decades the sounding of the gun by the Brown family has been the signal for the runners to exhale and finally do what they came to Hopkinton to do.

In 1897, race official Tom Burke organized the fifteen runners behind a line that he drew with his heel, raised his hand at 12:19 p.m., and shouted, "*Go!*"

Like warriors going off to battle, the runners cross the starting line to the ballad of drums and cheers. Virtually all competitors proceed with caution through this early stretch. The course takes them dangerously down Route 135 in the direction of Boston. They don't see any skyscrapers but rather a sharp decline and a blind turn at the bottom of the first hill. With adrenaline pumping, the runners must hold back and make an effort here to move smartly and safely. The start is very narrow: just under fifty feet, fitting only twenty-one bodies across. A disorderly start could result in injury or even death.

Greg Meyer, winner of the 1983 race, feared the start with a passion: "With the course starting on a narrow street and moving downhill, all of your training could be for naught with one trip over someone's feet. I wish I could fall asleep, and wake up somewhere in Natick."

No one would agree with Meyer more than Rob de Castella, the winner in 1986. One year after winning the laurel wreath, the defending champ from New Zealand stood ready for the gun. Strangely, when the clock struck noon, the designated time to start, the rope used to hold back the runners was still tied to a tree. Up on the podium, the starter fired the gun as was the custom, and the crowd surged forward, causing de Castella to trip over the restraining rope. Thinking quickly, a race official cut the rope with a pocketknife, avoiding further disaster, but not before the fallen champion had donated some of the skin from his knees and elbows to the streets of Hopkinton. Instinctively jumping to his feet, de Castella regained his form and went on to a sixth-place finish. Later he recalled that he "either had to get up or be trampled by ten thousand runners." The starting process has since been modified to avoid accidents like this.

The uniqueness and location of the race's start has been the cause of several disorderly starts over the history of the Boston Marathon bringing scrutiny upon the race custodians, the Boston Athletic Association (BAA). The combination of the occasional issue and the peculiar nuances of the course have sometimes proved to be a recipe for controversy. Following the 1977 race, winner Jerome Drayton of Canada crossed the finish line and turned back to face the course in a look of disgust. At the post-race press conference, he groused about starting the race on some suburban street, complained that there was no countdown before the gun, and when the gun was fired, he was kicked, grabbed, and almost pulled down, in fear for his life. "[At the] start I thought I was a goner in the first mile," he complained. "You're so frightened for the first two hundred yards—you can train for ten weeks and be done in ten yards."

As the race continued to evolve over the decades, the contingent of runners continued to grow. This increased field placed new and larger demands upon the BAA to ensure that the only combatant the runners faced was the course itself. These calls for improvement in the 1970s were personified by Boston Marathon guru Tom Leonard, who described the race as only he could: "The Boston Marathon is a vintage wine which should have a delicate bouquet. The race has a million-dollar audience and a twenty-five-cent field."

The calls for change were many, but race officials were slow to respond. Repeated complaints about the lack of crowd control, scarce water stops, irregular checkpoints, and the absence of timing devices evolved into frustration that eventually compromised the image of the race in the minds of the world's greatest runners. Inevitably this dissatisfaction resulted in declining numbers, both at the starting line in Hopkinton and on the sidewalks along the route.

In the early years, support and aid on the course was inconsistent, as officials assessed the cost and necessity. In 1915, they voted not to provide assistance along the course or to the runners in any form. On race day that year, temperatures rose to 87 degrees, forcing twenty-two of the sixty-four runners to drop out of the race. Runners were left to their own devices, forced to procure their own supplies and give them to their followers, who would then dole them out to runners along the course. In 1916, competitor William Kennedy secured his own supplies and then prior to the race, handed his refreshments to his assigned bike attendant for safekeeping. Later, when Kennedy ran through Mile 16, the *Globe* reported, "He asked his attendant for a stimulant only to find that the attendant had consumed the entire supply."

By the late 1920s into the '30s, the Great Depression had run roughshod over America. No entity was immune from the disease of financial ruin, and this included the BAA. Since 1888, the Boston Athletic Association had been the prominent athletic organization in the city. But the financial plague sweeping the country prevented members from paying their dues, and as a result the BAA was in arrears on taxes and delinquent on bank debt. Calls to underwrite the race were sent to the towns along the route, and even to the *Boston Globe,* but they went unanswered. By 1936, the BAA had $157,201 in assets and $231,097 in liabilities; they were insolvent, and subsequently forced to file bankruptcy under the statues of the New Deal, thus forfeiting their showpiece property on Exeter Street.

At the public auction of the club's assets, BAA official George Brown watched mementos of sentimental value walk out the door in the hands of strangers, including pictures from the first Olympics in 1896, and a variety of mounted animal heads, such as a walrus, gazelle, elephant, and antelope. Overcome by emotion, he commented, "I feel just as though my house was being sold after thirty-seven years." The following day's *Globe* eulogized: "[G]hosts of great athletes of the past may gather in the far corner of the gym and there drink a toast to the grand old club that was."

Somehow the nomadic BAA was able to sustain the race despite the loss of its clubhouse and the impact of a world war. Nonetheless, little by little, the allure of the race had diminished to the point where in 1964, with race expenses nearing $1,000, Walter Brown considered a radical change to the race in an effort to spark interest. The proposal he intended to present to a voting committee would suggest that the course be reversed—moving the start to Boston and the finish line to Hopkinton. The proposal eventually was tabled, but it spoke to the level of financial and legacy desperation the race found itself in.

By the 1980s, race director Will Cloney determined that his financially strapped organization was foolish not to leverage their race and its history for capital. To secure funding, he contracted with a fast-and-loose marketer by the name of Marshall Medoff. Medoff, a Mustang to Cloney's Edsel, was too fast for the BAA, and in turn manipulated an agreement in which he received every dollar he gathered in marketing dollars over an agreed-upon figure. The unevenness of the arrangement brought the matter to the courts, eventually jettisoning Medoff and forcing the resignation of Cloney, after thirty-seven years in the service of the race he loved. In the end, the genie had been let out of the bottle; the Boston Marathon was now exposed to the world of business. It was an unfortunate reality, but the race existed in a world where it had to partner with capitalists in order to carry on.

In the end, the BAA ended up signing a race-saving contract with the insurance company John Hancock Financial Services. The marriage ended up being an ideal one. John Hancock is a longtime Boston entity with roots as deep as the race itself. In 2013 alone, John Hancock helped to raise almost $8 million for local charities through their relationship with the race and its runners.

━━◦~◦━━

Down the hill, the road snakes its way left for the first half-mile, and then right. For runners who had been hydrating throughout the morning, the calming trees on their right not only help quiet their nerves but also may provide a spot for an impromptu bladder release. Marathoner and Orlando Magic executive Pat Williams calls this stretch of the course "the best fertilized."

For wheelchair competitors, their start is paced by an official's car to control speeds. In 1987, the lack of restraint allowed wheelchair competitors to reach speeds in excess of forty miles per hour in the first mile. Inevitably, as in any sport with committed competitors, the risk of success led to a heart-stopping accident in which chariots were flipped, athletes injured, and onlookers aghast. In New York, race director Fred Lebow

Like all athletes, wheelchair competitors face challenges and obstacles in their efforts to reach their goal, as pictured here in the 1985 Boston Marathon.
PHOTO COURTESY OF THE *BOSTON HERALD*

took a shot at Boston's "tolerance" of wheelchair runners, saying the BAA "is flirting with disaster."

The attractive opening descent can be treacherous to any of the runners. With thousands of lemmings all going in the same direction—at the same time, with the same purpose, and all hoping to be first—there are endless risky possibilities. Runners must watch their step, keep their elbows down, and stay patient. Some are forced to adjust their game plans and pace because traffic is moving at the speed of the IRS.

Prior to the implementation of phased starts that allow elite runners a head start, it was a free-for-all. Traditionally, there was always one young buck whose sole intention was to lead the race for the first mile before dropping out. This created a nuisance for the world's best. Bill Rodgers, a four-time winner, didn't particularly like the start when he was owning the world of marathoning back in the glory days of the late 1970s. "The descent at the outset gives runners who aren't necessarily world-class the opportunity to stay with the leaders long enough to be bothersome," he said.

While the elite runners are now allowed a separate and "clean" start, the "meat of the pack" runners jockey for position by jumping up on sidewalks and around parked cars in an effort to pass slow starters. At the back of the pack, runners move like rush-hour traffic on the Expressway (Route 93) in Boston—barely. Champion Jack Fultz sees value in the congestion; it forces runners to control their early pace.

At the halfway point of Mile 1, the course teases your muscles with a preview of the monster that lies ahead by making the runner shift from downhill braking to uphill grinding. In the last quarter of the first mile, the runners move by a nursery. Just beyond the nursery sits a barn from old Tebeau's Farm. From the 1920s to the 1940s, runners used to gather at this spot to change clothes and receive their pre-race physicals.

According to the United States Department of Agriculture, back when the race was first run, 41 percent of the workforce was employed in agriculture, using 21.6 million animals in their efforts. As of the turn of the century in 2000, 1.9 percent of the country's workers are farmers, relying on just 3 million animals.

Runners from the middle and back of the pack start to break into a jog after crossing the starting line in 1991. PHOTO COURTESY OF THE *BOSTON HERALD*

Mary Tebeau, an Ashland schoolteacher, eventually sold the land to the Mezitt family. The Mezitts—the largest landowners in Hopkinton, with over nine hundred acres—still work the land under the name of Weston Nurseries. Here they grow everything from Christmas trees to a special rhododendron that blooms for the race. Brothers Wayne and Roger Mezitt remember when the race started on their farm at a ledge called "Lucky Rock," so dubbed because of a streak of quartz that ran through the middle. Although they have fond memories of this day, their business suffers badly throughout the holiday because of the tight traffic control maintained around the race.

At the end of the first mile, the competitors can look over Mahar's Meadow to their left. The first chapter of their journey is complete; 25 miles and 385 yards to go. Hopefully the harriers at the back are approaching the starting line. In all, the runners have descended 130 feet in the first mile, the greatest drop of any mile on the course. The starting line is at the highest point on the route, approximately 490 feet above sea level. In the first four miles, the course falls over 300 feet.

Mile 2

It's a setup. It is so easy to be suckered in by this attractive course.
—John "The Younger" Kelley, describing the first half
of the Boston Marathon

The town of Hopkinton represents 1.8 miles of the racecourse, or 6.8 percent in total. The town's true contribution to the race is twofold: First, it serves as host to the world's most unique and hospitable start; second, it provides two miles of mostly downhill running, allowing the runner to test Sir Isaac Newton's law of gravitation; they serve as apple in a maniacal experiment, falling 165 feet from town common to the border with the next town of Ashland.

In the early steps of the race, the athletes move as a solid mass. Spectators waiting for the runners to come around the corner, or down the street, can hear and feel the oncoming stampede. The herd moves east in what appears to spectators as a mosaic of hats and bounding hair. This collection runs without distinction—it's one monstrous chain gang, buoys bouncing up and down on a rough sea.

Up until now, most runners have been unable to open up to a comfortable pace. Each step must be carefully placed to avoid another runner's foot. On the sidewalk, the contingent of spectators is mostly comprised of locals, as the streets of Hopkinton are closed to normal traffic at 6:30 a.m. The second mile continues with a series of quick-hitting ups and downs and an occasional house among the woods and fields that line the road. Halfway through the mile, the runners pass Clinton Street and its admiring residents.

Later in Mile 2, as runners begin to extend their strides, they also start to assess their pre-race strategy, deciding to either respect or ignore it. In that pre-race strategy one must decide whether they are going to run with consideration, or a lack of restriction. It's where the race can't be won but is sometimes lost. For the elite, it's critical to get to the early flats of Mile 2 before others do. This is especially true for the wheelchair athletes.

If a runner can't move in the shared cocoon with others, then they face the same fate as the slowest antelope in the Serengeti, with the course playing the role of the lion. Tardy wheelchair competitors left behind are forced to run Boston on their own as the lead group of wheelchair racers work together to break the wind and thus move faster. An elite wheelchair competitor who loses contact with the lead pack on the first incline are unable to draft off the front group, and thus faces the daunting task of running on their own. It has been estimated that separation from the pack here can add as much as ten minutes to a competitive racer's overall time. If you don't crest the first big hill back in Mile 1 with the lead pack, your day is probably over, so it is essential to push the envelope here. Five-time wheelchair champion Jim Knaub puts it this way: "If you make it to the top side of the first hill before everyone else, you have a great chance of winning. It's like God picked you up and dropped you in the lead, and said, 'It's your day.'"

The decision to run fast or deliberate, to run with the lead pack or let them go is a determination that has been mulled over and discussed for months leading up to the race. The decision is as simple as the riddle posed in Aesop's fable, "The Tortoise and the Hare."

> *Hare ran down the road for a while and then paused to rest. He looked back at Slow and Steady and cried out, "How do you expect to win this race when you are walking along at your slow, slow pace?"*

The methodical plodder sees the tortoise as wise and calculating. For the radical, it's all hare; the hare is the *essence* of running. It's putting one foot in front of the other without regard for winds or sun or competitors; if it's their day, it's their day. In 1941, the *Globe* wrote about a champion who ran at a pragmatic pace, similar to the tortoise, in the previous year's race. "Leslie Pawson showed everybody how to run this course last year.

He started away from that crazy fast early pace. He hung back until the leaders tired. Then he ran away from them."

While Pawson used pace to run to victory, others find that running with restraint is counterintuitive to the very act of running. The hare wants to run because *that's what the hare does.* The emboldened runner is like the Italian speedster Franco, played by Raul Julia in the 1976 road race movie, *The Gumball Rally.* As Franco prepares for the start of the race, he rips off his rearview mirror and declares, "What's behind me—it's not important."

The runner who wants to run without restraint is a piston-firing Corvette, not a peace sign–stickered Prius. The runner of haste doesn't spend his days worrying about global warming—he creates his own energy. These runners run hard because that's what they do. In their minds, all fables are open to interpretation. Morals of stories are subjective, hinging on the perception of the reader. The runner knows that the hare's only problem in Aesop's fable is that he *stops running.*

The incomparable Clarence DeMar runs toward one of his seven championships.
PHOTO COURTESY OF THE *BOSTON HERALD*

46

The greatest competitor in Boston Marathon history was a hare. Seven-time champion Clarence DeMar ran not to run but to win. He was wired to let his legs—not his brain—decide where to go, how to go, when to go. "I always annoyed marathon coaches by telling them that the main thing was to get there as quickly as possible and to let the styles chips fall where they would."

Clarence DeMar is the most underappreciated star in Boston sports history. Happy to be known as a humble print-shop worker, DeMar won his first Boston Marathon in 1911, and his seventh at age forty-two, in 1930, a staggering nineteen years later. Following one of his races, the *Boston Globe* wrote of the two-time Olympian, "[He ran] like a running brook." Like a brook he ran Boston thirty-three times, finishing every time, including a seventh-place finish when he was fifty.

DeMar might not have had polish but he had plenty of substance. His blue-collar, grind-it-out running form made up in effort what it lacked in style. With his left hand held out at his hip, pawing at the air as if a personal trigger to pronate forward, he ran with upright rigidity, symbolic of his uncompromising personality on the road. It was this type of running that endeared him to the locals who lined the sidewalks, unable to leave until DeMar passed by.

In his prime, DeMar might have won ten or more marathons but for a Boston doctor who was concerned about the echoing he heard when listening to the runner's heart. The diagnosis indicated that his heart—ironically, DeMar's greatest muscle—was deficient, and that his irregular heartbeat could be fatal. He warned DeMar that even stair climbing should be avoided, never mind marathoning. So DeMar dutifully skipped ten of the next eleven years of running Boston.

Eventually, the printer and his competitive gene grew tired of running back and forth to work as an outlet for his need to run, so he entered the race in 1922, claiming the first of five victories in that decade. The seven-time champion was once asked the name of the doctor who diagnosed his cardiac condition. DeMar answered, "I won't tell you his name, but he recently died of a heart attack. He must have been listening to his own heart."

Born the son of George Washington DeMar, Clarence grew up in a family that was impoverished, but still provided for him. He would fight in World War I, return home to earn an associate's degree in art at Harvard, and a master's degree from Boston University. He was quiet and almost introverted off the course—some would say recalcitrant, even unfriendly. DeMar didn't apologize for this perception, but tried to explain. "Many people, I'm afraid, think that I have a nasty temper while I'm running; that's because I wanted everyone to know that I don't want to be encouraged or interfered with while running."

It was on the course that he did his talking. Fiercely competitive, he trampled anything that got in his way en route to the finish line. In one race, as he ran through Coolidge Corner, DeMar was hit by a car. When he crossed the finish line, he realized that he had run the final miles virtually with a bare foot after the car had ripped most of his sneaker off.

In Clarence's mind the roads of the eight towns belonged to him on Patriots' Day. Once the gun sounded, he ran to Boston without any regard for anyone or anything. In 1930, DeMar ran through Wellesley and was almost offended to see competitor Hans Oldag running in the lead. When DeMar caught up to him, he asked, "Who are you?" DeMar went on to victory while Oldag finished fifty-seventh.

It wasn't just runners who drew the ire of DeMar. Two fans could attest to his intensity after suffering right crosses from the runner. One had asked for an autograph in the middle of the race; the other had poured ice water on the back of his legs to try to cool him off.

Clarence resided in the Greater Boston town of Melrose, Massachusetts, where he taught Sunday school and was a Boy Scout leader. After victories, he was more comfortable sharing the moment with his pupils and Scouts than the Brahmins of prominence, who, for one day a year, would be interested in keeping company with a mere printer. It was with the youngsters that he found sincerity.

After each race he would return home where the bells of Melrose would be rung in his honor. At home, his mother—who would listen to the race on a neighbor's radiophone that allowed radio transmissions over the phone—would treat her son to a champion's dinner. Afterward, Clarence would join his young friends at the local theater, or even play baseball with them on the sandlot where he would implore them to avoid smoking if they ever dreamed of winning their own marathons.

Clarence DeMar-velous, they called him. He once said, "I would be happy if I died while running." And he got his wish. Hospitalized with intestinal cancer, DeMar horrified his doctor by jogging in place in his hospital room. The doctor pleaded with him to rest, but DeMar continued on. Hours later DeMar died, a fulfilled man.

❦

Like DeMar, in 1978, Gayle Barron also ran like a hare. She showed up at the starting line of the Marathon with training sneakers instead of her running sneakers, assuming her run that day would be respectable but not winnable. As she ran, she felt light and relaxed, despite the fact that she was running in the lead. When she came upon friends who were there to support her, they beseeched her to slow down, as she was running beyond her means on that day. But *slow* wasn't in her nature. She would say later, upon reflection, "I said to myself that I'd run that pace as I could for as long as I could." After running through the tape as the women's champion, she said, "Can you believe it? I've never run that way in my life. I never, never would have picked me to win."

To run a marathon means that the enormity of the undertaking should be matched by the effort. This sentiment was echoed by men's elite runner, Andy Ronan, who said in 1991, "I'm here for it today, and if [anyone's] going to beat me, he's got to work for it."

To cross the finish line with more left to give, with more run in your legs, more fuel in the tank is considered by some to be disrespectful to the course and those who have run before. Some view it as a sin.

In 1978, Jeff Wells ran with great speed, but in the end, he had more to give. When he sat after the race with beef stew in hand, he felt guilty for finishing two seconds behind winner Bill Rodgers, and begged God for forgiveness. "I had too much left in me. I hadn't given out 100 percent as I had promised Him. And I didn't. I had too much left."

Jeff Wells never ran with the lead that day, but for those who have run the final yards of a marathon with no one in front of them, and the gleaming, unbroken tape in front, they claim something beyond victory. With that victory comes the knowledge that is bestowed upon those with a marathon championship on their résumé and a laurel wreath in their trophy case. From that point on, the runner runs with a level of confidence and chutzpah that other runners are simply not wired for.

It's the "been there before" attitude that allows the veteran to run the race without getting swept up in the challenge of the course or the threat of competitors. Boston Marathon champion Rob de Castella explains the core of his strategy: "I have a pretty simple theory, really. If you run as fast as you can, you should finish up there with a pretty good time. If you're fitter than others that day, you may win. If someone's with you the last couple of miles, then you've got to start racing. But I worry about that when it happens."

Past winners Geoff Smith and Jim Knaub concur with the "run for the tape" mentality. They will tell you that there is no such thing as a game plan. Both runners have a common strategy: Attack every inch of the course the same. Knaub says: "Go for broke from the beginning to the end. If it's not your day, then it's not your day." Smith agrees, and adds, "Line up and let's see who's best—whoever wins was the best that day."

While some run with a paced gait and others with abandon, there are others who run not against pace or competitors or even the course, but rather, against themselves. It's a self-calibrating mode that allows for the runner to run with a self-absorbed concern of singular intention and laser focus. John "The Younger" Kelley spoke of this approach: "I run against myself. I am the only one I must control and guide. I must run correctly without giving too much regard to what others are doing."

For months leading up to the race, runners digest, absorb, and discuss race strategy with everyone from the mailman to their psychiatrist, as well as in the pages of *Runner's World,* in chat rooms, on blogs, and inside books. Discussions run the gamut from what to eat to running technique, from the latest sneaker innovations to even how to sleep. The runner's brain can be overwhelmed by information overload, causing paralysis by analysis; sometimes all that has to be stripped away. Running should be about nothing but itself. As seven-time wheelchair champion Jean Driscoll puts it: "You've got to respect all runners, but you can't be afraid of them. I just put my head down and go for it."

At the end of Mile 2, the course continues to move downhill in a mostly residential neighborhood. House prices in Hopkinton had a median sales price of $485,600 in 2013. For 364 days, the neighborhood provides for good schools, low crime rate, and suburban living. On Patriots' Day, residential status in Hopkinton gets you a front-row seat for the world's greatest race—but it also comes with the foreknowledge that your front yard could serve as a makeshift Porta-Potty at any time.

Late in the mile, the course continues to wind downhill. At the 1.8-mile mark, the race moves from Hopkinton into the town of Ashland. On the left side of the course, the runners pass TJ's Food & Spirits, a restaurant and bar, which traditionally hosts a spirited party each Marathon Day, with their outside deck jammed and parking lot full.

After TJ's, the road leading runners to Mile 3 is flat and residential. By now, their breathing usually becomes more settled after the initial excitement—and adrenaline spike—of the start. As the runner approaches the mile mark, the sidelines are still crowded and festive.

To enjoy Boston, many runners hug the sides of the road to high-five fans who extend their hands in a gesture of New England goodwill. As the runners continue to move toward Oz, they must measure and assess. Mile marks are a great time to check in. They'd be wise to mind the recommendation of four-time winner Bill Rodgers, who suggests, "The toughest part is the early part. If you can survive the fast, early pace, your legs start to feel really light. You're running easily."

Mile 3

The journey is the thing.

—HOMER, *THE ODYSSEY*

BACK ON THE TOWN COMMON IN HOPKINTON, THERE IS A SIGN THAT reads IT ALL STARTS HERE. Not to be outdone, the town of Ashland posts a sign that reads IT ALL STARTED HERE. The two towns are nemeses in a friendly rivalry. The conflict was born from each town's contributions to the Boston Marathon.

Mile 3 starts off level as it runs through a residential neighborhood for the first two-tenths of the mile. In the third tenth, the road moves up only to fall for the rest of the mile, dumping the runners into Ashland center. Throughout the mile the route moves left and then comes back right, almost as if it were a driver overcompensating in the snow, causing rear wheels to slide back and forth. Halfway through the mile, the runners pass the local Knights of Columbus and the Ashland State Park. From there, the course moves downhill precipitously for the last half of the mile.

At approximately the 2.7-mile mark, the runners go by Steven's Corner. It is here where the race was started from 1899 to 1924, after starting in the first two years at a bridge outside a property known as Metcalf's Mill. Not until 1924 did the start of the race get moved back to Hopkinton.

The idea for the Boston Marathon was born in 1896. It was in this year that John Graham—coach of the Harvard track team and the US Olympic team, and a member of the Boston Athletic Association (BAA)—ventured across the ocean to watch the 1896 Olympic Games in Athens, Greece, with his friend Herbert Holton, a Boston financial agent.

There the two men witnessed a running event that pushed the limits of human performance. The event was a footrace of endurance to honor the legendary trek of Pheidippides, the Greek soldier who ran from Marathon to Athens in 490 BC to deliver the message that the Athenian army had conquered the Persians, exclaiming, "Rejoice—we conquered!" before dying from exhaustion. His death forever warned all would-be runners of the price a marathon can extract from the human body.

It was at that first Olympiad in 1896 that Greek runner Spiros Louis paid homage to Pheidippides by running to victory and national immortality. Along the course, gulps of wine propelled him forward to the finish line. After crossing over, he ran over to BAA officials, hugged them, and then kissed the American flag that they were holding before taking a victory lap around the arena, where he was pelted with flowers from the ladies in attendance. At the end of his lap, the contingent from the BAA honored the victor by chanting the ol' BAA cheer—three times.

In recognition of his victory, Louis was crowned with a laurel wreath and showered with gifts of appreciation, including tailored clothes, clean shaves, and free meals for a year, along with proposals of marriage and free working shoes for life.

Graham and Holton were so awestruck by the race that upon their return to Boston, they pledged to bring a similar event to their city. After much discussion, they mapped out a route to honor an American messenger worthy of comparison with Pheidippides—Paul Revere. The designed course traveled the same route as Revere's famous ride in 1775, in which he rode from Boston to Concord to warn Massachusetts colonists of the impending attack by the British.

Fortunately the road was clear in 1775, but it was not in 1896, when Holton and Graham attempted to trace the historic gallop. Their efforts were thwarted by the discovery that the bridge from Boston to Cambridge was closed for repairs (the nineteenth century's version of the Big Dig, Boston's seemingly never-ending bridge-and-tunnel project). Consequently, the two originators amended their plans and decided to follow the breezes of the Atlantic to their destination. They bicycled out the gate of the Irvington Oval race track onto Huntington Avenue in Boston, each man holding a Veeder cyclometer. The pair headed down Exeter Street, past the BAA clubhouse, and onto Commonwealth Avenue, and then rode alongside the Boston-Albany train tracks, which they used as a guide. (The tracks were an ideal escort because at the time, railroad engineers used the best technology available to map routes and track distances.)

They pedaled through town after town: through Boston, into Brookline, past Boston College, over the hills of Newton, through Wellesley, past Natick, over the train tracks of Framingham, and into Ashland. At this point Graham's cyclometer read twenty-five miles, while Holton's read twenty-four and a half. Here they dismounted, grabbed two rocks, and declared the spot the start of the first marathon—on a quiet dirt road called Pleasant Street, across from Metcalf's Mill, one mile from Ashland Center.

From 1887 to 1923, Ashland hosted the start of the race, a fact not commonly advertised by the people of Hopkinton. Eventually the starting line was moved down the street to Hopkinton, in 1924, to adhere to the accepted Olympic distance of 26.2 miles after the marathon had been lengthened during the 1908 Olympic Games in England to 26 miles, 385 yards. This was done to appease the sedentary and spoiled King Edward VII, who wanted the race to start at Windsor Castle and to finish in front of his royal box in the Olympic Stadium. The king did what a king does: He issued a proclamation. In the future, the start and finish lines would be moved intermittently to placate other voices—such as sponsors, municipal planners, and the swelling ranks of runners.

For over a century, the Boston Marathon has been cultivated, shaped, and accommodated by the likes of John Graham, Herbert Holton, King Edward VII, and John Hancock Financial Services, with the ultimate aim of creating and operating a sporting event that respected the needs of the city and the runners—as they honor the first marathoner, Pheidippides. All these years later, the runners continue to toe the line in solidarity with their many brothers and sisters, past and present, who have come to pay homage to the mecca of all marathons.

The course passes the entrance to Ashland Middle School on the left while still falling all the way into Mile 4. Overall the course plummets three hundred feet—almost thirty stories—in the first four miles.

The town of Ashland was best known for manufacturing clocks and watches to the designs of a local inventor by the name of Henry Warren. Warren created the first self-winding clock during the Great Depression. People moved to Ashland to find work in the prospering clock factory. In later years, the town, and Mr. Warren, thrived when General Electric joined Warren as a 49 percent partner. Time and clocks remain integral to the town of Ashland. The high school sports teams go by the nickname of the Clockers, and a clock tower stands in Ashland's epicenter, down the road in Mile 4.

By the end of the third mile, runners are getting used to the rhythm and the pace of the race. After a couple of miles, anyone in corrals behind the elite runners needs to practice patience by controlling their pace and navigating through walkers and slower runners.

For years Ashland was the spot where runners came in order to embark on their journey to Boston. It was on the bridge at Metcalf's Mill or at Stephen's Corner where the men pushed and carved out space in hopes of being the runner who would realize marathon glory hours later on the streets of Boston. Surrounded by race officials and gamblers alike, the runners would crouch, awaiting the gun as thousands of fans cheered them on, just as they did for the first Boston Marathon in 1897. As the *Globe* wrote, "The crowd at the Ashland station was good natured, and as it formed a line for the athletes to pass, the sleepy old town rang with the cheers of her lusty sons."

Mile 4

And a rock feels no pain, and an island never cries. *
—Paul Simon

Each mile on the course has its own characteristics—persona, even—and presents its own unique challenge for the runners. In the first steps of Mile 4, the runner moves downhill and to the right. It is here that the runners are introduced to ankle-high cement traffic islands that rise from the ground, often tripping unsuspecting competitors. The islands stretch for a tenth of a mile as the road reaches right. This protrusion is known as "Three Mile Islands" (even though they occur in Mile 4)—a nuclear metaphor that implies the danger if they're not properly navigated. Its obstacles enhance the degree of difficulty of Boston, making the event into a virtual steeplechase, and the course part of the competition.

This raised cement extension stretches for about twenty yards. Wheelchair competitors need to be especially careful rolling around the bend, as they may be traveling in excess of twenty-five miles per hour coming down the long hill approaching the first of the islands. Although the island early in the mile is well marked with cones and police tape, it can jump on the runner in a hurry—especially if you're drafting or following another competitor too closely. This is one of the spots in the race where being unfamiliar with the course can be a real disadvantage.

This threat was personified in the 1997 race, when German Silva of Mexico was already feeling the pressure of not only running as a pre-race

---

* © Paul Simon, 1965.

favorite, but also the responsibility of running on behalf of his town. If Silva won the laurel wreath that day, there was the prospect of procuring running water for his impoverished village of Tecomate. (After winning the New York City Marathon in 1994, he used his prize money to help his village obtain electricity.)

But the power of H_2O would be elusive. As Silva ran with the lead pack, his sight line was blurred by the Kenyan group running in front of him. The African runners had just left a water stop, but they failed to negotiate the first cement traffic island when Kenyan Charles Tangus tumbled to the ground. Silva, who was trailing the fallen Kenyan, attempted to hurdle over the tangle, but he was tripped up and taken down as well. With damaged legs, he picked himself up to finish a sad fourth. For those who are not able to negotiate the concrete islands, their day is permanently impacted by sadistic Mile 4.

At this juncture of the race, the surrounding area begins to become more commercial. The road continues on a downward grade, moving left before straightening and going right. At the 3.1-mile mark, there is a small shopping plaza on the left, occupied by your standard places of retail and business. You can smell the grease burning at Honey Dew Donuts on your right, and see kids licking ice-cream cones from Tasty Treat next door.

Because the town of Ashland has multiple perpendicular roads allowing fans access to the route by car or foot, many fans make their way out to the suburb to take in the race. This point marks the beginning of the growing crowds that greet runners with great enthusiasm and hospitality. Every runner is the recipient of attention and care from fans throughout the race route. It is an impressive display of goodwill in its purest form—people caring for others without previous acquaintance.

Every year since 1897, the race has served as a platform for the love affair between fans and runners—the fans, sincere in their adulation; the runners, sincere in their appreciation. Italian champion Gelindo Bordin, who won Boston in 1990, called the Boston Marathon his favorite race. "As a total experience, it's unparalleled," Bordin said. "The history behind it; the level of competition; the educated fans; the festivities of the day."

Boston Marathon fans are not only educated on the event and the sport, but also very protective of *their* race. Their attendance is not random; it's not impulsive happenstance that brings them to the side of the road. It's not because they saw helicopters overhead and heard sirens down the way. Boston fans come to view the race because it is a New England rite of passage. A fan that stands on the side of the road quite possibly could be the fourth or fifth generation of that particular family to do so. At that particular race, a fan could be standing with multiple generations, including parents and children.

The Boston Marathon isn't a road race for people with short shorts and sneakers; it's a family heirloom. It's a part of the community's identity. Year after year, decade after decade, generation after generation, families line the streets on both sides. Parents bring their kids out to the course to expose them to a positive and traditional pastime—a baptism in the waters of the Boston Marathon. When one lives in these parts, the Boston Marathon is a part of life. Marathoner Pat Williams is amazed each year to see the same faces in the same spots. He wonders, "Could these families lay claim to a piece of the roadside as a function of squatters' rights?"

New Englanders are traditionalists with parochial allegiance to any possession they perceive as theirs. It's this obsessive ownership and passion that the fans feel toward the race that occasionally causes them to give the impression they are more than just fans.

For months leading up to the race, the locals have been forced into hibernation by the snowy effects of blizzards and storms. Being trapped in the house by the sadistic blasts of a winter *nor'easter* means that by the time Patriots' Day arrives on the calendar, the antidote for cabin fever is the Boston Marathon. It's their race, and no official or member of the constabulary is going to discourage them from participating—although in 1905, the fans were so active along the course that "police tried to keep the interlopers out and made tackles that would do credit to Harvard–Yale football players."

There have been years in the race's history where fan zeal reached epic proportions—to the point that they actually impacted the outcome. Such was the case in the tenth anniversary race, when the *Boston Globe* wrote, "From Coolidge Corner to Massachusetts Avenue, the runners and attendants had to fight their way along practically, for they are mobbed. The police did everything in their power to keep the crowds back, yet each year the conditions become worse."

Keeping the spectators under control and ensuring the runners' access to the course was such a concern that in 1914, the *Globe* released a plea to all fans on the morning of the race: "Whether on foot or in automobile you witness the marathon today, lean backward in showing consideration for the lads in the race." The suggestions went on to read, "Don't slap a tired marathoner on the back. You may mean to encourage him but you really do him harm."

The race is so important to the people of New England that they want to protect its tradition. Just as they are linked to their descendants, they want the current race to be connected to those runs of days gone by. An example of such rigid defense of race tradition occurred in the mid-1980s. It was during this time that there were discussions of corporate sponsors and cash prizes in order to sustain the race and its rising expenses. The very prospect of professional intrusion triggered outrage, especially among the traditionalists. The disdain for the stain upon sports purity manifested itself on the course in 1986. Canadian marathoner Art Boileau was moving toward Boston in second place when a fan darted out of the crowd and began throwing money at him.

The fan base is sincere not only in their love for the race, but in their actual role within it. Words of encouragement, yells of how much farther a runner might have to go, cooling warm runners with garden hoses or slices of oranges—all speaks to the fan's role in the race. This is not a parade that they are passively watching; it's an event in which they are actively participating. From the open bathroom doors in Hopkinton to the screams of "One more mile!" in Kenmore Square, the spectators become part of the race, earning the undying appreciation of the runners.

Four-time women's champ Catherine Ndereba cherished such participation, noting, "Boston is my finest and my favorite milestone. I like the people and the atmosphere down there because they are very friendly . . . the fans are very welcoming."

Of course, some competitors might interpret the passionate involvement of fans as being as obtrusive as the hills on the course. Dick Beardsley, who finished second in the 1982 duel for the ages against Alberto Salazar, appreciated the fans' love of the race, but saw the overzealous as an unwelcome part of the challenge, which ultimately hindered his ability to run. "Boston [fans], they're much louder. They're much closer to the runners. At some points there is a ten-foot space in between two walls of people. You have the sirens, the police for miles. It seemed the noise was unending. It was so loud it hurt your ears."

Whether the marathoners want it or not, this is what Boston is all about. Runners, officials, fans, and the terrain of the city itself—all have a role to play. Every year following the race, the *Boston Globe* is inundated with letters to the editor from runners who are desperate to thank the million-plus fans who lined the course and served as that extra motivation the runners so desperately need in their battle to run Boston. Following the 1967 race, runner Bill Taylor wrote to the *Globe:* "To the people who lined the way from Hopkinton to Boston, for all the refreshments and sincere moral encouragement given all the runners—I was very much impressed, and felt like a hometown boy." This sentiment was echoed in another note to the *Globe* from "Forty Runners from Northern California": "We wish to express our heartfelt thanks to all of you from all of us. You spectators of this race make it what it is, simply the finest race ever . . . Your cheering was an inspiration, to say the least. We couldn't have done it without you."

The mile turns flat and straight as the course moves briefly through a residential neighborhood before creeping past an old burial ground, and then a school on the left. At the next set of lights, marking the Main Street intersection, the runners pass the spot where the old Central House and the Columbia House were located. In the early 1900s, it was at these places of lodging that runners received their physical exam and pre-race meal of steak and eggs. Most didn't finish their plates because of nervous stomachs.

In 1928 seven-time winner Clarence DeMar didn't suffer from that problem. Prior to the race—in which he won his sixth championship—he devoured two prunes, two hard-boiled eggs, oatmeal, two pieces of toast, and a glass of milk. In current days the pre-race meal, compliments of the

BAA, is held the night before on the grounds of Boston City Hall, and the fare is pasta, and more pasta. (The 2013 menu included tomato basil pasta with chicken meatballs and four-cheese lasagna with mushrooms.)

Back in the days when DeMar was winning races and Ashland was the hub of clock-making, the runners would pass the Ashland Clock Tower on their left, later in the mile. This large timepiece was mounted on a commercial building called the Ashland Technology Building. At the top of the structure's face sits a giant clock facing kitty-corner to the race. During the days when there were no clocks along the race course, DeMar used the clock to check his pace early in the race. As the runners pass the clock nowadays, they hardly glance up at the old dinosaur; they all have digital watches and numerous clocks along the route to remind them that they should have trained harder.

Jack Fultz used to take advantage of the tower's timepiece to help him with his splits. During the dark days in which the race administrators lacked proper resources, the racecourse still had no clocks. As result, he used his placement in the race as a timer. He knew that if he was running in the top ten, then his splits were consistent with what he needed to run a good race. It must have worked, as the twenty-seven-year-old took home the wreath in 1976 despite 100-degree heat that had the crowd hosing down the runners to cool them off. The *Boston Globe* called it a "race of attrition," and it became known as the "Run for the Hoses." The *Globe*'s Jerry Nason concluded with a classic understatement: "If you had the choice of a day to run 26 miles, 385 yards, it would not be April 19, 1976."

Continuing down the road, the runners enviously sneak a peek at the Dairy Queen ice-cream shop on the right side of the road. This is one of those spots where you see a complete nutritional polarization between the runners and the spectators, many of the latter apparently regulars at the establishment (although on hot race days, Dairy Queen has been known to see the occasional marathoner at its window).

At the end of the mile, the runners pass Tom's Auto Body on the left. Because the property is raised above the course, the location serves as a perfect vantage point for fans and journalists. In the late 1800s, the Perini family, who are known in New England for owning the Boston Braves and Perini Construction, owned an estate on this site that was the envy of the town. The mansion had a fishpond in the shape of a fish, cathedral windows, and Old Man Perini's favorite toy—a baby grand piano. On spring and summer days, Perini used to enjoy sitting in his house up on the hill with the windows open, treating the town to a piano concerto.

Along with its many other amenities, the Perini estate was the first house in Ashland to have electricity. This blessing proved to be a curse when a nor'easter blew into town. The blizzard, accompanied by blustery winds, ignited a fire at the Perini mansion that burned the estate to the ground. As the old man reviewed the damage, he was overjoyed to find that his pride and joy, the baby grand piano, had survived to be played another day.

The town of Ashland was itself named after a rich country estate. A town incorporator who admired Senator Henry Clay adopted the name "Ashland" from one of Clay's three properties in Kentucky. Previously known as Unionville, Ashland was incorporated in 1846 after acquiring land from the three surrounding towns, including Hopkinton. Ashland is in close proximity to three major thoroughfares, Route 9, the Massachusetts Turnpike, and Route 495. In 1900, the town was occupied by 1,525 residents, and now has over 16,000 Ashlanders. The town stretches thirteen square miles, with more population density than their rival, Hopkinton.

At the end of Mile 4, runners need to remain focused and stay to the right. In the middle of the course there is yet another traffic island rising from the ground, forming the second half of the Three Mile Island sandwich. Runners are relieved to survive this mile, and look forward to the comparatively boring setting of Mile 5.

At this point runners start to gain their stride and stretch it out, glad to be checking Ashland off their list and moving on to Framingham. Any thoughts of stepping off the course and calling it a day at this juncture would raise the ire of the demanding spectators, who won't accept this decision. This sentiment was shared by local marathoner Mark Coogan, who said, "Boston is the only marathon where you can't walk off the course. The fans are going to push you right back out there."

Mile 5

No man is good enough to govern any woman without her consent.
—SUSAN B. ANTHONY

IN THE FIRST STEPS OF MILE 5 THE RUNNERS CONTINUE RIGHT, AS THE traffic island extends from the previous mile into the next one. Beyond the islands, runners can look to the left and see the refreshing sight of Bracket Reservoir, which stretches over the next mile, flowing into the Framingham Reservoir. After the runners slide past the cement protrusion in the middle of the road, the course moves up a hill and to the left.

At 4.2 miles, the road continues to hook left like a John Daly drive. The course leaves Union Street and forks left up a slight incline onto Waverly Street, past Ashland Landscape Supply on the left. In the past, the shopkeepers posted the names of friends and associates running the race on a display board outside. It is here that runners have to shift muscles to work the uphill. The increased exertion begins to warm them as the rising sun causes many to peel off layers and toss their sweatshirts, hats, and gloves into the parking lot.

Back in 1967, on a cool, overcast race day in Ashland, runner #261 decided to leave on a gray sweatshirt. But it wasn't the sweatshirt that was of interest; instead, what was underneath captured the attention of fellow runners, race officials, and the entire sports world. This was the late '60s, and America was in the midst of radical shifts and upheaval. No longer were society's conformities just blindly accepted; change was in the air. The country was losing men in Vietnam, leaders were being assassinated, minorities were standing up for their rights, and women were no longer accepting the imbalance and inequities being presented to them at work,

Jock Semple feels the wrath of Kathy Switzer's running companion, Tom Miller, in the 1967 Boston Marathon as Semple attempts to rip Kathy's number from her Jersey. Women were not allowed to "officially" run the Boston Marathon until 1972. COURTESY OF THE TRUSTEES OF THE BOSTON PUBLIC LIBRARY

home, and even on the sports fields. So as #261 ran under the gray skies of Ashland, it was apparent to all that the first numbered female runner was in their midst.

With the entire country seemingly involved in some form of change or protest that spring, the Boston Marathon was not exempt. Kathy Switzer was not primarily a rebel or a troublemaker, or even a feminist—she was, in her words, an athlete "in pursuit of a goal." Prior to the 1967 race, the college runner had submitted an application for entrance into the historically all-male event as K. V. Switzer. She had come to Hopkinton to challenge herself athletically, just like everyone else. In the process she became the first numbered woman ever to run the Boston Marathon, thus putting the Marathon and the entire sporting world on an irreversible course toward equality. As runner Sara Mae Berman would say some years later, "Women are human beings—not pregnancy machines."

Switzer's run came one year after the trailblazing trek of Roberta Gibb Bingay. In 1966, Bingay was the first female runner to ever run Boston, even though her request for a number had been denied by the BAA, on the grounds that "women were not physiologically capable." Nonetheless, she showed up in Hopkinton in a hooded sweatcoat hiding her black bathing suit, white shorts, and brother's sneakers. Earlier that morning Bingay was conflicted when she left her house in Winchester, just outside of Boston. It was her dream to run Boston, and she knew she could do it; the only question was, would her father, and Boston, *let* her run it?

Earlier in the day, when her dad had discovered her intentions, he'd stormed out of their home, furious, without providing his blessing. Bingay wouldn't be denied, however, and went on to complete the marathon in just over three hours, finishing 124th out of 400 runners that day. When she crossed the finish line, Governor Volpe shook her hand. The BAA, on the other hand, wasn't as congratulatory; they chose to ignore her historical run by casually stating, "Ms. Bingay did not run in the Boston Marathon; she merely ran over the same route as the official race."

In the following day's papers, Bingay was referred to not as athletic, but as "pretty," and "blonde with blue eyes." When reporters asked her father about the landmark achievement, he proclaimed with a change of heart, "Oh, we knew she could do it." This was just hours after he had lambasted her for even trying.

A fellow runner who ran alongside Bingay was an assistant professor of classics at Yale University by the name of Erich Segal. After finishing the race, he was asked by the *Boston Globe* what he thought of Ms. Bingay's run. "For ten miles I saw nothing but those beautiful legs," he said. "I should have asked her to dinner." Erich Segal, who went on to write the hit novel, *Love Story* (turned into an even more famous film), defended a woman's will to run Boston: "If we have to preserve male superiority through legislation, we are in trouble."

The urge to run Boston is a magnetic feeling, felt by many in New England and around the world, and of course, this long included women. Bingay was the first to break that glass ceiling, but the interest from women to run Boston dates back to 1915. In the same year that an initiative to grant women the right to vote was denied by Congress, George Brown of the BAA received a letter from the Boston neighborhood of Hyde Park; the sender "want[ed] to know if ladies are permitted to run in the marathon, and if not, why not? For women now have the same rights as men. If ladies are permitted to run, please set aside a dressing room for them. We are going to run anyway."

Brown stated that they would be able to run, but not with the registered runners; they could start fifteen minutes behind the male runners, along with those that doctors judged not fit to officially compete. "[The BAA] would abide *this* year by the AAU [Amateur Athletic Union] bylaws that still frown upon the entrée of women into general athletics." This indication that Brown would consider such participation in the future turned into fifty-one years of deliberation. Later that week in Dorchester, two women were spotted training in bloomers, blouses, and leather gymnasium shoes.

After Bingay ran in 1966, race administrator Jock Semple—whose wife had divorced him years earlier partly because of his commitment to the Boston Marathon—once again was facing the dangerous crossroads of his race and women. The *Globe* reported, "Jock Semple was in charge of keeping 'babes' off the course." He was later quoted as saying, "They will run over my dead body!"

One year after the historical run by Bingay, Switzer took her spot with the other runners at the start. Race director Will Cloney walked among the competitors to confirm that they were registered. When he reached Switzer, he placed his hand on her shoulder, checked the number on her sweatshirt, and pushed her back behind the snow fence with the other runners. In all the chaos Cloney didn't realize that he had just sent through the first numbered woman ever to run the race.

After the gun was fired, the numbered men and women trotted through Hopkinton and into Ashland. With each step Switzer took toward Boston, word spread like neurons firing to every fiber in the race and back into its history: *There was a woman running Boston with a number.* These neurons soon fired to the brains of Jock Semple and Will Cloney, who immediately sped off in the press bus to stop the renegade.

While the bus caught up to the intruder, five miles into the race, Switzer wasn't concerned about being apprehended; she instead was focused on her own vanity. "I couldn't wait to take off my old gray sweat suit," she said, "and show off the beautiful running suit that I had on underneath. I wanted to prove that a woman athlete didn't need to be masculine or a tomboy, but could be feminine and an athlete."

The year before, Switzer had garnered media attention in an Associated Press story about a woman runner who was competing in the half-mile for the men's track team at Lynchburg College in Virginia. The story stated that the runner had some unusual statistics (34-25-37), and that she was going to play the accordion in the talent portion of the Miss Lynchburg beauty contest later that week. Other interests were listed as tennis, karate, and fencing.

While contemplating the pros and cons of looks versus warmth, Switzer may not have noticed that the flatbed truck carrying the photographers—along with the press bus that also contained the two red-faced race officials—had arrived on the scene. The bus pulled to the side of the road, and Cloney and Semple disembarked, determined to remove the official number that mockingly hung on the front of the genderless sweatshirt.

Little did these defenders of chauvinism know that they would have to get by Switzer's muscle-bound boyfriend, Tom Miller, a collegiate hammer thrower who was running side by side with his girlfriend. Semple got to her first ("Cloney tried to catch her first—he was too bloody slow," Jock later recalled) and yelled for the woman to "get out of my race!" Unaware of Miller's presence, he reached for Switzer and began to pull off the number 261. Instinctively, the runner's boyfriend knocked Semple to the ground, introducing the race official to the brawn he used in the hammer throw, allowing Switzer to escape and proving that chivalry is not dead. Semple later claimed "that he never hit the ground," and that, "if Cloney wasn't so fat and slow he would have been to the girl before I got there and did what I did and then women wouldn't hate me."

With Semple flying through the air, Switzer and her Syracuse posse continued down the course. An enraged Semple would later call the group a "close-knit bunch of scoundrels," stating that the "Syracuse bunch would never run in this race again."

But on that, the scoundrels kept running. The next miles were sad and eerie. "Everyone was silent," Switzer told me. "The only sounds you heard were the quarter-sized snowflakes hitting the leaves of the trees above and the runners' feet pounding the pavement." Switzer did what any focused marathoner would do: She kept putting one foot in front of the other—but in her head she was confused. "I was embarrassed and mortified. I was treated like a common criminal when I was only hoping to run a race," she said. Switzer would finish the marathon that day; in the process, she would change the race—and women's sports—forever.

At the post-race press conference, Cloney and Semple were rabid. "I am surprised that an American girl would do something like this, and go someplace where she wasn't invited," Semple fumed. For her "rogue" run of twenty-six miles, Katherine Switzer was eventually banned from the Amateur Athletic Union (AAU) on the following four counts:

- Running without a chaperone;
- Fraudulent application (Switzer applied for her number using the initials of her first and middle names; 267 out of 700 applicants did the same that year);
- The AAU did not permit women to race distances over one and a half miles; and

In an effort to look both athletic and feminine, Kathy Switzer runs the first 4 miles of the 1972 Boston Marathon in a lovely black-and-white ensemble.

- She ran in an all-male race (although that was not stated on the application).

Forty-eight years after women were granted the right to vote and three decades before Title IX amendments ensured women equal rights in sports, Switzer's run would be both historical and ostracizing. In the end, her run and the picture of the confrontation gave women an irreversible foothold in American sports. Very few, if any, athletic endeavors have had a greater impact on women's efforts for equality in athletics.

Following the race, the fallout was epic. Debates raged at the BAA and in the newspapers. In the *Globe,* sportswriter Bud Collins wrote on behalf of women runners in Boston. "The gals, bless them—let them in," he argued. "The Boston Marathon is Boston's finest sporting event because of its wide-open nature. It's embracing of every man, demented and daring, the heroes and the hopeless."

It wasn't until five years later that the BAA finally relented and allowed women into "their" marathon. The marathon's bylaws now allowed women runners in, but that didn't mean the BAA would commit resources to them. The female contingent found this out in their inaugural race, as they were on their own for timing, splits, and getting soap and towels for their post-race "locker room."

During the 1972 race, Kathy Switzer was determined to win—and look good doing it. Despite the heat, Switzer appeared at the starting line decked out in a beautiful white tennis dress over a black, full-body leotard. After passing the famous location where race officials had accosted her five years earlier, Switzer began to overheat. Desperate, she was forced to run off the course into a gas station, where she grabbed the women's room key and a steak knife that the station gave to customers who purchased a full tank of gas. In the dark gas station bathroom, Switzer began to cut and mend. Some minutes later she emerged with the tennis outfit pinned up—no legs to her leotard, and no socks—and continued on.

Despite the pit stop, Switzer finished third, behind Nina Kuscsik and Elaine Pederson. Kuscsik's win crowned her as the first official female

Kathy Switzer wearing the remodeled tennis outfit in 1972—pinned up, no legs to her leotard and no socks.

winner, with a time of 3:10:26, which placed her 410th out of the field of 1,081 runners.

In all, there were nine women contestants in 1972, including Kathy Switzer and Nina Kuscsik. The women runners were well received by the fans on the sidewalks, from start to finish. Runner Elaine Pederson would later say that the challenge was eased by the crowd's enthusiasm. Four decades later, in 2013, 11,606 women would enter the race, representing 43 percent of the entire field.

The nine ladies went down in Boston Marathon history for their trailblazing runs; they would be joined by the likes of four-time winner Catherine Ndereba and three-time winners Rosa Mota of Portugal; Uta Pippig, a medical student from Germany; and Fatuma Roba of Ethiopia, as the great women runners of the Boston.

After the landmark years of 1966, 1967, and 1972, women's marathoning evolved gradually, until 1984, when two-time Boston Marathon champion Joan Benoit Samuelson captured the hearts of women and men alike with her dramatic gold medal victory in the first-ever women's Olympic Marathon in Los Angeles. During that period, women made up 10.5 percent of all marathoners. Three decades later that number has just about quadrupled for the Boston and New York Marathons, and trends show that the numbers are steadily climbing.

Halfway into Mile 5, up until its end, the course snakes back and forth, left and right, testing the runner's rack-and-pinion steering. In the final steps, there is a mixture of residential, commercial, and undeveloped land. It's too easy to feel indifferent during this stretch, and runners must bear down in order to stay focused. Back in 1907, reports stated that the runners ran into Framingham with dirt up to their ankles. For the first three decades of the race, witnesses would say that the dirt of Ashland would create a human dust bowl, kicking up a cloud that absorbed the runners into its haze. Runners were said to enter Framingham with soiled faces and tired legs.

In the final tenths of the mile, the runners have a chance to genuflect when they pass the Sri Lakshmi Temple at the Framingham-Ashland border. The temple draws Hindus from all over the Northeast. With a mailing list of over eight thousand, worshippers come from as far away as New Jersey to shed their shoes and pay homage. On the temple's magnificent tower, which rises fifty feet into the sky, is a statue of Lakshmi, the goddess of wealth. At her sides are the *dwarapalaka*—the female gatekeepers. It is only fitting that they continue to keep watch at the end of Mile 5, the site of the battle for female equality at Boston.

Mile 6

After the five-mile mark, the runners' brains are busy with calculations as they divide five into their time and then multiply by twenty-six and round up to account for the last 385 yards. The route has been fairly easy to this point, with adrenaline helping runners with their pace for the first thirty to forty-five minutes. By Mile 6, runners should be ahead of their intended splits, both because of the downhills and the early excitement. Runners who are new to the Boston Marathon can easily fool themselves into thinking that they can maintain this pace for twenty-one more miles, but the veterans know all too well that this optimism is off the mark. In fact, more runners than not will see splits trend up as the Newton Hills give way to the Citgo sign in later miles.

The early steps of Framingham offer the runners the first of many tugs-of-war that will happen that day between the mind and the body. They rejoice that they have passed the first real benchmark of the race, but at the same time they realize that they haven't even completed a fifth (a mere 20 percent) of the course. The devil on the runner's left shoulder starts to debate with the angel on the right. With more than twenty-one miles to go, and the easiest part of the course in the past, it takes a calm

73

mind and a well-trained body to take the next step and pretend that the ten-mile mark is just around the corner. Of course, it is not.

During the 1898 race, the *Globe* reported that "Framingham greeted runners with gongs and ringing of bells. The road was dusty from Ashland, causing the runners to run in a cloud." Luckily, the crowds start to increase in size and passion. Five miles into it, the runners are starting to crave the much-needed "Looking good!" or "You can do it!" provided by sidewalk supporters.

At the beginning of the sixth mile, the course moves uphill and to the right before leveling off through a wooded, residential neighborhood. The course then makes its way from residential to commercial. On the left, marathoners may notice diners stepping out of the landmark Italian restaurant LaCantina's (founded the same year Shigeki Tanaka won Boston, in 1951) with meatballs on their forks and *amore* in their heart for the runners.

Two-time Olympic champion Abebe Bikila and fellow Ethiopian Mamo Wolde follow the signs to Boston in 1963. COURTESY OF THE TRUSTEES OF THE BOSTON PUBLIC LIBRARY

After bending right, the runners get a brief respite with a short descent past another commercial area, before another right-hand bend and a slight uphill. Through this section, trees provide some temporary protection from either sun or rain, offering the runners a moment to gather themselves. Up ahead, the increasing noise signals a tumultuous welcome around the corner.

In the last half of the mile, the runners pass over the intersection of Route 135 and Winthrop Street. This area proves to be an ideal viewing area, where fans stand five or six deep to get a look at the competitors, drawing the runners to them like magnets. This is one of the areas on the course where the athletes are greeted like prodigal sons (and daughters), returning home. It's an amazing feeling for both elite runners and ten-minute milers to be celebrated like Tom Brady or Lionel Messi by an adoring crowd.

This crowded intersection tends to put smiles on the runners' faces and reinvigorate their spirits as they continue down the route. As they return salutations, they must pay attention, because the big right turn from a half-mile back is reversed here with a huge left turn that stretches for a tenth of a mile through the intersection. This curve in the road appears to have been molded for the sole purpose of straightening out the marathon course: For the next four miles, the route remains straight and relatively level.

In 1660, the deputy governor of the local colony, Thomas Danforth, Esquire, was compensated for services rendered to the Crown with a grant of 250 acres of land in the western section of the colony. Over the years, he added 15,000 additional acres, which he combined to create Danforth Farms. In 1700, the area was incorporated as the town of Framingham in honor of Danforth's hometown in England, called Framlingham (the "l" was dropped somewhere over the Atlantic Ocean).

Today, Route 135 in Framingham is primarily a commercial area with a scattering of modest homes. In 2013 the average home cost $319,500, in a town that stretches over 26.4 square miles and has a population of 68,318. The town hosts 2.57 miles of the race, or 9.81 percent in total.

It's here—in the third town of the race—that many begin to bid farewell to the runners they befriended back in their corral, at the starting line. After five miles of running and the traffic of competitors starting to spread, runners naturally begin to fall in line with those of similar talents and abilities. It's possible that runners in lockstep in Framingham could still be side by side as they enter the gates of Boston, twenty-plus miles down the road.

It's during these miles of Framingham (and later Natick) that runners began to clique together into groups that match their comfort level. This includes runners who have aspirations of victory. It is at these seemingly irrelevant segments of the course that the seeds of historical challenges are planted. Within this stretch, as the amateurs fade away, the world's greatest runners begin to size up the competition and determine how best to be the one who heroically breaks the tape on Boylston Street.

Within the pack, the elite runners are busy assessing their opponents and calculating strategies. Bill Rodgers used to look forward to this stage of the race to throw a surge at the pack and shake off pretenders. By contrast, some runners like to glide along in the pack and bide their time; the front-runners shield them from the wind and relieve them of the psychological burden of having the lead with so many miles to go.

Amby Burfoot, the 1968 winner, compared the security of the pack to "a comfortable, cozy nest." But Uta Pippig doesn't care whether she runs in a pack or by herself. "I am confident in my abilities and what I can do," she says. "Although, if in a pack, I respect everyone in that group. I feel solidarity with the other runners. I appreciate the physical and emotional investment that they have made in order to run in this race. Although I might not know some of the runners in my pack, I must respect them, because at that moment they are the same distance from the finish line as I am."

While the lead pack is sometimes an amicable group, the 2000 contest between Ethiopian runner Gezahegne Abera and multiple Kenyan runners proved to be more of a border battle than a road race. It was during this race that the usual pack-running tactics, in which the leaders work together to conserve their energy, degenerated into a shoulder-knocking, arm-pushing tussle that sent the Ethiopian tumbling to the ground halfway through Mile 10. As he picked himself up, blood poured from his elbow and leg.

Sixteen miles later, Abera was literally nosed out at the finish line by Kenyan Elijah Lagat, with both runners recording a time of 2:09:47 in the closest finish in the race's history. Following the race, Abera complained that the Kenyan runners (especially Lagat and Moses Tanui, who finished third) had "ganged up" on him, pushing and shoving him throughout the race, and then working together to beat him at the end.

It's here—while appraising other competitors—that the physical joins forces with the cerebral. While the legs beneath the runner turn, the runner himself must switch his or her focus from the road ahead to the runner nearby. This takes insight, deduction, and a keen understanding of the tangible indicators that differentiate between fresh and tired, hunter or hunted. It could be the labored breathing, changes in the pigmentation of the skin, or something as simple as the alteration of one's running form.

In 1903, Sammy Mellor ran up next to Canadian Jack Caffery and used both running skill and gamesmanship to pass him. As the *Globe* reported, "Mellor trotted over to Caffery and eyed him from head to heel. A few sarcastic remarks, and Mellor jumped in front."

Like a duel, the act of competing mano a mano on the streets to Boston is fueled not just by legs but by emotion, manipulation, and, sometimes, intimidation. It was said that during the glory years of the Japanese runners, the 1950s and '60s, that the contingent from the Far East used to run as a group, helping each other to move forward through drafting, encouragement, or shared strategy. This type of communal running was evident if they were running alongside competitors from a different country. It was then that they worked together to eliminate that runner from contention. As a team, they were known to circle the other competitor and force him to run at their pace, in isolation from the freedom of the course. Step by step they would grind the runner down, forcing him outside of his comfort zone and trapping him in their bubble. Eventually, the victim of the Japanese team would be forced to drop back so that he could see the whole course and run at a pace that was agreeable to the bullied runner's capability and strategy.

Gamesmanship and intimidation can also backfire; it depends on the makeup of the runner. Some competitors are fueled by the intensity of the competition—challenges actually help to propel them forward—while others might cower in the safety of trailing runners. Aggressive manipulation is tricky, and it behooves one to know the intended target.

In 1936, in the hills of Newton, defending champion John "The Elder" Kelley had closed a half-mile gap on the leader, Tarzan Brown. Brown, a mercurial sort, was as unpredictable as he was gifted. Depending on the day, a challenge might convince him to quit, while on another day it could cause him to sprint. On this day Kelley moved up to Brown's side, riding the momentum, and tapped him on the shoulder. Kelley told him, "I will take it from here."

This attempt by Kelley to demoralize the Narragansett Indian actually had the reverse effect, serving as *motivation* for the tiring runner and consequently sending Brown on to victory. Whether to run, to bait, or to remain back are all calculations that a potential champion must assess during his or her run. It's not who is the fastest; it's who *gets to Boston* fastest.

Stalking one's prey takes the heart of a lion. To patiently sit in the weeds figuring out exactly when to strike is a skill that separates the hungry from the fed. In 1971, unemployed Colombian Alvaro Mejia ran Boston for the first time. For miles he ran on the back shoulder of pre-race favorite, Pat McMahon. Mejia was unfamiliar with the course, so he decided to allow McMahon to lead the way while he followed. As the trail runner, Mejia could draft off McMahon's experience on the hills and run the tangents for the five corners along the course.

Mile after mile, McMahon anxiously felt his competitor's breath and wondered when Mejia would unveil his 4:04 mile speed. The Irishman knew the outcome was inevitable; he knew he wouldn't be able to outrun his opponent. At one point he was conscious of the fact that there was only chance to claim victory. "Toward the end I figured there was only one way I could beat him—trip him."

McMahon didn't trip him; not exactly. When they took the last corner—just 385 yards from the tape—Mejia reportedly elbowed McMahon into the crowd and sped away, leaving the trailblazer to watch the Colombian run across the line.

It is unnerving to always be the prey. The challenger runs from behind with a clear view of what lies ahead, while the leader runs, wondering not *if,* but *when.*

In 1968, Amby Burfoot ran with the lead but wasn't able to enjoy it. Behind him, the early spring sun was setting in the west. Also behind him was the source of most of his anxiety and fear. "I couldn't see Bill Clark, but I could see his shadow out in front of me," he said. "It was like a ghost or a spirit haunting me. I was trying to get away from this guy. He wasn't there, but his shadow was; I couldn't get away from [it]. I was running to get away from this apparition."

The lead runner has "nothing to fear but fear itself," as FDR once said—that, and of course, the trail runner. Just as Burfoot experienced, trail runners don't even have to be seen—just perceived. It can be the shadow or the source of the shadow. This is the essence of competition: sensing that shadow.

Marathoning is akin to a giant poker game taking place on the streets of Greater Boston; a player endeavors not to fold, but instead to flush his competitor with a full house. The game is full of fake surges, risks, smarts; it's the ultimate battle of wills. Some competitors like to take the measure of their opponent across the felt table, while others would prefer to silently hold their hand and hide their intentions behind mirrored sunglasses. In this game, as well, the stakes are real; the consequences of victory or defeat are significant in both prestige, and—in these days of prize money and sponsorships—lucrative.

In the 1940s, the ace was Gérard Côté. The five-foot-three Canadian won Boston four times during that decade. Having refined his skills as a snowshoe running champion, Côté was bold and brash, never afraid to challenge, annoy, or win. With his two gold-capped teeth, Côté loved to sport a smile of both confidence and insolence. Before one race, he was so sure of himself that he ordered brandy, wine, and cigars to be delivered to his Lenox Hotel room, and then invited the press to his post-race victory party. As he ran the final yards to victory, he looked up at his friends in the window of his room at the Lenox Hotel and gave them the signal to have his beers ready.

In 1948 Côté was thirty-five, and his better days were behind him. His legs were tired, but he still had guile. He spent most of the race running side by side with Tufts University student Ted Vogel. Throughout their run he kept telling Vogel not to worry about him (because he was an old man), but to focus on the runners behind them who were coming up fast.

Running through Wellesley and toward Newton, they continued to run in step with each other. Côté kept assuring Vogel that he (Côté) didn't have much left. But as Boston got closer, Côté turned from supportive older brother into fierce competitor. For miles he had been setting Vogel up; now he was ready to strike.

Côté knew that the legs beside him were younger and faster, but he was a Canadian World War II veteran, and had lived through the heat, sand, and pain of the African campaign; Vogel lived a life of homework, socials, and professors. Côté believed that he would thrive in conflict and Vogel would melt.

As they ran the hills later in the course, Côté went from running side by side to taking position behind Vogel. As they ran, the Canadian would continuously step on the back of Vogel's sneakers. To avoid the annoyance Vogel would change his stride, forcing Côté next to him. Then Côté changed tactics and started to cut back and forth and in front of Vogel, forcing him to stop and alter his strides.

Still neck and neck on the back side of the hills, Côté would take cups of water and toss them over his head, hitting Vogel, gradually sending the college student over the edge. Finally, after passing through Cleveland Circle, Vogel had had enough. He ran up alongside Côté and offered the Canadian runner the opportunity to settle their problem in the middle of Beacon Street. Côté smiled his gold-tooth smile, ignored the offer, and ran on to victory.

The race in 1948 was the personification of the dual challenges of the Boston Marathon: runner versus course, and runner versus runner. Both force athletes to go beyond their limits. This is what draws people to the race—to witness an event that, when it was first run, resulted in the death of a Greek warrior.

When Spyridon Louis won the marathon at the first Olympics in Athens, the crowds were so taken that they showered him with flowers. One year later, when John McDermott won the first Boston Marathon, the fans were so overcome that they carried him around the track on their shoulders. While these runs have their places in history, there was no marathon in the history of the sport that matched the 1982 duel between Alberto Salazar and Dick Beardsley.

In that year's marathon the two runners ran side by side from Hopkinton to Boston, fending off each other, fans, potholes, buses, and policemen. In the end, the two went down as the authors of the greatest race in the history of the Boston Marathon.

What made the contest so special was that there seemed to be no strategy at work—just primal running. As one runner placed his foot down, the other did the same. Step after step after step, each man refused to allow the other to move in front. It was Ali-Frazier on the streets of Boston.

When they came into Wellesley Square, an intoxicated fan took a swing at the runners. His fist barely missed Beardsley and struck Salazar in the stomach, knocking the wind out of him. Salazar regained his breath and continued stride for stride into Kenmore Square. Here another drunken fan grabbed at Beardsley's shirt, impeding his stride yet again. Beardsley shook the fan off just in time to be sideswiped by the press bus, which the runner pounded with his fist in frustration.

Continuing down Commonwealth Avenue with barely a mile to go, Beardsley stepped in a pothole so deep that spectators lost sight of his foot. (This was a blessing in disguise, as it shook out a cramp that Beardsley had been hobbled with for some miles.) Escaping the pothole, he moved onto Hereford Street in pursuit of Salazar, who was in the lead. Beardsley would not only have to catch him but also circumvent the ten motorcycle policemen waging their own battle to get next to the leader. From Hereford to the finish, Beardsley was twice blocked by a motorcycle and was actually hit by one, forcing him to push away the motorcycle and its officer. As they made the turn onto Boylston Street, the crowd was brought to such a fever pitch that television commentators couldn't hear each other, so they all ended up yelling and cheering at the same time. Salazar seemingly had victory in hand only to have Beardsley come back over and over again. Salazar finely went on to win the race by two seconds, with a time of 2:08:52. They turned and hugged and held each other up.

With Mile 6 coming to an end, the seeds of competition are just blooming. The friendly banter that occupied runners in the bucolic environs of Hopkinton is now replaced with steely focus and purposeful adrenaline. Up ahead, a form of transport other than running awaits the runners, and serves as yet another obstacle in the steeplechase of Boston.

Mile 7

You know what the three most exciting sounds in the world are? Anchor chains, plane motors, and train whistles.
—GEORGE BAILEY, *IT's A WONDERFUL LIFE*

IN THE EARLIEST STEPS OF THE SEVENTH MILE, THE COURSE DELIVERS runners to the ten-kilometer demarcation. Many runners take this opportunity to review times on their watches or on course clocks to assess their pace. At this juncture, the route runs straight ahead and flat, allowing the runners to pound the pavement and continue the process of self-examination. If the runner has any ailment or malady at this point in the race, then they are subject to the third town's axiom: "If you're hurting in Framingham, you're dead."

Starting in Ashland: From Metcalf's Mill, down Pleasant Street, across the steam railroad tracks, to the trolley tracks, and then follow the electric line straight through South Framingham.
—FROM THE 1897 *BOSTON GLOBE*'s COVERAGE OF
THE INAUGURAL MARATHON

In the nineteenth century, Framingham became an important railroad hub because of its location halfway between the cities of Boston and Worcester. In 1834, train tracks were laid through South Framingham from Boston because the people on the main stagecoach road (now Route 9) didn't want the dirty, noisy trains chugging past their homes.

Those very train tracks inject themselves into the race, becoming part of the challenge in the race's seventh mile. In the first tenths of Mile 7, runners tend to relax their stride and have begun to run freely when they come upon the first set of dissecting train tracks. These raised rails have been known to cause havoc, and thus runners need to return their focus to DEFCON 1—highest alert. Runners, and especially wheelchair competitors, need to maneuver carefully to ensure that they hit the tracks either to the left or to the right, as the rails crown in the middle.

Most veterans of the race are aware of the rise and act accordingly, while some hit the tracks aggressively, like Jim Knaub, who approaches them with one mind-set: "Just hit them and hope for the best. It's either your day or it isn't." This strategy of attack can have consequences, however, as two-time men's wheelchair champion and pre-race favorite Andre Viger discovered in 1988. While rolling with the lead, Andre rotated over the protruding tracks at full speed and suffered a flat tire. By the time he was able to mend the damage, he had lost contact with the lead pack, along with the comfort of drafting with the leaders. His lead disintegrated into an eventual sixth-place finish, costing him money, glory, and one tire.

On the left side at the 6.2-mile mark is the old Framingham train depot. The building was designed by H. H. Richardson in 1883, and built according to his "Richardsonian Romanesque" preference at a cost of $62,718, the equivalent of $1,458,558 today. Richardson is the same architect who was responsible for Boston landmark Trinity Church, with his trademark "massive stone walls and dramatic semicircular arches," which stands just yards from the race's finish line. The train station is still functioning, and houses both a depot and a popular restaurant destination. Like TJ's in Ashland, the bar hosts a loud and festive Marathon party that spills out into the street. Its very presence teases runners, as the smell of barbecued ribs crosses over the route while the DJ cranks tunes that turn coeds into drinking, dancing partiers. The runner, however, is left to dance his or her own dance, with no partner and no beer.

In the nineteenth century, six train routes used to run through this bustling station, moving west to Worcester and east to Boston. In 1885, the station received and dispersed over a hundred trains a day. These days, the tracks mostly carry commuters into Boston, with newspapers in hand and dreams of five o'clock on their mind. Years before, the station served as a launch for the soldiers from nearby Camp Dewey as they went off to

Gérard Côté (left) and Tarzan Brown battle for the lead as they pass the Framingham train station in 1939.

fight in the Spanish-American War, World War I, and World War II. At this very platform, mothers, wives, and children stood with tears in their eyes and waved good-bye, praying that someday the train would return, carrying their loved ones once again.

The train station not only serves as an emotional landmark, but it was also designated as one of the race's checkpoints despite its unconventional location in the race. Checkpoint locations were originally selected for officials' easy access and to provide watering holes for the attendants' and spectators' horses. Officials would take the train from Boston out to Framingham to oversee the race and place checkmarks next to the names and numbers of runners. After the last competitor passed, officials could jump back on the train and arrive in Boston fifty-five minutes later for the finish, and the first bowls of beef stew.

Runners came to despise the odd placement of checkpoints because it made it difficult for them to calculate split times and keep track of their pace, but the BAA and race traditionalists defended them for their historical significance. It wasn't until 1983 that runners won the battle of common sense over tradition, and the checkpoints were moved to mile marks and at kilometer intervals.

In 1959, John "Jock" Semple was one of these administrators, and, as was typical, the hot-tempered Scot with a shrill brogue overstepped his authority in an effort to sustain the race's integrity. He was tracking runners as they passed when an incident of jocularity almost landed the BAA race official in jail. While placing a check next to the name of a runner that was moving past, Semple was infuriated to see a spectator wearing a mask and clown shoes run out of the crowd, drawing laughs from both the masses and the runners. Enraged at the "blasphemy," Semple leapt at the individual, grabbing the mask but missing the clown. Semple rolled into the gutter with mask in hand while the clown ran down Route 135, clomping his giant shoes to the delight of onlookers. A policeman approached the red-faced race director lying on the ground with the intention of arresting him for assault, but was persuaded against it.

Jock Semple did more to give color and identity to the Boston Marathon than any other individual in the hundred-plus-year history of the race. Born in Glasgow, Scotland, the raging Scot traveled across the sea to Philadelphia at age eighteen. In 1929, Semple hitchhiked to Boston to run in the world-famous marathon. He ran that year, and eighteen more times, finishing in the top ten six times (his personal record was 2:44:29).

Eventually Semple traded Philadelphia for Boston and joined the BAA. The marriage between Semple, who would become known as the cardinal of the race, and the Boston Marathon was a special union. Semple treated the race as a classroom and the runners as its students. He demanded that the pupils be attentive and respectful, but when he spoke, his cantankerous demeanor was more scolding than educational. Whenever a potential runner requested an application to run in the race, Semple was known to loudly demand: "Are you *sure* you can run twenty-six miles?" Runner Ken Parker of Canada looked forward to being yelled at as almost part of the experience. "It was an honor to be yelled at by Mr. Semple," Parker said.

Jock passionately administered the race from 1947 to 1982. And though he will be most remembered for his failed extrication of Kathy Switzer, the race wouldn't be the premier event it is today without his contributions. Jock died in 1988 at the age of eighty-four, but many swear that they can still hear the echoes of his abrasive brogue back in Hopkinton, commanding that the runners adhere to protocol, run with honor, and conduct themselves with dignity.

❧

Validating the premise that no mile is irrelevant in the Boston Marathon, it was in Mile 7 that a runner once made the greatest game-changing move in the race's history: In 1911 a Native American from Canada made a bold move and barely made a train.

Thomas Longboat was an Onondaga Indian from Ontario, Canada. He was a world-class runner known to disrespect his gift, as was evident in his training habits—or lack thereof. Instead of nurturing his talent, he lived a life of sloth. In an article written in the *Cincinnati Enquirer,* his habits were chronicled. "During what is supposed to be his training time," the reporter noted, "the Indian smokes six to eight black cigars a day and drinks all the liquor he sees fit."

When Longboat arrived at the starting line earlier in the day for the 1911 Boston Marathon, he was afflicted with tuberculosis, but he convinced the doctor performing pre-race physicals that he was healthy enough to run. The doctor relented and allowed him to toe the line.

One hundred and fourteen runners stood on the starting line that day, and though it was spring, brutal winter conditions greeted the runners. At the sound of the gun, the runners moved as one—as though running together would shield them from the slippery sleet and painful winds. As they ran through Ashland into Framingham, the runners dipped their heads, setting their eyes upon the mud and dirt in front of their feet. With heads down, the athletes focused on their form and dreamt of warmth. Except one—Thomas Longboat.

Simply on talent alone, a sickly Longboat was able to run within the collective pod of the lead pack. As the leaders ran through Framingham, most runners had their heads down, perhaps dreaming of a hot toddy or a warm bath, but Longboat picked up his head and eyed a train that appeared to be switching tracks. As he ran further, he realized that the freighter train that had been moving parallel to the course was now working itself across the route. In an instant, Longboat decided to make a run for it and attempt to beat the train. In full sprint, Longboat sacrificed his legs and wind; with nineteen miles still to run, if he could beat the train, he knew the race would be his. If he didn't make it, he would have expended significant fuel and would most likely waste away on the course's later hills—or perhaps even be hit by the train. The sprint was more than one hundred yards, prompting one of his competitors to mock, "That crazy Indian; he won't finish the race."

When Longboat arrived at the tracks, witnesses reported that the locomotive had beaten the Indian and the trailing cars were now blocking the course. Not discouraged, Longboat searched each car until he found an open door. He then jumped into the car and out the other side.

Decades later, in 1973, marathon spectator Harry Augusto, who had witnessed the event, recalled the bold maneuver: "I was fourteen at the time, and the fact that I saw Tom do this has always stayed with me. I was amazed he took the chance he did."

Longboat was now the only runner on the Boston side of the train; on the other side of the tracks stood 113 impatient challengers, including the two pre-race favorites. Frustrated and stiff, Longboat's competitors were forced to wait for the train to pass while the Canadian took advantage of his good fortune (and brave move) and ran through the day's snow to the finish line.

The *Globe* wrote the following day, "Longboat's victory makes him the greatest of marathon runners. It is the more extraordinary that he competed with 101 white men, [only] 52 of whom finished. The Redman never has been the equal of the Caucasian in physical strength or endurance, and Longboat, lean and lithe, is the rare exception of his race."

Such insensitive references to nationalities or race weren't uncommon for the time. What was acceptable in print or word was much different back then—a time that included casual references to "Redmen," "Japs," and "Krauts." It wasn't until the 1960s that societal norms compelled writers to be more sensitive in communicating runners' origins or heritage.

Throughout the history of the race, obstacles along the course have inhibited runners and added to the challenge. In a review of the 1911 race, BAA officials were not only conscious of the train's role in the race's outcome but also observed that those who were riding horses to view the race had shown cruelty to their transport. In response, police were asked to give "special attention [to] reckless drivers of carriages who beat their horses to make them keep up."

Demands upon the horse were excessive, as riders were challenged to secure the same vantage point that they had been granted in past races. But 1911 was also the beginning of something else on the road with superior speed, protection from the elements, and durability—the automobile.

The evolution of the car was advancing so fast in the first part of the century that by 1911, it was being introduced into mainstream society. The Boston Marathon, with its 100,000 fans, was the perfect forum in which to publicize the automobile, with the race serving as a virtual commercial for the product. "The thousands of spectators were impressed by motor cars," the next day's *Globe* noted. "[It was as] great a day for the cars nearly as for the runners."

It was inevitable that this toy of the affluent would become more than just a curiosity. By 1914, cars were so prevalent that on race day, runners were less worried about horse droppings and more concerned with the choking fumes as they navigated past the new machines. The fact that runners now had to worry about being run over only added to the difficulty of the marathon experience. The traffic and hindrance posed by automobiles was so suffocating for the competitors in 1914 that the infuriated Massachusetts lieutenant governor, Edward Barry, threatened to propose legislation that would make the race a ward of the state, thus allowing him to forbid cars from the course.

Such efforts to police the automobile traffic were futile; cars remained on the course at the peril of runners. In 1923, Clarence DeMar was hit by a car in Coolidge Corner; Tarzan Brown in 1936 and Stylianos Kyriakides in 1946 were both almost killed by cars while in the lead, almost costing them their historical runs. In 1938 five reporters were traveling in a car at such a reckless pace, trying to stay with the leaders that their car flipped over, almost killing them. (They later showed up at the finish line looking like battle-wearied soldiers.) In 1940, fan Katherine Sullivan was hit by a car, thrown into a tree, and administered last rites. She would be rushed to the hospital where she would recover. Automobiles were so prevalent on the course that the spectators had trouble seeing the runners because of the "blue and black cloud from the autos' oil and smoke." In fact, in 1946, there were so many cars on the course that the fans couldn't see the runners at all, their vision impeded by the cars, including those driven by BAA officials. Fans were so frustrated and outraged by this violation that they dubbed that year's race "The Marathon Nobody Witnessed."

Throughout the history of the race, various forms of interference have added to the challenge of an already-difficult course. While horses, cars, and trains played a significant role in the race's history in the first half of the century, the 1940s and '50s were the decades of the dog.

In 1947, South Korean Suh Yun-Bok was running with the lead through Newton when a fox terrier ran onto the course and knocked him to the ground, ripping skin from his legs and laces from his sneaker. Suh was so shocked that when he stood up, he experienced a rush of adrenaline—and despite his flailing shoelace and bloody legs, he ran on to victory.

Fourteen years later, a dog once again interfered with the leaders, this time costing an American the championship. For ten miles into Newton Lower Falls a rogue black dog had stalked leaders Fred Norris, John "The Younger" Kelley, and Eino Oksanen. For some reason it was in the depths of Newton that the dog decided to jet across the course at the three runners. Oksanen was quick enough to avoid the canine, but not Kelley, who was knocked to the ground. As Kelley lay bloodied and upset, the trailing media bus was now driving directly toward the fallen runner. With Kelley in peril, fellow leader Fred Norris of England stopped, grabbed Kelley, and pulled him to safety. The lost valuable seconds cost both Kelley and Norris, and Oksanen ran on to victory.

Local sports writer Bud Gillooly would write that the dog was a "son of a bitch," while writer Harold Kaese supposed that the mystery dog, who aided Finland's Oksanen, had "boarded a Finnish freighter disguised as a submarine sandwich."

Clarence DeMar once had to "dropkick a dog" in Natick, while in 1962, former champion Paavo Kotila was forced to spend energies searching for a stick on the hills of Commonwealth Avenue to fend off a dog that had been stalking him for more than three miles.

It was incidents such as these that compelled the BAA to take action once again in a desperate effort to protect the runners. Administrators of the race begged dog owners to leash their dogs until the race's conclusion, while a mobile MSPCA (Massachusetts Society for the Prevention of Cruelty to Animals) contingent traveled the course, looking for dogs to incarcerate. Dogs became less of a problem after this, although, sadly, dogs would again become a part of the race decades later because of their bomb-sniffing abilities.

❧

Challenges that went beyond the running itself have forever been woven into the fabric of the Boston Marathon. In 1938, with twenty-four miles to go, a motorcycle crashed into runner Leo Girard, injuring both of his knees. After receiving medical care for his badly cut knees, elbows, and shoulder, Girard jumped back in the race and climbed into ninth position, before falling back and finishing fifteenth. In 1947, during the twenty-first mile, Lloyd Barstown was knocked out of the race—while in third place—when he was run over by a bike. In 1978, champion Jack Fultz was run off the course by the media bus.

But no runner in the history of the race had a more challenging journey in running Boston than Sunita Williams did, in 2007.

Sunita Williams had looked forward to running Boston ever since qualifying for the race at the Houston Marathon. She had circled Patriots'

Day on her calendar, with plans to be standing on the starting line—but only if she could get out of work. Sadly, astronaut Captain Williams's stay on the space station was extended, forcing her to forgo her Hopkinton visit.

Determined, the forty-one-year-old Sunita decided to run twenty-six miles from 220 miles away. With sneakers on and a harness attached to keep her on her treadmill, she ran with the bib number 4,000, finishing in four hours and twenty-four minutes. Writer Aly Adair noted that while she ran, the space station orbited the Earth three times, roughly 76,000 miles.

The rest of the seventh mile carries on along the same plateau. The route is almost completely commercial here. At the 6.8-mile mark, the runners again have to cross train tracks; of the three sets of tracks, these are by far the most treacherous. Even cars move to the right as they proceed over them.

On the left side of the course, over the tracks, are the remains of the brick factory of E. W. Dennison. In 1897, Dennison moved his gum label and box factory from Roxbury to South Framingham. The factory, which employed over two thousand workers, was world-famous for baggage labels. The skeletons of the old factories make this section somewhat haunting, but the runners appreciate this stretch for the level topography and the helpful tailwind that traditionally blows here. The latter allows wheelchair racers to sit up from their aerodynamic crouches and enjoy the ambience of the course and the support of the spectators.

Edgar Allen Poe once wrote, "Never to suffer would never to have been blessed." The soul and glory of running Boston comes not in the smooth miles on the course but in the hills, train tracks, potholes, and dogs. The torment along the way allows the earnest runner to look back at the course from the finish line and feel that he or she has traversed something enormous.

With Framingham coming to an end, Pat Williams always says to himself, "Just make it to Natick."

Mile 8

I would prefer even to fail with honor than win by cheating.
—Sophocles

Mile 8 begins on a level and straight road with the Boston-Framingham train tracks on the left, running parallel to the race route. In the old days, spectators could watch virtually the entire race by boarding the local train to Boston and securing a seat on the right side of the car where they could peer out the window, their view broken only by the occasional horse-drawn carriage parked on the side of the road. These days, so many trains clog the tracks from Framingham to Boston that the runners move much more efficiently than the trains do, leaving the trains—forced to wait for switches and stops—behind.

The eighth mile is mostly wooded, with an occasional house, vacant lot, or business. After flat running over the first four-tenths of the mile, the runners are confronted with a little tester of a hill that stretches a tenth of a mile. Greg Meyer, the 1983 winner, points to this hill as a spot in the race where runners can assess their condition: "You'll have a good idea at this point if it is your day or not. This incline certainly makes an impression on the runners." Some know this slight rise as "Heartburn Hill" (not to be confused with the more treacherous Heart*break* Hill later in the course).

Up the hill and down, the runners pass the halfway mark of the mile and run into the town of Natick, the fourth town on the route, which hosts 16 percent of the course. The town of Natick covers just over sixteen square miles in area. Its population, just over 33,000, is almost doubled on race day; the marathon essentially consumes the town.

Natick is an Indian word meaning "place of hills." Native Americans settled in this area in 1651 with the help of Puritan missionary John Eliot, who was known as the "Apostle to the Indians." Over the ensuing years, the Indians built a prospering town here while Eliot preached to them. In 1675, during King Philip's War, English settlers took the village by force, laying claim to the attractive area. They then shipped the "Praying Indians" to Deer Island in Boston Harbor out of fear of retaliation. Many Native Americans died from illness and starvation on the barren and exposed island.

It's out in the woods of the Natick suburbs that the runners have swum far enough from shore that their fluid stroke may turn into a thrashing tread. In Natick, the athlete is far from the glare of Hopkinton and miles from the spotlight of Boston. For some, the insecurity begins to take residence in their consciousness around now. It's at this point that the fragile ones are susceptible to moments of weakness—in both body and mind.

For those who allow doubt to creep in, a choice presents itself. Whether out of a desire for personal gain, a fear of failure, or embarrassment at failing one's supporters, some runners choose the easy (and shorter) path of deception. Runners who cheat the race and insult the marathon's long-standing integrity—and the noble run of Pheidippides—are part of the race's history. The Boston Marathon, like all of society's institutions, is not immune to deceit and fraud.

The first documented deception at the Boston Marathon occurred in the 1909 race. It was in Mile 8 that Howard Pearce, seemingly unnoticed, and believing that he was hidden from scrutiny, decided to stop running. He climbed into a carriage and was chauffeured into Boston, eighteen miles down the road. When he arrived in the city, he disembarked from his transport and picked up his run. As he approached the finish line, Sergeant Crowley of the Boston police—alerted to the runner's fraud by judges of the race who yelled to the police through their megaphone to stop him—blocked him from experiencing the glory of crossing the line, pulling him from the course as only a Boston policeman can.

Pearce's attempt at Boston followed the controversial 1904 Olympic marathon in St. Louis five years earlier. American Fred Lorz was overcome by cramping in Mile 15 and was forced to surrender his Olympic dream. Dragged off the course, he was carried to the last mile by vehicle. Fully recovered, he emerged from the carriage and ran the final steps, breaking the tape as the apparent victor. The very site of an American claiming victory brought the home crowd to a state of delirium. After crossing the finish line, he was whisked over to Theodore Roosevelt's twenty-year-old daughter, Alice, who placed the laurel wreath on his head. As Alice prepared to present him with the gold medal, it was discovered that he had failed to complete the course, and he was immediately disqualified. Deafening cheers turned to shouts of disapproval and disgust.

Seven years after Pearce's attempt at unearned glory at Boston, A. F. Merchant claimed fifth in the 1916 race, only to be later stripped of his credit when a Boy Scout along the course, who was serving as an attendant, reported that Merchant had actually left the course and traveled to Boston by alternative means. The accused vehemently denied the allegation, only to have the boy's story validated by another runner.

As the years passed, the temptation to cheat still hovered over the population of marathon runners. In 1979, Oscar Miranda ran a record Masters time of 2:16, only to find out that he wasn't identified at any checkpoints. His explanation—that he ran with his shirt off, where his number was attached—was disproven and he was disqualified. So was the married couple, Suzanne and John Murphy, in 1997; they both failed to show up on surveillance cameras situated at checkpoints along the course. Both had won their age group and improved their personal records. In all, sixteen runners were washed from the record books that year.

~~~

While Fred Lorz's prank at the Olympics was egregious and other disqualified runs were shameful, the runs of wheelchair competitors Kevin Smith and Jennifer Brown in 2000 were simply reprehensible. After finishing the race it was discovered that they were not disabled at all; instead, they were able-bodied "competitors." They claimed that they had done this before, back home in Canada, in an act of camaraderie with Kevin's disabled brother, Kelley. Their act compelled the BAA to add words to their application that had once seemed self-evident: "Able-bodied individuals may not participate in the Wheelchair Division."

These moments of deceit are part of the history of the race. But no fictional run is more infamous than Rosie Ruiz's in 1980. Ruiz—born Maria Rosales in Havana, Cuba, before resettling in New York City—chose marathoning (or the *appearance* of marathoning) as a vehicle to bring attention to herself. After obtaining New York City Marathon credentials through fraudulent means, she convinced her boss to pay her way to the Boston Marathon, for which she had secured an official number.

In Hopkinton, she started the race with the other competitors, only to peel off the course soon after. She reentered just past Kenmore Square, a mere one mile from the finish line. It was from there that she dashed to the finish line, crossing with a time of 2:31. It would have been the third-fastest female time in Boston history—if it were real.

All along the course, people told Canadian runner Jacqueline Gareau that she was running in first. Even television commentator Kathy Switzer, who was following the women's race in the media truck, yelled to Gareau close to the twenty-two-mile mark, "You're in the lead!" When Gareau turned onto Boylston Street, just yards from her greatest moment, she was shocked to hear the announcer refer to her over the PA system as the second-place female runner. But how could this be? No one had ever heard of Rosie Ruiz.

Bill Rodgers asked Ruiz on the podium, "How are you? *Who* are you?" Her scam was eventually exposed: Ruiz had not been spotted at any of the checkpoints; two Harvard students saw her jump back in the race at Kenmore Square; her shirt was almost dry at the finish; and her knowledge of running was elementary. At the press conference, analyst Kathy Switzer grilled her on topics such as intervals and training. Ruiz was vague and unresponsive. She was eventually stripped of the championship, but she refused to return the winner's medal.

Ruiz remained true to her conviction that she did not cheat. The BAA and the *New York Daily News* both offered her an opportunity to prove that she was capable of such a feat. The BAA offered her a number for the following year's race, while the newspaper pledged to pay her $1,500 if she could come within thirty minutes of her purported time from 1980. Both offers were declined, leaving Rosie with both a wreath and a ring of doubt that would circle her indefinitely. Her name would forever be synonymous with cheating and the Boston Marathon. Bill Rodgers would later say, "Think of the most famous marathon runners—Pheidippides and Rosie Ruiz—one dropped dead, and the other was crazy."

Jacqueline Gareau, who had been cheated of her championship glory, flew in from Canada a week later and ran the final two hundred yards in a pair of jeans. Two hundred people cheered her on; afterwards, Bill Rodgers held her arm up in victory. Later, she visited the Eliot Lounge, where Tommy Leonard was ready for her with a bottle of Dom Pérignon on ice and the Canadian flag flying solo over the bar. When she walked in, one of the bar patrons got on the piano and played her country's national anthem, "O Canada." Leonard later said, "There wasn't a dry eye in the house."

The cheating that goes on in the Boston Marathon is further proof that the race is subject to all of society's shortcomings, vulnerable to the seedy side of the world that orbits around it. The Boston Marathon community respects the efforts of the competitors; they show up and cheer out of respect for the difficult feat being performed by the runners. The runs of Ruiz, the Murphys, and other cheaters are aberrations. They insult Boston, its history, and its people. As Henry David Thoreau wrote, "Rather than love, than money, than fame, give me truth."

At the end of Mile 8, the skyline of Boston is still just a dream to the runners, a mirage in the desert—but every step brings them closer to the City upon the Hill.

Mile 9

And if I really wanted to understand the Rarámuri, I should have been there when this ninety-five-year-old man came hiking twenty-five miles over the mountain. Know why he could do it? Because no one ever told him he couldn't. No one ever told him he oughta be off dying somewhere in an old age home. You live up to your own expectations, man.

—Christopher McDougall,
Born to Run: A Hidden Tribe, Superathletes, and the Greatest Race the World Has Never Seen

For the previous three miles, the runners have been treated to a pancake-flat course, allowing them to settle into a consistent pace with limited downshifting or upshifting. Mile 9, on the other hand, hits the runner like a sneaky uppercut. The mile starts on the crown of an incline only to dip before jumping up again. There are inclines at the beginning and again toward the end of the mile. Here the route passes by a combination of commercial enterprises on the left and wooded lots and a residential stretch on the right.

For the wheelchair competitors and hand cyclists, it's between Miles 6 and 11 where the game of cat and mouse is played out. Drafting and false surges are all part of competitors' strategies that are played out between Hopkinton and Boston.

The history of runners with disabilities participating in Boston dates back to 1906, when Sam Pavitt ran the first of his ten marathons. Although the participation of disabled runners didn't capture the attention of the marathon community until 1916, it was prior to that year's running that the *Boston Globe* titled a pre-race article TWO DEAF-MUTES IN THE MARATHON.

Back in March of that year, applicant Harold Parker was the first runner to petition the BAA for a number to run. Parker was confident in his abilities and his will to compete, despite being hearing impaired. When race administrator George Brown simply asked Parker, "Can you run the race?," Parker responded with the answer of a champion: "Yes, I will do it if I have sunshine heat over my face, cold water, lemon, sponge." He continued, "I ought to be a good sport around the world. I told my folks and they will hope."

When Brown asked further, "Why do you want to run in the BAA race?," Parker replied, "Because I shall win!" Parker would go on to run Boston in 1916 and in the future. In 1919, he would break three hours, and finish fourteenth.

This is the essence of Boston: a commitment to accept the responsibility to honor the Greek hero of centuries past; to run in the footprints of those who passed these miles before; to respect the challenge with passion and great sincerity. Ever since Harold Parker and Sam Pavitt ran Boston, it has been apparent that it's not the consistency of the human anatomy that qualifies a runner to run Boston, but instead the strength of the single muscle that pounds within the chest.

> When can their glory fade?
> O the wild charge they made!
> All the world wondered.
> Honor the charge they made,
> Honor the Light Brigade,
> Noble six hundred.

In "The Charge of the Light Brigade," brought to life in the words of Alfred, Lord Tennyson, it was the troops' belief in their purpose and their unconditional commitment to the cause that propelled them forward. Runners run because it is in their blood to run. They run because they must. They run not because they are the same as everyone else, but because they are not. Runners are different by nature. They represent a minority, and exist within a community of unlike parts but similar hearts.

Runners with disabilities have shown up on the starting line of Boston for decades, determined to run because their pounding compasses told them to. In 1929, visually impaired runner Manny Costa ran Boston; Al Ventrilo did it in 1969 with the aid of a guide runner, while his seeing-eye dog waited for him at the finish line.

To run Boston, one doesn't need legs or vision or hearing or other conformities. Instead, the only requirement needed to conquer the twenty-six miles of Boston is *the will to do so.* This premise—that the power of the human will is capable of delivering a runner to Boston—was personified best in 1970, when Eugene Roberts positioned himself on the starting line.

Roberts returned from Vietnam with two things: a Purple Heart, and the inability to walk. After stepping on a land mine, which killed five men from his company, Roberts returned to the United States a changed man, but determined to show that he was still the same. He came to Boston that year, choosing the Marathon as the forum to prove that he would not be hindered by physical limitations.

In preparation for the race, Roberts practiced both pushing in his hospital wheelchair and hand-jockeying (using his two hands as crutches and pulling the body forward) to figure out which approach would be more efficient. Before the gun sounded, Eugene had only completed three miles in training by hand-jockeying and just one mile by wheelchair. Roberts and his brother decided on the wheelchair; they ended up making history, becoming part of the legacy of the Boston Marathon and stirring countless fans along the route to tears.

Four hours into their run, after climbing up Heartbreak Hill and arriving at Boston College, the shadows of Boston's skyscrapers lay just around the corner. On the sidewalk, students from the Heights of Boston College were so moved by his effort that they decided to join him for the final miles.

Some five miles later, Eugene became the first wheelchair athlete ever to complete the Boston Marathon. In just over seven hours, the Baltimore native finished the race by getting down out of his chair and using his two hands to pull himself across the line. Alongside the courageous warrior were his brother and the crowd of Boston College Eagles, who had joined them in a chorus of "Praise the Lord!" as they covered the last mile.

It was no longer about what was seemingly impossible but about what was literally possible. It was for this very same reason that wheelchair-bound Bob Hall challenged the BAA five years later with the proposition to formally consider him a runner and be presented a medal. "If I finish the race in less than three hours, will you recognize my run?"

No BAA official was confronted with—and ushered in more change—than race organizer Will Cloney. Granted, sometimes he did so with great reluctance, but, like the world of which he was a product, he eventually acquiesced to the flow of history and the push to reshape the race. So when Hall ran the race in 2:57, he was presented with a BAA medal and in turn catapulted the wheelchair competition into the mainstream of running.

Two years later, the *Boston Globe* would write (using the language of the times), "[C]rippled contestants will join the race and will start fifteen minutes early." Race director Will Cloney commented on the milestone addition to the event: "I'm trying an experiment. I figure this is a community event, and I'm softhearted. Covering a course in a wheelchair isn't running a marathon, but they're so ambitious—so dedicated."

Four decades later, athletes with disabilities have become an integral part of the race, with four distinct categories within this field:

- push-rim wheelchair
- visually impaired
- mobility impaired
- hand cycle

In the 1980s and early '90s, Jim Knaub of California was the king of the road in this division, with five championships. His approach of attack—going for broke on every piece of the course—made him a favorite of Boston. Knaub's philosophy is to always be moving on to his next challenge, his next victory. As proof of this, whenever he wins a race, he always finds a child in the crowd to hand his trophy to; to him, an award is a way of looking back. Knaub looks at the race not as an athletic event over roads and bridges, but instead, a spiritual experience over something much bigger. "The Boston Marathon is a race that is not competed against other athletes but raced against a supreme being," he said. "The Boston Marathon is bigger than life. It's a feeling like no other."

Along with Jim Knaub, two other male wheelchair greats form a triumvirate of dominance: Ernst van Dyk of South Africa, who owns the Boston Marathon record of nine championships, winning them all in a span of only ten years, from 2001 to 2010, like Bill Russell's Boston Celtics in the 1960s; and Franz Nietlispach of Switzerland, who has five Bostons to go along with his amazing fourteen gold medals in the Paralympics.

The Boston course presents unique challenges for wheelchair competitors. Besides the exhausting distance, there are significant impediments between the start and finish that wheelchair competitors must be conscious of, including potholes, manhole covers, uneven pavement, and train tracks. The course is always ready to show its teeth to the competitors, warning them not to lose focus—*never* to lose focus.

For wheelchair competitors, the risk of the course's many obstacles is magnified by the fact that they can reach speeds of forty miles per hour. They spin at such an aggressive pace that injury and accident are always a threat.

In 1987, Jim Knaub hit a groove in the road at thirty-five miles per hour, knocking his wheel off and causing the infamous pileup at the start that year. In 1979 Cindy Patton crashed flying down the black diamond hill into Newton Lower Falls and was taken to the hospital, in critical condition, later to recover. In 1989, Pat Holley rolled over a sewer cover in Kenmore Square and was flipped, landing on his side and breaking his shoulder. In 2003, Krige Schabort couldn't avoid a seven-year-old who ran onto the course, sending the child to the hospital.

But despite the risk of injury that all athletes face, eight-time women's wheelchair winner Jean Driscoll approaches the race with the strategy that the best defense is a good offense. She takes advantage of the flat miles into Natick to soften up her competitors. When it's her turn to lead, she aggressively picks up the pace, forcing other members of the lead pack to push their limits to stay in contact—which may cost them dearly on the infamous hills ten miles down the road.

Jean Driscoll broke Clarence DeMar's record of seven championships in 2000, with her eighth championship in eleven years. After winning her seventh, it would take three exhausting—but memorable—duels with friendly rival Louise Sauvage (who has four championships of her own) to finally capture her eighth laurel wreath and make history. She holds the Boston Marathon course record, 1:34:22, which she set in 1994.

Jean sees Boston as the ultimate event—"Bigger than the Olympics!"—and thus treated the training like it was a religion. Every year she began her training regimen at the University of Illinois (a trailblazing institution in the study and training of disabled athletes). It was there that Jean pushed herself to improve the ever-important strength-to-weight ratio, which calculates how well a person pulls his or her own body mass. While preparing for the 1996 marathon, the 112-pound champion bench-pressed 200 pounds. This strength gave her the physical and mental ability to attack the hills instead of fearing them. Two weeks before the race, Jean would travel to the south shore of Massachusetts to train on the area's hills.

After claiming one of her eight championships, Jean was invited to run with President Clinton. During the run, the president from Arkansas remarked, "You have the best-looking arms in America."

❦

As the runners continue through Mile 9, they run past an auto dealership now named Chambers Motorcars of Natick. Traditionally, employees and their families have been treated to a barbecue on race day, causing pungent smells to waft across the course and over the runners.

Throughout the course, on sidewalks and in front yards, and even sometimes up in trees, fans gather to watch the race, welcome spring, and share a day of community. For years, spectators have cheered the leaders, encouraged those behind, and wished all well. But over the history of the race, certain runners have captured the attention and hearts of all those who watch. In the early days, "Old" Pete Foley ran into his seventies, against doctor's orders and the BAA's permission. The crowd stood and waited and cheered loudest for Foley, as they did for Clarence DeMar and John "The Elder" Kelley in their formative years.

Team Hoyt: The father and son team of Dick and Rick Hoyt inspire all who witness their quest to meet the challenge. PHOTO COURTESY OF THE *BOSTON HERALD*

But in all the history of the race, no runners have captured the hearts of those who love the Boston Marathon more than the tandem of Rick and Dick Hoyt.

Team Hoyt is a father-and-son team that has become one of the most inspiring stories in the history of the Boston Marathon. Rick Hoyt, the son, was stricken with cerebral palsy as a child. An avid Boston Bruins fan and a Boston University graduate (class of '93), Rick loved athletics, but his disabling disease and his confinement to a wheelchair restricted his participation. That is, until his father Dick, at the age of thirty-six, was prompted by his fifteen-year-old son Rick to run in a road race together back in 1977. Running with his dad opened up a whole new world for the younger Hoyt. As Rick said, "When I'm running, I feel like I've never been handicapped."

Dick started out running around the block while pushing Rick in an old wheelchair; eventually they graduated to road races, marathons, triathlons, and Iron Man competitions. (During the swimming segment of triathlons, Dick incredibly pulls his son in a small rowboat with a rope held in his mouth.) Going through these endeavors as a team, Dick and Rick formed an extremely tight bond. They now share their pain and triumphs together as a team. As Dick pushed his son through the streets of Hopkinton and all the way into Boston, another bond formed—between Team Hoyt and the Boston Marathon fans. With this new passion, Rick's sense of humor also blossomed; after each race, he takes the opportunity to remind his father that he beat him by one second.

Past the smell of chicken wings and ribs, the runners are now in the final steps of the mile as they run through the Speen Street intersection (named after John Speen, a Native American who first built on this land in the early 1700s) and bend left. The runners toward the end are greeted by the beginning of Fiske Pond on their right and Lake Cochituate on their left. At that point, trees that protected runners from the right give way to the waterways that expose them to all weather conditions, including beating sun, crosswinds, and, in some years, driving rain or snow.

If the runners can push through the ten-mile mark up ahead, compared to the sparse gatherings that saluted them along Mile 9, they are in for a giant welcome.

Mile 10

If you are going through hell, keep going.

—WINSTON CHURCHILL

MILE 10 BEGINS WITH A WINDING RIGHT BEND AT HORSESHOE CURVE; then the road hugs Fiske Pond on the right and the train tracks and Lake Cochituate on the left, for three-tenths of the mile. This stretch of the route is best known for traversing the Henry Wilson Historic District.

Henry Wilson was the vice president of the United States from 1873 to 1875 under Ulysses Grant. As a young man with only ten months of education under his belt, Wilson came to Natick, Massachusetts, from New Hampshire. He found employment in a local shoe factory, educated himself by reading over a thousand books in his spare time, and then turned his attention to politics. Given the nickname "Cobbler" by his adversaries, Wilson became a US senator before moving on to the White House. Known as a friend of the soldier and common man, Wilson gave away most of his money to the needy; he died in office, leaving a humble personal estate.

Even though Wilson has a whole district named after him, he's actually the second-most popular citizen of Natick, next to Heisman Trophy–winning quarterback Doug Flutie. Flutie was a football star at Natick High School before moving on to Boston College, where he will forever be remembered for throwing the legendary "Hail Mary" pass against the University of Miami, beating the defending national champions as time expired on the clock in 1984. After college, Doug moved on to the pros, where he became the most prolific player in Canadian football history and an All Pro in the NFL.

After leaving an open area at the end of the lake, where the runners are exposed to the random weather of April, the course works its way up a slight incline for two-tenths of a mile, toward the protection of West Central Street. Uta Pippig enjoys this part of the route. "For some reason, I look forward to this small hill," she said. "I don't know why. Maybe it's the way it twists back and forth. But I know it's up ahead, and I am excited to get there."

At the top of the hill, West Central Street (still Route 135) straightens and begins to move through the residential portion of the Henry Wilson Historic District. Here, magnificent trees line the road on both sides, providing the athletes with a natural protective tunnel as they parade toward Natick Center. Over the years nature has ravaged the trees with ice storms and disease, but they endure, rising dramatically toward the sun, their tops meeting over the road like a marine honor guard crossing swords at a wedding.

In 1909, Lucy Child, a resident of Framingham, aptly described the site as "a row of stately trees which fling their arms across W. Central Street, forming a green roof in the summer and a brown arch in winter." In the late 1800s and early 1900s, this segment of West Central Street was used for buggy rides on spring and summer afternoons; in the winter, the street was scraped, rolled, and roped off so that the affluent could race their horse-drawn sleighs here each afternoon. The sleigh rides of the early 1900s were competitions that took place on the same streets as the Boston Marathon. The winter events depended upon the elements, including snow and freezing temperatures. The Marathon, on the other hand, never has the luxury of waiting for appropriate conditions. Often, the weather joins forces with the course itself to stretch the challenge of the 26.2 miles.

Since the moment Tom Burke raised his hand in 1897 and yelled *Go!*, there have been two critical variables that factor into each runner's quest: his or her physical condition, and the weather. On the morning of the very first race, the *Boston Globe* reported: "The race will run, rain or shine." And for a hundred-plus years, it has continued to do so.

During the week of the race the smart competitors don't read *Runner's World* but rather *The Old Farmer's Almanac*. Tailwind or headwind, sun or overcast, cold or hot—they are all elements that can make the difference between success and failure, personal best and survival. From blizzards to heat waves and everything in between, runners on Patriots' Day have endured all of it. Index readings in 2007 and 2012 differed by an astonishing 65 degrees. The 2007 race had wind chills of 25 degrees Fahrenheit, which included a fifty-mile-per-hour headwind; five years later, newspaper headlines spoke of "scorching" heat, as temperatures flirted with 90 degrees.

The runner's ability to adapt to such conditions is one of the single most important factors in determining how (or whether) one arrives in Boston. In the torrid 1927 race, Clarence DeMar ran to his sixth victory by deviating from the melting pavement and traversing the course upon its sidewalks, while defending champion Johnny Miles stayed on the bubbling streets and was eventually driven to Boston in what was described as "pitiful" condition.

In high-temperature years such as 1902 and 1976, prudent runners paced themselves under the sweltering sun instead of going full speed, often stopping on the side of the road to be refreshed by the hoses of neighbors, compelled to be supporting characters in the day's drama. In 1976, triple-digit temperatures had ignited brush fires throughout the state of Massachusetts and threatened the health of the runners, leading the *Boston Globe* to print a "how to help heat stroke victims" article the morning of the race. High temperatures benefit those who are willing to amend the day's game plan of structured splits and instead customize their run to the day's elements. This approach was personified by the winner that day in 1976, Jack Fultz, who decided early in the race to actually sacrifice minutes of his run to not only drink water, but also to stand beneath makeshift showers on his way to victory.

Those who run without regard for the inevitable effects of the heat and sun ultimately pay the price. In 1909, 91 of 164 runners dropped out of the race, allowing a mill worker who toiled every day in 100-degree temperatures, Henri Renaud, to come from fifty-third place in Framingham to first in Boston. In 1916, it was so hot that the newspaper reports described the failed attempt of Edouard Fabre to defend his championship as "cooked" and "baked." One year after his failed defense of his championship, Fabre prepared for the heat by rubbing cold iodine on his chest because of what was described as "unpropitious conditions." He would wilt yet again on Beacon Street despite a desperate attempt to cure his failing condition by eating a raw egg that his attendant procured at a drugstore along the course.

It was in Mile 10 in 1938, with the temperature approaching 80 degrees, when the heat and discomfort prompted past winner Tarzan Brown to surrender his lead in order to take a swim in the refreshing waters of Lake Cochituate. Only after being cooled sufficiently did Brown return to the race and finish in fifty-first place. Later asked about his decision to sacrifice a shot at the first-place trophy, he retorted, "Sooner or later, they [trophies] get black and you have to throw them out," Brown said. One year later, Brown returned to Hopkinton and proceeded to set a Boston Marathon course record of 2:28:51 on the way to his second laurel wreath.

While Tarzan's reaction to the weather was as extreme as the conditions themselves, it's the resourcefulness of DeMar using the sidewalk or Fultz spending time under a hose that secured their victories. In 1917, William Kennedy draped an American flag over his head to protect against the sun on his way to the tape; forty-one years later, Franjo Mihalic of Yugoslavia wrapped his head in a Lenox Hotel napkin, only to discard it feet from the finish line so as not to be photographed with his makeshift kerchief.

The intensity of the Boston Marathon combined with torrid conditions only adds to the race's difficulty. In 2012, temperatures were predicted to rise to such levels that the BAA offered qualifying runners deferment of their well-earned number in order to forgo the risk of running. John Powers of the *Globe* memorably wrote that day, "For more than a century, this marathon has been Mother Nature's diabolical test lab."

Following the 2012 race, runner Kathy Hardcastle, who chose running over deferment, described the conditions on the course as actually hotter than what the thermometer read. "With crowds on both sides, you've got all that body heat of people screaming and shouting," she said, "and that of the runners inside the running tunnel, [which] creates a temperature that's actually much higher than the real temperature." Like the sentiment in the postman's creed—"Neither snow nor rain nor heat nor gloom of night"— the Boston Marathon is not deterred by weather. It does not begin because the conditions are right; it begins because the calendar says it is time.

In the increasing warmth of a beating sun, runners—just like car engines that are not properly cared for—can overheat and stall. When the conditions are reversed, and the readings on the thermometer fall, the car struggles to warm, maneuver, and function. In the famous runs of both Thomas Longboat—who jumped through the freight car of a train in 1909—and Kathy Switzer, in 1967, the runners competed beneath falling snowflakes and biting winds.

Some aren't built to run in the cold, like Frank Wendling, who in 1925 actually left the lead pack to sip on tea and warm his hands at the Woodland Hotel in Newton. Others like Bill Rodgers actually thrive in the cooling conditions. As race guru Tom Leonard once said about the four-time champion, "If he puts on his white gloves—look out."

Mile 10 continues through the Henry Wilson Historic District. At the intersection with Taylor Street, just past the half-mile point, runners in a far more urgent race used to pause from their journey to rest. The Edward Wolcott estate, on the left side of the road, sheltered runaway slaves in the 1800s. With twenty-one rooms, the mansion was the most impressive property in the town, but its real stature is due to the tunnels that ran from the rear of the estate to the Boston-Albany train tracks, one hundred feet away. Fugitive slaves who jumped from passing trains and made their way underground to the estate would receive food and shelter here before continuing on to Canada.

Boston has long been a beacon for tolerance and acceptance. Throughout the mid-1800s, abolitionists, including William Lloyd Garrison, Wendell Phillips, Henry David Thoreau, and Lucy Stone would convene in the Marathon town of Framingham to rally, strategize, and raise funds for their cause. The famous 54th Regiment of the Civil War, comprised of all black soldiers, hailed from Boston, and it was Bostonian William Carney who became the first African American presented with the Medal of Honor. It was in Boston and its outskirts where Harriet Beecher Stowe, who wrote *Uncle Tom's Cabin*, Frederick Douglass, Harriet Tubman, Martin Luther King Jr., Malcolm X, Louis Farrakhan, William Monroe Trotter, and President Barack Obama (a Harvard alum) once all resided.

Next, the runners pass the Forest Street intersection, where sits another house connected to a dark chapter in American history. Major Daniel Henry Longfellow Gleason lived at 71 West Central Street, on the left side of the road, after serving in Washington, D.C., during the Civil War. Gleason is famous for his intimate connection with the assassination of Abraham Lincoln. When Gleason was working in Washington, one of his associates attended secret meetings where a plot to kidnap President Lincoln was discussed; one of the individuals present at those meetings was John Wilkes Booth. When he learned of the plot, Gleason warned officials, but to no avail. The kidnapping plan turned into murder, and after the assassination, authorities turned to Gleason for help hunting down the culprits. With his assistance they tracked down Booth, but the others escaped. Gleason died in Natick in 1917.

With the Mile 10 demarcation visible in the distance, the runners are rejuvenated by the sight of such a critical juncture in the race. Although this milestone is another benchmark on the long list they've already conquered, they are tempered by the fact that the race isn't even half finished. Nevertheless, it is an opportunity to take satisfaction with one's efforts while focusing on the challenges that loom ahead.

Many recreational runners call it a day here at the ten-mile mark. In 1927, 23 percent of the competitors walked off the course rather than keeping on and fighting the sun. A good number of the early participants, mostly bandits (those without a number), enjoy the pageantry of the start, get in some exercise, and then drop out after ten miles for a beer and some chicken wings, rather than a PowerBar and sixteen more miles. At house parties and celebrations taking place on the town common there are always signs and shouts to take one's mind off the grind of the course. In Natick, a sign once read SHORTCUT TO BOSTON, with an arrow pointing toward kegs of beer.

Champion Rob de Castella used to say, "If you feel bad at Mile 10, you're in trouble. If you feel bad at Mile 20, you're normal. If you don't feel bad at Mile 26, you're abnormal."

Mile 11

Mankind must put an end to war before war puts an end to mankind.
—PRESIDENT JOHN F. KENNEDY

AS SOON AS RUNNERS CROSS OVER INTO MILE 11, THEY CAN SEE THE steeple of the First Congregational Church rising above the treetops of West Central Street, leading the athletes into the town center. On the steeple's face sits a clock. It's on the face of a clock that the runner is exposed to truth. From a runner's very first race, it has been the tick of time that has played the role of judge and jury. Time doesn't lie. Fast or slow, paced or reckless, the clock gives testament to the runner's performance. This is why Bill Rodgers always looked forward to Natick. "There are two things that excite runners," Rodgers said. "They are people and clocks—you've got both here."

Two-tenths into the mile, the runners cross the Route 27 intersection and arrive at the Natick Commons. It was here that the Great Fire of 1874 destroyed half of the town center in just six hours, including the post office, Congregational Church, the fire station, and the brand-new shoe factory. For years, this point not only served as an ideal viewing location for fans of the race, but also as the second checkpoint (prior to their movement to more-appropriate locations on the course).

Like Hopkinton, Natick Center has a village-like feel to it. It's the small-town America that you see in pickup truck commercials or in country music videos. On the left, runners pass by two church steeples during this mile—one for Protestants and one for Catholics. The First Congregational Church, which was originally built in the 1850s, sits on the left side of the intersection. Opposite the Congregational Church is the Natick Common, which was dedicated in 1856. Thirty years later the Soldiers' Monument was built to honor the eighty-nine Natick soldiers who died in the Civil War. This area is usually busy with a concert on the bandstand, mothers with babies, and teenagers playing Hacky Sack.

At this point West Central Street becomes East Central Street, but remains Route 135. Both sides of the road offer welcomed and needed fan support. Runners might not feel worthy, but by this point in the race they are starting to crave the yells of encouragement to assure them they are "looking good" and to "keep going." The presence of the spectators and their supportive tone is like an emotional water stop; after all, despite being surrounded by thousands of people, marathoners can get lonely.

However, sometimes fans along the sidewalk extend things too far. Such was the case in 1985, when John "The Elder" Kelley was running through Natick in what was the *fiftieth* anniversary of his first championship. As the patriarch of the race waved to the crowd and smiled at the shouts of praise for his six-plus decades of Boston running, a vendor ran up to him and patted him on his back. The vendor was selling buttons displaying Kelley's face. Kelley was not amused. Kelley later said, "Would you believe it? I'm hurting and this son of a bitch is trying to make money off me!"

John "The Elder" Kelley, from the local town of Medford, ran Boston for six decades, winning races in both 1935 and 1945. He ran the race over *sixty* times, finishing second seven times and third once—all following his very first race that he dropped out of because of blisters. After his 1935 win he commented on all the attention he was receiving for his accomplishment. "This is fleeting fame," he said. "No one knows it better than I do. I will live the same, feel the same, and think the same. But boy, it sure is a swell feeling to be the Marathon winner."

Kelley was once told by a reporter that if he had run during today's era of professionalism and prize money, he would have won more than $1,000,000 for his eighteen top-ten finishes. To this Kelley humbly responded: "Different times, different values. I ran for the love of it. My good friend Ted Williams, baseball's greatest hitter, was asked the same question. He responded that he once begged Red Sox owner Tom Yawkey to cut his $70,000 contract because he had a subpar year. We both had a passion!"

A smiling Johnny "The Elder" Kelley runs down Commonwealth Avenue to his second laurel wreath in 1945. © RUNNING PAST

In the absence of prize money, Kelley worked several jobs, including painting houses and toiling for Boston Edison. Loved and admired throughout the running community, John is a member of the Track and Field Hall of Fame, and was named the Most Prolific Runner of the Twentieth Century (he has competed in more than 1,500 races, from Boston to Japan). The five-foot-three, 145-pound runner will forever be linked with the Boston Marathon; he embodied the pride, endurance, and tenacity of the race as much as anyone who has ever competed in it.

In 1942, Kelley lamented the day he wouldn't be able to run: "When it comes time to quit it will be with regrets, because I've had a lot of fun and won a lot of races and associated with the swellest bunch of athletes in the world." He could not have known he would run it another fifty years—running his last one in 1992, and living to the age of ninety-seven.

In Kelley's obituary in 2004, none other than marathon authority Bill Rodgers was quoted as saying: "He *was* the Boston Marathon."

Many runners use the words and cheers from the crowd to propel themselves forward; in fact, they even prompt such well wishes by having their name or affiliation written upon their shirt. Over the last century, a wide range of causes, from Pro Life to No Nukes, have been advertised from Hopkinton to Boston on the chests of sweating athletes. In 1965, runner John Marchant printed words on his T-shirt not intended for fans but rather for his fellow runners. On his left shoulder he wrote PASS, and on the right he wrote DON'T PASS. In 1983 Fred and Paula Palka ran with shirts that read JUST MARRIED.

As the runners run by the throngs of spectators, many of the athletes use the forum (and the platform) of the race to express who they are as individuals. Multiplied by thousands, the race can turn into a giant costume party or parade, much to the dismay of some of the traditionalists, including the ornery Jock Semple. For him Boston was a race, pure and simple, not an event.

Nevertheless, runners have always used the race as a stage to add their personal piece of color to the race's history. Crowd-pleasing characters who have run over the years include the Viking, Superman, Groucho Marx, the Blues Brothers, Kermit the Frog, a rhinoceros, an astronaut, and—of course—the obligatory runner with the beer-can hat—in which the beer dangles forever four inches in front of the runner, thus giving him something to run for.

Moving through Natick Center, the race route continues flat and straight with a slight bump at the 10.4-mile mark. On the left side of the road, a new police station, fire station, and library represent the contribution of Natick's taxpayers. Halfway through the mile, the runners run in front of the stairs of St. Patrick's Church. It is here where babies are carried to their christenings, brides beam the smile of newlyweds, and caskets are carried—these life events known as hatch, match, and dispatch.

Runners work toward the end of the mile where Nick's, the popular Natick ice-cream and hot-dog place, used to stand on the right. Nick's was best known for its Saturday-night gatherings of classic 1950s automobiles, especially Corvettes. For years the Boston Marathon marked opening day for the ice-cream establishment. Outside, they would dress the place up for the big race with balloons and American flags. If you were in need of ice cream some Saturday night, you could drop by—just not in your minivan.

Past a tricky little intersection with Union Street on the right, runners veer left and continue through the final tenths of the mile. On the right, the runners pass the courthouse and, at the 10.7-mile mark, the Natick Battalion Armory. The Armory was built to honor the veterans of the Spanish-American War, in which America flexed its muscles and dominated Spanish forces to resolve conflicts over the island of Cuba and neighboring sovereigns. After much saber rattling, war commenced in the spring of 1898 after the USS *Maine* was sunk—an act of hostility that forced President McKinley to declare war against Spain.

This occurred in February of that year. In Boston, the BAA and those who supported the race had to decide whether it was appropriate to run the second annual Marathon with war imminent. For the first time in the race's young history, the world around the Boston Marathon would impact the race—but it would be far from the last.

The race *was* run that year, and for the first time, officials realized both the power and importance of the Boston Marathon. By running Boston that year, while war was on the horizon, it demonstrated to people that although the citizens respected those about to enter the fray, life must go on.

So as the sons of Massachusetts mustered at the train depot in Framingham for deployment, the race went on. Fans lined the course along the side of the road, cheering the runners, albeit with heavy hearts, many of them remembering the pain of the Civil War four decades earlier. "Natick women and girls shook American flags hysterically," the *Boston Globe* reported, noting that there was a spirit of patriotism that enveloped the event.

Fortunately, the Spanish-American War was over in just three months, with the Americans scoring a decisive victory. Fifteen years later, the Boston Marathon, like the rest of the world, would again suffer from world conflict on a much grander scale. In World War I—dubbed the "War to End all Wars"—America went to Europe, including 168 members of the Boston Athletic Association, who knew that war took priority over all. "We believe that the entire energy and resources of the organization should be concentrated on the task of winning the war," the BAA announced.

As the war waged on, the death toll touched every corner of the world. In all, sixteen million people perished, including 1914 Boston Marathon champion James Duffy. The *Globe* wrote, "As Pheidippides gave his all for his country, so too have marathon heroes of later years laid down their lives for the honor of their countries, and will continue to offer and sacrifice their youth—their lives."

The BAA was so concerned about the overwhelming effect of the war on the community that there was a heated debate about whether to run the race in 1917, the year America entered the conflict. Opinions focused on both respect and security concerns; the organization issued a statement to explain their reservations. They were considering canceling the race "because of the tenseness of the American situation at present [and] because of the trepidation with which the flower of American manhood looks out upon the future."

The race went on that year, and was won by Boston's adopted son, William Kennedy, who before the race implored American runners to "[e]ndeavor this year, above all others, to prove to the world that America is supreme in all branches of endeavor." Later that day when he ran through Coolidge Corner with the lead, the bricklayer passed masons working on a building, who saluted him by clapping bricks together. The newspaper would write the next day about the runner who ran to victory with an American flag around his head. "He won a remarkable race," the paper reported, "and carried Old Glory to one of the most popular victories achieved in this or any other country."

The question to run or not was again debated in the following year, 1918. This time, the BAA changed the tradition of making it an open race and instead dedicated the marathon to the American military by organizing a twenty-six-mile relay race for sixteen service teams. During the run, participants carried batons with a message inside that the runners read to the crowd at the finish line. "We will fight to the limit, and we expect you to buy [Liberty Bonds] to the limit."

The winner that day was the Camp Devens team, who ran in their "khaki suits and leggings with government-issued shoes," beating the Boston Naval Yard in their "spic and span white suits."

The Allies were victorious in Europe, and those who were fortunate to survive the trenches, including Clarence DeMar and William Kennedy, returned to America, believing the world had been freed from tyranny. Sadly, the war to end all wars didn't end all wars.

In 1941, America again went to battle in Europe and Asia, and again the Boston Marathon community was committed to the cause. Larry Brignolia donated his statue of *Mercury*, which he had received for winning the 1899 race, for scrap metal. In 1942, the race was moved to Sunday by Governor Saltonstall, "to keep war work proceeding without moment of slow up." Jock Semple, Gérard Côté, Johnny "The Elder" Kelley, and countless Marathon personnel and runners fought for the Allies, while the Women's Defense Corps used Patriots' Day to put on demonstrations on bomb drills and air raid preparation.

Prior to the 1943 race, the runners were led down the course by an armada of army vehicles (each of which had their cost publicized to justify the $13 billion loan the government had taken out for the war effort). Two years later, in 1945, John "The Elder" Kelley returned from the war and won his second Boston, the same year his brother was killed in Japan.

America once again proved victorious in Europe and the Pacific. In 1951, six short years after the Axis powers had surrendered, Japanese runner Shigeki Tanaka would come to Boston and—despite the raw feelings that still consumed the country—be treated with great respect from the crowd, the officials, and the field. Tanaka lived twenty miles from Hiroshima, and remembered seeing a flash of light and smoke on that fateful morning. Ten hours later, victims of the bomb walked into his village with their clothes burnt off, only to die soon after their arrival. Ten days later,

Tanaka and his neighbors would be summoned to Hiroshima to help search for survivors.

Tanaka would go on to win the Boston Marathon that year. Following the race he was hurt to read of himself referred to as "Atomic Boy" in newspapers under headlines of JAP WINS BOSTON, and jokes that they needed a Geiger counter to track him. Before he left town, he was interviewed by the American Civil Defense about what he saw on the day the bomb leveled his city. Despite the offensive words in the paper, the people of Boston treated him warmly, and as one of their own.

The nation, looking to heal scars that affected both its bodies and minds, embraced this period of peace from the late 1940s into the early '50s. Inevitably, the call of war would soon sound again as the threat of Communism drew Americans back into conflict in Korea. As a result of the politics of the war, runners from Korea, including prior Boston Marathon champions Ki-Yong Ham and Suh Yun-Bok, were barred from running Boston during the years of the conflict. In 1979 the BAA would again make a political stand by banning applicants from South Africa as a protest against apartheid, until the heinous policy was lifted.

As one war ends, it seems that the embryo of future hostilities is conceived; only a period of germination separates one from the other. From Korea, the war machine moved to Southeast Asia, in a war that changed the United States and the lives of a whole generation of Americans. It was within that conflict, the Vietnam War, that the twenty-two-year-old son of BAA race director William Cloney lost his life, as did 58,000 other Americans.

Eugene Roberts returned from the fog of Vietnam without the use of his legs but determined enough to complete his landmark run of Boston in his wheelchair. Pat Messore of Natick was inspired to run Boston after reading about the race while stationed in Southeast Asia in 1972—one year before the race was won by conscientious objector Jon Anderson.

The Boston Marathon can't hide, nor is it immune, from the world around it. From the second year of the race to the current day, the race has not been able to separate itself from the reach of war, its horrors and realities. In Iraq in 2009 the BAA helped to organize the "Boston Marathon in Iraq," 5,771 miles away from Boylston Street, at Camp Adder. Spear-headed by Jack Fleming at the BAA, the race organizers provided med-als and certificates for four hundred runners stationed at and around the base. Sergeant Derek Miller would win the men's race with a time of 3:01. Four years earlier he had toed the line in Hopkinton but had dropped out before finishing; after the "Boston Marathon in Iraq," he was more deter-mined than ever to return. The winner of the women's race was Specialist Janelle Drennan. In the closing miles of the race she started to slow, but was motivated by the words her father had taught her: "Keep going—keep fighting." The race occurred just two years after Boston Marathoner Andrew Bacevich was killed by a roadside bomb in Iraq, reminiscent of when 1914 Boston Marathon champion (and Olympian) James Duffy had died in World War I, almost a year to the day from his victory.

From Hopkinton to Cuba to France to Asia to Iraq and then to Boston, the world's greatest race isn't just twenty-six miles of roadway, but instead, a transcendent event that exists *within* those miles, in the people's minds, and in the hearts of all who dare to run. Through war and storm and even terrorist attacks, the race goes on, as proud as it was when John McDermott was carried on the shoulders of admirers back in 1897: determined, resolute in its purpose, steadfast in its cause.

❧

Mile 11 continues past the armory out the back side of Natick. The route continues straight and up and down on ascents and descents of little consequence. For the last three-tenths of the mile, the road is lined with mostly houses and some small businesses that are blocked from conducting business on the day of the race. The runners push for-ward, looking forward to Wellesley women and the adrenaline rush that accompanies them.

Mile 12

Now I know I've got a heart, because it's breaking.
—L. FRANK BAUM, *THE WONDERFUL WIZARD OF OZ*

THE ROUTE CONTINUES THROUGH NATICK, PAST A MOSTLY RESIDENTIAL neighborhood with the occasional business mixed in at the start of Mile 12. Along this part of the course, house parties are popular and the fans are polite. The twelfth mile is relatively quiet, but more demanding than appearances would lead the runner to believe. The homes are comprised of colonial, gambrel, and split-level houses occupied by middle-class families. The crowds are somewhat sporadic but well-meaning; the runners get a push forward as the spectators look up from their hamburger or hot dog to wish them well. The mood is relaxed even though the topography is anything but. With more significant miles still ahead in the distance, runners might be lulled into a sense of indifference—until they discover that Mile 12 is more than just the relaxed flats of Framingham. They are wise to heed Jim Knaub's maxim: "There is no such thing as an unimportant mile."

To make it to the final stretch on Boylston Street, runners must respect each step along the course. Even during the quiet moments, when the ranks of lawn-chaired grandfathers thin out and the screams of beer-slugging college kids temporarily subside, the runner's mind drifts away from the sights and sounds—even the running itself. At these times, the race seems more like a daydream than a concentrated effort.

For the first two-tenths of this mile, the course moves up and slides left. The rise at the beginning then falls for a tenth before jumping for the next three-tenths of a mile. This is the first real up-and-down the runner has experienced since way back in Ashland. Now is a good time for runners to test-drive those muscles in their legs that will allow them to grind uphill and then flow and brake downhill.

At the 11.7-mile mark, the course bids adieu to Natick and enters into the affluent town of Wellesley. Here, the runners are guided east by the same train tracks that escorted the founders of the race a century ago. The course dives down for a tenth of a mile at a spot where, back in 2002, one runner ran with a heavy heart. He carried with him a Mass card, an American flag, and the responsibility of running for another.

That year, for almost thirteen miles, Henry Staines, along with his marathon partner Diane Geehan, joined the ranks of thousands running toward downtown Boston. As they ran from Natick into Wellesley, the burden of the challenge was beginning to weigh upon Henry. There was still more than half the course to traverse, and completion was in doubt. As he continued to put one foot in front of the other, he looked to the left of the course and saw a relief station.

Assigned to the aid station was a local fireman, there to provide first response. With no pressing needs at the time, the civil servant was cheering on runners when he spotted Henry running by with the American flag sewn into his shirt. For a brief second, they caught each other's attention, prompting the fireman to nod and give the tiring runner a thumbs-up. It was one of those moments along the course that profoundly moves a competitor and pushes him forward.

Henry needed all the help he could get. He was running not just for himself that day, but for his best friend as well. Eight months prior, Henry and lifelong friend Jerry Dewan were out on one of their many long runs. During those miles the two men often discussed life, sports, and work. On September 9, 2001, the two friends sat down and discussed the idea of running Boston together that coming spring. Both excited and committed to the idea, they pledged to each other that they would be in Hopkinton together the following Patriots' Day. Boston would be more than a race for the two friends; it would be the gateway to the next phase of their friendship, and their lives.

The two parted ways on Sunday, September 9, 2001. Jerry had to work on Tuesday, although he didn't consider it work; his vocation was a family calling. Since he could remember, Jerry had longed to follow his grandfather, father, two uncles, and three brothers into the brotherhood of firefighters. Despite his outstanding test scores, attempts to secure a job in Boston proved futile, so he traveled to New York where he was granted a position in the city department. It was not just any department—he was assigned to Ladder Company 3 in Manhattan's East Village, one of the oldest fire companies in the city. His boss was living legend Paddy Brown, a highly decorated Vietnam veteran who had returned home to New York to become one of the most daring and courageous firemen the city had ever seen. His record of achievement and level of valor were so great that reality and folklore merged into one in Paddy Brown.

When Jerry arrived at the firehouse that Tuesday morning, he changed into his fire gear and hung his clothes on his assigned hook. On the chalkboard, Jerry was listed for duty next to his corresponding assignment for the day. It wasn't long thereafter when the alarm came in. There was a fire at the World Trade Center. When Ladder 3 arrived at the New York skyscraper, the top floors were already engulfed in flames. Jerry, along with the rest of the team, jumped off the truck and made their way inside Tower One and up Stairwell C. Floor by floor, they hustled while others came down. When they arrived at the fortieth floor, Jerry and the men started to organize stranded workers, guiding them to safety with a calmness and professionalism that instilled confidence in those terrified souls who had to descend into God knows what. Many of those people came down to safety even as the firemen kept moving up to help more people, only to have the building collapse around them. They were doing what firemen do—helping others. It is what Jerry was born to do. This moment was in his DNA: a fireman, a brother, a son, a grandson, a hero.

At home in Boston, his friend Henry sat helpless, staring at both the television and his phone. He texted and called Jerry over two hundred times that day. Weeks later, officials would declare Jerry, Paddy Brown, nine of their brothers from Ladder 3, and 332 other firemen dead.

As others would report, the men from Ladder 3 died taking part in the greatest evacuation in United States history, saving over 25,000 lives. Their death was not in vain; it was the ultimate sacrifice, conducted in the most harrowing of conditions. It was one of those rare moments that validate one's purpose on this Earth: to help others, positively impact the world around you, live a life of consequence. Jerry and his brothers will forever live in the hearts of those they saved and those inspired by courage. Some weeks later a woman who survived the World Trade Center collapse would identify Gerard "Jerry" Dewan as the fireman who had led her and twelve of her coworkers to safety.

Following the attacks, the country, Jerry's family, and his friend Henry lived in a state of shock. There was no body for the Dewan family to claim, but in an effort to seek closure, they held a memorial service. It was empty, unfulfilling—Jerry wasn't home. Then, two weeks before Christmas, the family was notified that the workers at Ground Zero had found Jerry's remains. As Jerry was taken from the site, all the workers there stopped, stood at attention, and saluted a true American hero. His body was escorted home to Boston by his brothers of Ladder 3. Standing at attention when the body arrived at the funeral home was his friend Henry Staines. The family now had closure, but Henry still had a pledge to fulfill: to run Boston.

On Marathon Day 2002, Henry ran with American flag embroidered on his shirt and Jerry in his heart. The thumbs-up he received from the fireman during Mile 12 inspired him to carry on, knowing that Jerry was truly running with him that day. With a new bounce in his step and the weight of his friend's presence, Henry ran with a renewed purpose. During moments of doubt or discomfort, Henry would take out Jerry's Mass card and read it:

> *No farewell words were spoken.*
> *No time to say good-bye.*
> *You were gone before we knew it,*
> *and only God knows why!*
> *Gerard, we love you.*

Carrying that flag and card, Henry ran through Wellesley and over the hills of Newton and into Boston. When he arrived at Kenmore Square, he was met by Jerry Dewan's nephew, Kevin Gilligan. Henry stopped and hugged Kevin. Both had tears streaming down their faces. Then Kevin reached into a bag and pulled out Jerry's fire helmet, which was found next to the fallen fireman at Ground Zero. Kevin then looked Henry in the eye, handed him the helmet, and implored him, "Bring Jerry home!" Henry took the helmet and carried it aloft, running as if on air. It was just as they had promised each other eight months earlier—two eternal friends, running as one.

Down Boylston Street, Henry would stop one more time to embrace Jerry's sister Maureen. Again emotion would wash over him as she hugged him and then handed him an American flag to run the final steps. With Jerry's helmet and American flag in hand, the crowds on the sidewalk were delirious. With the pain of loss and the satisfaction of a promised pledge soon to be fulfilled, he ran those final steps not alone but with the support of all those who lined Boylston Street, the Dewan family's love, and with his friend not a memory but with him. With flag held proud and Jerry's helmet in his hand, Henry stepped across the finish line, looked to the sky toward his friend, and became overwhelmed in emotion. Henry's running partner Diane hugged him, saying, "Jerry is watching us right now; you did it!"

Back at the firehouse in Manhattan, Jerry's name remains on the chalkboard with his assignment, which he did so well, and his clothes still hang on the hook, right where he left them. He is always on call, always a fireman, always a friend.

Since the genesis of the Boston Marathon, runners have been running for others. Some do so in memory of loved ones, some for support, and others for inspiration. But in 1989, the BAA instituted a grassroots program to use the Boston Marathon for the service and improvement of the community. That year the American Liver Foundation and the race teamed up to raise money to assist in their efforts to meet their mission. Runners would earn a number in exchange for funds they would raise on behalf of the charity.

A quarter of a century later, thirty-five charities now form a network of organizations that have been granted numbers from the BAA; in turn, they have parlayed those race entries into $140 million in donations, helping people to help their fellow men and women, and giving the race even more purpose. Since 1897, it was never just about the miles from start to finish. The destiny of the race was always about so much more. Pheidippides ran not for a medal but to serve the community of Athens, as do thousands of runners every year in Boston, using running as a vehicle to reach out to others and to make the community a better place.

Most of the runners who run on behalf of a charity do so because they have a loved one who is somehow associated with the cause. In 2013, Joey McIntyre of the New Kids on the Block ran for the Alzheimer's Association in honor of his mother, afflicted with the debilitating disease, who raised nine McIntyres. In all, he raised $40,000 from family, friends, and fans of the music group. Later in the race, his sisters brought their mother out to the course. When Joey looked her in the eyes, twenty-three miles into the race, he saw in them the love that only a mother can have. He kissed her and ran on to Boston.

Like McIntyre, women's soccer great Kristine Lilly ran Boston in 2013 for the greater good. Kristine had played her sport at the highest level, winning two World Cups and two Olympic gold medals as a member of the USA Women's team. When she retired, she dreamed of running the Boston Marathon. She had stood on the sidewalks of the race in years past and been moved by the spirit and will of the runners. As part of her quest, she sought out a charity to partner with and give back. After researching the different causes, she chose Children's Hospital in Boston, running in tribute to a young girl who had lost her life to cancer. When Kristine ran through Wellesley she came upon the parents of the girl. She stopped to embrace them before continuing on. In all, she raised $21,000 that day for a girl she had never met, but now held in her heart.

At the end of the mile, as both the elite and charity runners collectively run toward Mile 13, they all start to hear the first faint echoes of a faraway din. Veterans of the race know that they are just yards away from

126

Three-time champion Les Pawson (left) and two-time winner Johnny "Elder" Kelley were fan favorites in the 1938 race because of their running skills and the fact that they both hailed from New England. COURTESY OF THE TRUSTEES OF THE BOSTON PUBLIC LIBRARY

the rallying cries of the women of Wellesley College—and the much-needed boost that their support and enthusiasm brings.

However, it can also add a distraction.

John "The Elder" Kelley, patriarch of the Boston Marathon and local hero, always warned of the need to stay focused at this juncture of the race. With the impending excitement in the next mile, he believed it was essential to stay within your game plan and not push yourself too early. He knew this from personal experiences that may have cost him two championships: "Running past the girls at Wellesley College, your mind tells you one thing, but your legs do something different. I was always impatient both in life and in running, and it cost me dearly later in the course."

As the course moves into Wellesley, the road widens to four lanes, and the speed limit goes up to forty-five miles per hour. The road drops for two-tenths of a mile until the mile mark, then rises over what is one of the most trying inclines on the course. Fortunately, you won't know you are running uphill, thanks to the women of Wellesley College.

Mile 13

"Why did you do all this for me?" he asked. "I don't deserve it. I've never done anything for you."
                    —E. B. WHITE, *CHARLOTTE'S WEB*

THE BEAUTY OF THE BOSTON MARATHON IS THE WAY THAT EACH MILE takes on a life of its own and has its own personality. Mile 13 is particularly special, as it is here that runners for over a century have been feted by the "bells" and "fair maidens" of Wellesley College. Many competitors point to the uphill at the all-women's college as the embodiment of the race—strangers, acting as friends, giving selflessly to the runners, committing their hearts and lungs to the cause.

The mile continues its upward climb, which started at the end of Mile 12. In 1904, it was said that the runners "could recognize Wellesley College by the lofty spires." The hilly terrain tests the quads and spirits of even the top athletes. When the most prolific landscape architect of his time, Frederick Law Olmsted Jr. (son of the famed designer of Central Park), was working on the college's design, he saw the location as problematic because of the "complex topography."

Wellesley College was founded in 1870 as one "Seven Sisters College" to serve as a "female seminary . . . [to] prepare women for great conflicts for vast reforms in social life." In the first years of the institution, 704 students paid $250 to attend the school. Currently, there are 2,204 undergraduates from 62 countries who pay $57,042 a year in tuition. The school is ranked in the top ten nationally for liberal arts schools, according to *US News & World Report,* boasting such illustrious alumnae as former First Lady and Secretary of State Hillary Rodham

Clinton, journalists Diane Sawyer and Cokie Roberts, former Secretary of State Madeleine Albright, and Katharine Lee Bates (class of 1880), author of "America the Beautiful."

In the late 1800s, there was a four-story factory situated near the Wellesley College campus. Town benefactor Horatio Hollis Hunnewell did not feel that industry was good for the image of the town, so he simply bought the factory and donated the land to Wellesley College for dormitories. Currently the college is the town's largest employer, with over 1,200 workers. Despite its educational mission and prestigious history, Wellesley College is best known to marathoners as the high-water mark on the course in terms of shrieks and screams.

Since the first race in 1897, the women of Wellesley College have hurried through lunch in order to stand on the old stone wall outside Cazenove, Pomeroy, and Munger Halls in time to encourage, inspire, and deafen the passing athletes. Runners need to stay disciplined in this stretch, known—for obvious reasons—as the "Scream Tunnel."

Like Johnny Kelley, Uta Pippig warns of the need to stay within yourself as you run past the campus. "I appreciate the support we receive as we pass the college. I don't let it excite me to the point of running faster than my capabilities. I use it more as a boost to my energy level, which I can then utilize somewhere later in the race." Uta has truly experienced the pinnacle of sound as she has cruised past the women of Wellesley: Although the Wellesley students cheer on all the runners, they reserve the highest pitches for the female competitors. And no runner in the history of the race has received a more riotous greeting than an athlete in white shorts and a black top in 1966. That runner, Roberta Gibb Bingay, was the first woman ever to compete in the marathon. As she passed the students of Wellesley College, she heard them cry, "It's a woman! It's a woman!" Thinking back on the passionate response, Bingay would later say, "It was like I was setting them free."

Former school president Diana Chapman Walsh was a student in 1966 when Bingay ran by, and she remembers the landmark moment. "A ripple of recognition shot through the lines, and we cheered as we

Les Pawson tries to focus on the duty at hand as he runs past the women of Wellesley College in 1940.

never had before," she said. "We let out a roar that day, sensing that this woman had done more than just break the gender barrier in a famous race."

Three decades later Bingay returned to Wellesley as the guest of honor at a rally held at the school prior to the hundredth running of the race. A number of current world-class runners waited in line to obtain her autograph. Over the years, Bingay has felt somewhat slighted by the massive attention given to Kathy Switzer for her run the following year, 1967. There is no question that Bingay—running in a black bathing-suit top, her brother's white Bermuda shorts, and a pair of boys' size-six Adidas sneakers—was the original trailblazing woman of the Boston Marathon.

Over the years, elite women runners from marathons past and present have participated in the John Hancock Financial Services "Women on the Move" Rally, first held in 1985. These rallies at Wellesley have provided an opportunity for top women runners to be recognized for their contributions to the Marathon, while at the same time thanking the students for theirs. The rally features clinics and speeches from elite runners. Past speakers include three-time champion Pippig, Olympic champion Valentina Yegorova of Russia, and New York City Marathon champion Tegla Loroupe of Kenya.

Former Wellesley Athletic Director Louise O'Neil speaks eloquently about the rewards that come out of meeting challenges as she describes the mission of the college:

There is no limit to what a woman can accomplish if she has confidence in herself and a determination to make her visions and goals a reality. Every day women from Wellesley College work a little harder and come a little closer to achieving these goals. Members of the college community encourage students to take chances to break down barriers, which stand in our way, and to embrace success.

Wellesley College students adding their decibels to the famous "Scream Tunnel."
© KEVIN R. MORRIS

In his landmark book *The Complete Book of Running*, Jim Fixx wrote, "The modern world's most appreciative marathon fans [are] the girls of Wellesley College." While Fixx's statement is likely, the feeling is mutual. Female runners appreciate the support of their sisters, while the male runners can't help but be seduced by the screeching song of the sirens. Tommy Leonard of the Eliot Lounge in Boston (where runners used to "rehydrate" and talk running) always enjoyed the run past Wellesley, as he noted in the book, *The Boston Marathon*. "These girls, I love them when they come out," he wrote. "They're all good-looking chicks. I try to make dates. See you at the Eliot Lounge, but none of them show up—I'm 0 for 21."

For over a century, the contributions of Wellesley College have been such an integral part of the race that the *Boston Globe* committed coverage to its annual reporting of the race. A sampling of the Wellesley tradition through the years of the Marathon:

The Scream Tunnel: Wellesley Through the Years

1897—"As the runners passed Wellesley College, several young girls received them."

1899—". . . a bevy of beautiful girls are gowned in fashionable varicolored gowns sitting on a stone wall."

1902—"Pretty college girls at Wellesley who had assembled along the highway to cheer on the tired runners, had flaunted their dainty kerchiefs and class colors in the face of the heaving panting leaders."

1904—"[Runners] were generously applauded by a coterie of pretty girls sitting by the roadside."

1905—"Fair Wellesley students were on the college grounds as the leaders swept past, and the girls seemed to enjoy the spectacle."

1907—"Wellesley college students gave the runners a great cheer. . . . Thomas Longboat caught sight of the girls waving to him. He grinned broadly and nodded his head."

1916—"On the hill leading up to Wellesley College, the fair collegians stood along the road within the grounds. They smiled at runners, but only a few took notice of the men following in the motorcars who tried to get a flirtatious twinkle."

1928—"The girls gave a cheer. Runner Joie Ray came along and smiled and laughed at the students. He was seen to wink once or twice, but he kept going as the girls smiled back. He ended up collapsing at the finish."

1934—"Leaders passed the Gothic Building of Wellesley College where the fair undergraduates turned out by the hundreds to applaud the laboring runners."

1942—"Anthony Allen of the Playboy Athletic Club of Lawrence bowed when he got to Wellesley College and gave the girls a big smile."

1943—"No girls—Easter Vacation."

1961—". . . greeted by girl with sweatshirt that read USA NECKING TEAM."

1970—"Wellesley College students were following more serious pursuits. There was scarcely a girl in front of the college."

1977—"Vin Fleming, a dishwasher at the Eliot Lounge, thought it was a bigger thrill to pass the girls at Wellesley College than to finish fifth."

1988—"Runner Michael Goldstein was so thrilled by the Wellesley students that he decided to turn around and run the stretch again."

1995—"The majority of the Wellesley College students wore special edition Wellesley College T-shirts as part of a promotion by Nike. Students also displayed shirts with their own personal endorsements. One shirt read WELLESLEY COLLEGE GIRLS HAVE BEEN ON TOP FOR 120 YEARS, and another proclaimed WELLESLEY COLLEGE IS NOT A GIRL'S SCHOOL WITHOUT MEN BUT A WOMEN'S SCHOOL WITHOUT BOYS."

1996—"The cheering began at 12:25 when the first wheelchair contestants began to roll by. It reached a crescendo shortly after 1:00 when the first pack of a dozen male runners approached, and it remained constant for more than three hours."

2000—"Signs outside the college read KISS ME, YOU'RE HALFWAY THERE, and RUN LIKE A FAUCET."

2002—"The festivities included a nonstop music broadcast by the college's radio station and scores of signs on both sides of Route 135, including, ALMOST THERE, BABY and AN ENERGY BOOST! WELLESLEY'S WOMEN!"

2008—"The so-called Wellesley Scream Tunnel is so loud, runners say they can hear it from a mile away . . . Their lung workout begins when the first racers, the hand cyclists, enter the Scream Tunnel around 10:15 a.m."

2010—"Senior Lee Ung held a sign that said she majored in kissing."

2013—"That's when it begins to happen," said runner Patrick
Brannelly. "You reach the Wall of Sound—the extraordinary
women of Wellesley College, waving placards and screaming your
name, who give you a new burst of energy. Before you know it,
you're halfway home."

———

At the beginning of Mile 13, the anticipated struggle slowly becomes a reality. The route is increasingly hilly, and the tough half of the course still lies ahead. Some climb the hill with their heads hung low. Thankfully, the runner discovers within this mile an oasis of relief: the gates of Wellesley College. The runner arrives and realizes that the legend of Wellesley College is not hyperbole; if anything, it's understated. It is here that the quiet miles turn into a tsunami of well wishes, screams of encouragement, and pleas for a kiss.

For this brief interlude, in the virtual middle of the course, the perpetual pitch of the students is intense. The runner might wonder if Wellesley applicants have to send in recordings of themselves screaming along with their transcripts and SAT scores in order to gain admission. Their effort is so genuine and selfless that the runner leaves Wellesley College with their spirits lifted, and with a renewed commitment to finish. To stop now would be to betray the women of Wellesley's trust, and no one wants to let them down; the only way the runner can repay them for their love is to dig in and concentrate on putting one foot in front of the other.

In the closing tenths of the mile, the competitors bid the students goodbye, hopefully with new smiles on their faces. The encounter is so heartwarming that it once provoked a runner back in the 1930s to ask, "Is this heaven?"

With the train tracks still on the left and the grounds of Wellesley's campus leading the runners up on the right, the route continues uphill until the 12.7-mile point, where it dips, only to once again climb all the way to the end of Mile 13, through the gates of Wellesley Center. This is where the course flattens out and the echoes of exultation still reverberate, where the cheers continue to inspire, where the runner learns further that they are not just embarking on a physical endeavor, but a spiritual one as well.

Mile 14

Believe you can and you are halfway there.

—Theodore Roosevelt

After scaling the last steps of Mile 13, the runner moves into Wellesley Center, past the aesthetically pleasing shops of Central Street. For the other 364 days of the year, Range Rovers and Mercedes pass through the streets, while shoppers with bags in in their hands and discretionary income in their pockets poke in and out of places like The Cheese Shop, London Harness Company, and dueling cafes selling lattes and finger sandwiches. The town's main thoroughfare doesn't host warehouses and shoe factories like previous miles. This town serves as the home of the affluent and the commerce hub of the wealthy.

Since the early 1800s, this town has leveraged its capital to its advantage. The Wellesley Historical Society contains many accounts of the town's history. One from the 1800s noted the town's ability to use its considerable wealth to its advantage by claiming, "Wellesley was getting a reputation as a town that gets what it wants. Might was right. There was no problem too big [that it couldn't] be solved with money."

The town was named after Isabella Pratt Welles, wife of the town's largest benefactor, Horatio Hollis Hunnewell. Along with his wife's maiden name, Hunnewell also gave Wellesley much land and financial support.

Out on the course, though, there is no class system based on wealth—just a hierarchy of speed, endurance, and experience. Those familiar with the route know that Mile 13 is not for deciding between Bleu des Causses and gorgonzola, but instead, for checking off another significant benchmark on their run. It is here in Wellesley Center that the runners cross over the literal halfway point of the course. With each step, they get closer to the finish than to the starting line. Inch by inch, Boston gets closer, and runners gets closer to realizing their dream of that final run down Boylston Street.

After taking a moment to note the benchmark, the runner must be conscious of an important change to the course. Between the quaint brick- and stucco-faced buildings, the town has made the streets pedestrian-friendly by extending walkways and thus compressing the race route. In the previous mile, the course provided runners with four lanes on which to spread out, but now, as they enter the town, they'll be unceremoniously forced to squeeze into two. Three-time winner Uta Pippig reminds herself when running through Wellesley to run with caution. "As you move past the halfway mark, the road narrows," she explains. "It's not a concern, but I am aware of it."

With careful footing runners carve their way through the town center. The halfway benchmark can provide some runners with a surge of renewed energy; however, for those with tiring legs and slumping shoulders, the halfway point could be a cause of discouragement. After all, half of the course still lies ahead—and it's the more difficult half, filled with miles of up- and downhills, not to mention the duress of the cumulative effect of the miles already run.

Just steps earlier, as the runners were passing the gates of Wellesley College, they welcomed the noise from the women as the decibel level drowned out their doubt. But at this point the ladies are gone, replaced by golf claps and time for quiet reflection. It is during these moments of rumination that the distressed runner must take part in the mental tug-of-war between uncertainty and confidence. Outwardly one pushes forward, but internally, the power of apprehension starts to creep across the bridge that separates mind and body.

Following the 1995 race, a *Boston Globe* article discussed this phenomenon of the tiring runner and the corresponding effect it has upon his mental well-being. Within the piece, runner Joe McCusker spoke to the sense of dread that overwhelms hope. "It's like *The Old Man and the Sea*," he said, referring to the classic Hemingway novel. "He thinks he got a big marlin, but he doesn't have the marlin, because they keep taking bites out of it . . . that's what the Marathon does to you. Little bites all over."

It is during these moments that runners need to remind themselves why they toed the line thirteen-plus miles earlier. Everyone has a personal reason for going out to Hopkinton on the third Monday in April. Some run to win; some run to be part of the 1 percent; some run because the course "is there," while others run for a cause, to honor a friend, or simply to pay homage to the world's greatest race.

At heart, the runner runs because at some crossroads within their existence, their soul told them they must run. Therefore, the question intrepid runners must ask themselves is a simple one: "What possessed me to travel to the starting line this morning?" It's here, during these moments of doubt, that they must examine *why* they began to run in the first place. It's within the answer to this question that they will find the motivation to push forward.

Lead runners make their way through the end of Wellesley Center with attendants accompanying them on bicycles. © RUNNING PAST

The motivation to continue to run can be found within the original decision that compelled the runner to first start running. Because in that first instance, when the desire first bubbled to the surface, the runner saw the world with their legs and not just their eyes.

"Why run?" is not just a question for the doubting amateur; the elite must ask it as well. The two greatest champions in the history of the race, Clarence DeMar and Bill Rodgers, nurtured their craft of running because of something more elemental: They had to get to work somehow. Rodgers grew up running, but returned to his gift when his motorcycle was stolen and he had no other way to get to his job. While DeMar and Rodgers ran to their places of work, Alberto Mejia of Colombia ran *after* losing his job as a metalworker. After getting laid off, he had nothing else to do, so he trained with laser focus in the weeks leading up to his 1971 Boston championship.

Others run because they are physically required to do so. Quite literally, they run to live—or to live the way they want to. Gayle Barron, winner of the 1979 race, had only been running for ten years when she captured the championship. The only reason she started to run was that she liked to eat, and couldn't continue as a newscaster if she didn't find a way to neutralize the calories. While Barron ran to maintain her physical status for her job, Elijah Lagat of Kenya had to lose weight to live. He had never been interested in running until at age twenty-five, his doctor told him he had to lose twenty-five pounds or die. He ran, and won the 2000 race.

Others use running as a catalyst to save their spiritual and emotional being. For some, running can be an outlet that separates them from the mental traps that restrict—and sometimes paralyze—their lives. Back in the 1970s, chain-smoking Patti Catalano decided to turn her life around while sitting in a drinking establishment where she had turned to escape the shackles of a harmful family life. It was in running that she felt free—that she found purpose and direction. Catalano would go on to become one of the greatest American female runners in history. She won the Honolulu Marathon three times, finished second in Boston three times, and set American records in almost every running discipline—including the marathon.

The commitment to reverse the course of one's life is a process that requires muscles besides those found in one's legs. The stagnant have to flex the muscle of the soul. In 1989, New Zealand runner John Campbell confessed that he had lost his way. Depressed over failed business ventures and a crumbling marriage, he realized that his life was in flux. "My life was in shambles; I was going nowhere," he admitted. Campbell turned his attention back to running with a renewed focus. In 1991, he came to Boston and posted a Masters (ages forty to forty-nine) record of 2:11:04. He is now considered by many to be the greatest Masters runner of all time.

Physical and emotional limitations have provoked some to take to running; they do it to stop the spiral of depreciation. These runners run in search of catharsis and release. Professional race-car driver Michael Waltrip spends his workday traveling at death-defying speeds in a million-dollar vehicle, sometimes separated from his competitors by mere inches. Turning or braking at the wrong time could have fatal consequences. So when he searched for an outlet to take him away from NASCAR, he found running. In 2000, he decided to run the Boston Marathon just hours after being part of a multicar pileup at Talladega. Waltrip ran to help deal with the pressures of drafting, hairpin turns, and extremely perilous speeds. It was in the rhythmic steps of solitude that he was able to decompress from the pressures of a hectic life.

Nine years later, another runner was determined to run Boston and find peace of mind. Like Waltrip, Patrick Harten was also desperate for quiet solitude. He had to run Boston or run somewhere—anywhere. Patrick Harten, an air traffic controller at LaGuardia Airport in New York, is compelled to run because of the stress of his job. From his "office" each workday, his decisions on the job can have massive consequences.

A normal day's duties for an air traffic controller are stressful enough, but on January 15, 2009, Patrick Harten took a call from the pilot of US Airways flight 1549—Chesley B. Sullenberger. "Sully" Sullenberger was the pilot of a flight leaving LaGuardia Airport in New York that struck a flock of Canada geese, causing both engines to fail. The last thing Sully said to Harten that day was "We're going to be in the Hudson." And into the Hudson River the plane went. Through the heroic efforts of the pilot, the plane slid along the winter whitecaps of the river, coming to a cozy rest and allowing all 155 passengers to survive.

Harten would be party to one of the greatest flying feats of passenger flight history. The air traffic controller would be grateful for the magic of his pilot, but was traumatized as a result of witnessing what seemed like certain tragedy. He would be obligated to speak to Congress about that day. "I believed at that moment," Harten told the congressional committee, "I was going to be the last person to talk to anyone on that plane alive." He would turn to running for escape.

In 2009, the air traffic controller submitted an application to the Boston Athletic Association to run the Boston Marathon. Upon being granted entrance, Harten had one more request of the BAA: He wanted to run with the race number 1549, in honor of the US Airways flight that had landed so softly in the Hudson River. The number was granted, and Patrick Harten ran Boston in 2:47:19. When the air traffic controllers union heard of their member's run, they wished him good luck and then good-naturedly jibed him to "watch out for the water stops."

Running allows people from all dangerous and stressful walks of life—air traffic controllers, race-car drivers, working mothers—to carry on. The runner doesn't get on the couch in a therapist's office; the runner takes to the road.

It takes time for some people to recognize the fact that in running they can find fulfillment that they can't find in other pursuits. In 1899, as Boston Marathon attendant Thomas Hicks watched Lawrence Brignolia run to the laurel wreath with a time of 2:54, he was convinced he could run faster. Five years later he would win the marathon Olympic gold medal in St. Louis and finish second in Boston.

Winner of the 1921 Boston Marathon, Frank Zuna, began running after being surprised by how easily he outpaced a New York policeman who broke up his illegal card game. Women's champion Allison Roe began as a high jumper. Before her jumps or after landing on the mat, she would watch the runners making their way around the track and be envious; they just seemed *happier*.

Lisa Larsen Weidenbach (now Rainsberger), the 1985 champion, started as a competitive swimmer, even qualifying for the 1980 Summer Olympics while she was still in high school. She switched to running because she felt it was a freer form of athletic endeavor than her time in the Olympic-size pool. "There was an excitement in reinventing myself," she said, "being at the bottom and having to work myself up the ladder." She remains the last American woman to win the Boston Marathon.

Running allows runners to literally or figuratively travel to places that other endeavors can't take them. Two-time champion Geoff Smith's first passion was soccer, and following his beloved Everton team in England; he turned to running almost by accident, when he discovered that his fellow Liverpool firemen stopped for a pint after their team runs three times a week. Whatever runners' motivations may be—beer or spiritual contentment—Mile 14 provides them ample time to think about why they are out there.

~ ◆ ~

Up ahead the course continues to travel toward Boston in front of more shops and cafes while moving downhill and turning left. At the 13.4-mile mark, the runners move past the Wellesley town hall and a small duck pond on the left. Across the street, just before the halfway point in the mile, runners say good-bye to Route 135. For almost fourteen miles Route 135 has escorted the runners over the course; now it passes the baton to "Route 16 East—Cambridge/Boston."

Moving left, the runners pass in front of St. Paul's Church—which sits on the right—where they can bless themselves and thank God for the countless gifts that the Almighty has bestowed upon them, if they choose to do so. The very fact that the runner is able to run, whether in sneakers or in a wheelchair, means that God has shone the light of fortune upon them. It's a reminder that running is much larger than listening to a playlist on one's iPhone and hitting the road. It is the opportunity to talk with oneself, perhaps align with one's spiritual side. All along the course, the runner moves past houses of faith: Catholic, Protestant, Jewish, Hindu, or

Muslim. It is so important to keep in mind that although you run alone, you don't have to be alone while you run.

Ultimately, whatever your religious tendencies, to move forward, one is best served by bringing forth his or her spiritual side. Running, when done right, can be an opportunity to become reacquainted with one's blessings. The marathon is an exercise in overcoming a challenge no different than the other tribulations in life. The race is a living metaphor. It's where character is formed and the soul is strengthened. At the runner's lowest moment—whether in the race or in life itself—seeing things in perspective can only help him or her continue forward.

In 1985, Joe Michaels ran Boston after surviving seven heart attacks, carrying with him the philosophy that helped him to endure in life and on the course: "The secret to life is hope."

~ ~

Across the street from St. Paul's Church sits a stone monument that commemorates the first-ever high school football game that was played on November 30, 1882, when the town of Wellesley beat neighboring Needham, 4–0. The road now straightens for a stretch, allowing the runners to once again take inventory and determine whether they should amend their expectations, either positively or negatively.

The route moves up and down with subtle rises and welcomed descents. The train tracks continue to shadow the runner on the left. On the right at the end of the mile marker is Hunnewell Field, named after the town benefactor. The runners soon come upon the infamous hills— where they may begin conversations with themselves, lost loved ones, or perhaps with the Supreme Being. All to pull them forward to the Promised Land.

Mile 15

When you come out of the storm, you won't be the same person who walked in. That's what this storm's all about.
—HARUKI MURAKAMI, *KAFKA ON THE SHORE*

MILE 15 IS THE CALM BEFORE THE STORM, THE LAST "PLACID" MILE IN which runners can work out a cramp or adjust their game plan. After this mile ends, the runners discover that the first fifteen miles were nothing but a dress rehearsal. After Mile 15, it's game time; ring announcer Michael Buffer might as well be standing at the end of the mile, yelling, "Let's get ready to rumble!"

Wellesley, the fifth town along the Marathon route, is such an ideal place to live that it used to be known as the Village of Contentment. Years later the name of this utopian enclave was changed because the town's most prominent benefactor wanted the town named after his wife, Isabella Pratt Welles.

A 1906 article said of the town, quite optimistically: "Pleasant paths for long, lonely strolls. . . . Wellesley, a residential village with no manufacturing, has long been noted for its pure water and invigorating air. It is believed that this fine village is absolutely free from all evil influence which tend to corrupt youth."

The former executive secretary of Wellesley, Arnold Wakelin, appreciates the Marathon and is grateful that his town can contribute to the event. "It's a privilege for the town to host the race and the halfway point," he says. "The marathon acts as a precursor to spring and good weather. With the contribution from the BAA, we are fully capable of living with any inconveniences. On a personal note, it is amazing to see the runners still coming by, one and two hours after the winners have finished."

For the 2014 marathon, the Wellesley community is going one step further and planting daffodils along the marathon route, with the plan to cover as much of the route as possible. According to the website The Wellesley Report, "Dozens of volunteers have begun planting some 26,000 daffodil bulbs along the Boston Marathon route, 10,000 in Wellesley alone as a living memorial to those who were killed or injured during the 2013 race."

At the beginning of Mile 15, Hunnewell Park, with its baseball fields and tennis courts, extends along the right-hand side of the course. On the opposite side, the railroad tracks continue to run parallel with the course, offering viewing for those on trains and temptation for tiring runners. At this segment of the route, the wheelchair competitors need to be cognizant of a change in the surface that might cause their wheels to jump and their spinning to have increased resistance. The unevenness of the road surface only adds to the challenge and necessitates that runners in wheelchairs exert additional energies just past the halfway point of the race. Eight-time champion Jean Driscoll spoke of the distinctive tarmac in this mile. "For some reason, you can't stroke as fluidly at this section," she says, "so you have to bear down more than you should through a level stretch."

With eight separate towns from start to finish on this point-to-point course, the route has different pavements, sewer systems, and road design; this makes each town, each mile, each stretch of ground separate and unique. The smart runners know this, prepare for this, and show respect for it; the importance of every step and spin from Hopkinton to Boston is not just a cliché—it's the difference between finishing and not.

Since the first year of the race, the towns along the course have been partners with the BAA, responsible for overseeing their miles and ensuring that the course is in appropriate condition. (As early as 1911, it was noted in the *Globe* that the "towns are responsible for watering the road.") The fact that each town is accountable for their contribution serves as a great source of pride for the towns and their residents, as well as helping to make the Marathon a true communal event. Though the BAA runs the event, each town is empowered to put its personal stamp upon the race.

As with any partnership, there have been power struggles. Over the history of the race there have been incidents of some towns trying to use leverage to guarantee that their town was properly acknowledged. In 1910, the parks commission of Boston threatened to block the race after the grass along Commonwealth Avenue was trampled by fans watching the previous year's race. It was only after Mayor John "Honey Fitz" Fitzgerald, John F. Kennedy's maternal grandfather, interceded that the race went off as planned. Seventy-one years later, in the days leading up to the 1981 race, the town of Newton called the BAA and threatened to block the race unless they were compensated for the $15,000 in police costs. The BAA found the means to compensate the town, saving that year's race and laying the groundwork for towns to receive funding to host the race. In 2013 the BAA paid out $858,000, with Hopkinton and Newton getting the most money ($85,000 each) through corporate sponsorship.

At the half-mile point of the mile, the runners pass the Wellesley Hills train station and the local post office on the left. After the depot, there is a variety of commercial buildings and businesses leading up to the Unitarian Universalist Society Church and the sixty-five-foot Wellesley Hills Clock Tower, built with the famous Wellesley field-stone. In years past, the bells of the tower were rung to greet the runners. In one of the many traditions that have fallen away because of the current size of the Marathon, the field is now far too large to continue to do this; it would be impractical to keep ringing the bells as 26,000 runners made their way past.

As this mostly level mile ends, the runners approach a multi-street intersection dotted with stores on all sides. On the left is Marathon Sports, where the entrepreneurs take advantage of their namesake event to hand out PowerBars and to fit sneakers on individuals who, they hope, will be inspired and subsequently pledge to run the next year's race. In front of the downtown Boston branch of Marathon Sports on Boylston Street is where the first of the two bombs went off in 2013, prompting the store's employees to react with courage despite the danger and mayhem. Owner Colin Peddie told *Runner's World*: "Our staff was very much involved in the recovery efforts. It was a war zone, with our staff pulling people into the store and doing triage on them." A woman reported that a tourniquet administered by a Marathon Sports employee ended up saving her arm.

The runner moves through Wellesley Hills and comes to a fork in the road seven-tenths into the mile. The runners remain left, continuing on Route 16 East. To go right would bring them onto Route 9 East, which actually serves as an emergency alternate for the course. For decades, the BAA has prepared for the worst but always hoped it wouldn't have to face it. Race officials have always been mindful of the potential for a calamity—anything from a water main break to a sinkhole to a bomb. Race director Dave McGillivray calls this contingency "Plan B."

In addition to planning course deviations, officials have to be sure that the town has adequate police and fire coverage. Complicating this measure is the fact that fans form a human wall along the course, meaning fire trucks and other emergency vehicles have to be placed strategically on both sides of the route in critical sections—although the Natick fire chief has said that if an emergency did arise, requiring additional units, the race would be stopped to let them cross. A more-typical emergency involves a marathoner stopping in at the local station with dehydration or blisters.

Ever since 9/11, the threat of a terrorist incident has been considered a distinct possibility. Prior to the 2002 race, officials implemented a dragnet plan in hopes of protecting runners and fans alike. On the racecourse, off-duty policemen ran the race, serving as virtual undercover officers, while three helicopters above blanketed the route in search of—or perhaps to discourage—nefarious behavior. On the ground, trash cans that could act as bomb receptacles were removed, while radar detectors scanned the city for potential nuclear devices. This effort was further supported by Boston SWAT teams and bomb-sniffing dogs.

Tragically, despite the best efforts of all emergency personnel, police, and firemen, everyone's worst fears were realized in 2013 when two bombs were ignited near the finish line at Boylston Street. Race and civic officials had to implement what everyone had always hoped would remain a plan and never an action.

—◦—

The runners work their way across a bridge that travels over Route 9. At the beginning of the bridge, there is a substantial bump, which forces the runners to pick up their feet and the wheelchair competitors to cross carefully. On the left sits the Wellesley Hills Congregational Church; it was here in 1996 (during the race's centennial) that Knoxville runners Denise Dillon and Edgar Walters stopped in the middle of the race to exchange wedding vows—alongside family and a string quartet. At a local flower shop, Ed changed into a tuxedo top and Denise into a wedding top. "To run this far was an effort," Reverend Craig Adams told the couple, "but the contest you face beyond the finish line is going to be even greater." The newlyweds kissed and returned to the course to finish the race.

The course then continues through a mostly residential neighborhood allowing for some of the runners' last relaxed steps. The competitor who is unfamiliar with the route probably enjoys Mile 15 as a level, forgiving stretch of running. But for those who are acquainted with the course, this stretch only produces fear and apprehension. It's the quiet before the storm. At the end of the mile, there are no breaks, no fun, no high-fiving fans, no dancing to the music from house parties—just outright pain. Here four-time winner Bill Rodgers used to assess the situation again and adjust his strategy. With the steepest downhill of the race approaching in the next mile, good downhill runners like him prepare to attack.

If John "The Elder" Kelley is the patriarch of the Boston Marathon, then Bill Rodgers must be its archangel. While individuals like Brown, Semple, DeMar, and Switzer introduced the race beyond the running world to the globe, Bill Rodgers is almost single-handedly responsible for bringing the globe to the running world. From 1975 to 1980, Rodgers won four Boston Marathons, four *consecutive* New York City Marathons, and the Fukuoka Marathon in Japan. During one incredible six-month stretch in 1977–78, Rodgers won all three of those races, achieving the Triple Crown of marathoning in what was one of the greatest athletic feats of all time. In all, he won twenty-two marathons. Twice during his reign over the running world, Bill graced the cover of *Sports Illustrated*, further introducing the sport to the masses.

A talented runner at Wesleyan University in Connecticut, Rodgers roomed with 1968 Boston Marathon champion, Amby Burfoot. Toward the end of his college days, and after graduating in 1969, Rodgers took an indifferent approach to his gift; in his senior year, he actually gave it up entirely. Smoking half a pack of cigarettes a day and drifting between jobs, Rodgers was forced back into running when his motorcycle was stolen; he had to get to work on foot. He regained his passion for the sport, and eventually won the first of four Boston Marathons in 1975. "When I won Boston in '75, my life changed," Rodgers admitted.

In the years following Rodgers's first Boston championship, an estimated 25,000 Americans finished marathons. Since then, the number has grown exponentially, to over 551,811 in 2011. The running boom that he helped to ignite eventually provided a comfortable living for Rodgers, as he went on to own two running stores and a running clothing line; in addition, he also receives stipends to appear at races and running clinics.

Famous for his swinging left arm and gloved hands, the five-foot-nine, 128-pound Rodgers broke onto the scene in the mid-1970s, and ended up becoming athletic royalty, especially in Boston, sharing a spot on a very short list of Boston legends that includes Larry Bird, Ted Williams, and Bobby Orr.

❦

As the runners move toward Mile 16, some will run with trepidation. It is ahead that the eye of the storm awaits. The prudent do not run toward danger but away, but no one ever accused a marathoner of being normal or prudent. The marathoner by nature is a risk taker, more interested in functioning within the eye than outside of it. It is within the storm that they can challenge themselves to run where few dare to venture. Others steer clear of the storm, afraid to explore. The intrepid don't, or won't, run because it is too hot, or too cold. They need family time or private time at the house. They need to rest their weary legs or save their fresh legs; let blisters die down or avoid new blisters. Too early, too late, too wet, too dry, too many carbohydrates, too few, full moon, half moon, can't run on days that end with the letter Y, etc.

Maybe it's the endorphins, or maybe it's just in the true runner's nature to run toward the storm. Perhaps the marathoner simply knows that the answers lie there. With head down and resolve in his or her heart, the runner keeps putting one foot in front of the other. Into the storm.

Mile 16

We find after years of struggle that we do not take a trip; a trip takes us.

—JOHN STEINBECK, *TRAVELS WITH CHARLEY*

THE NIAGARA RIVER IS A THIRTY-FIVE-MILE TRIBUTARY THAT FEEDS water from Lake Erie into Lake Ontario. As the water flows from the source, it moves at a speed of one or two feet a second. When the current reaches the crest of the American Falls, the controlled flow gives way to an awesome cascade of waters which spills over the ledge at speeds of sixty-eight miles per hour, pouring more than six million cubic feet of water into the bottom basin every minute.

At the top of Mile 16, the runners travel the first third of the mile at an even pace on an even course. It is here, like the movement of the Niagara River, where the runners flow inevitably toward the coming fall. Running past the white picket fences of a residential neighborhood, the athletes move forward in a state of either fear or denial. Either way, there is no turning back. The runner moves forward as if in a barrel, ready to go over the falls. From the crest of the mile to Newton Lower Falls below, the runner plunges one hundred feet, or 30 percent farther than the waters at the American Falls at Niagara.

Over the edge, and a third into the mile, the runner descends down the course for over a half-mile, past Walnut Street, which adjoins Warren Park. Each step on this slope obligates the runner to place his or her foot on the accelerator and the brake at the same time. It is this need for discrete manipulation of legs and their related muscles that separates the Boston Marathon from every other race in the world. Ironically, it is the downhills that have the greatest impact on the runners, not the upward hills of running lore.

At this point on the course, good downhill runners can separate themselves from competitors. Until now, race tactics have been limited to occasional surges on the flats of Framingham and Natick. This black diamond slope allows runners who can stay on their toes and use gravity to their advantage to roll.

In the very first race in 1897, J. J. McDermott took over the lead on this downhill, passing popular local runner Dick Grant of Harvard, who would see his lead vanish; this would cause Grant to collapse to the ground, calling for the water cart to provide assistance.

A well-timed surge by a runner in the lead in Mile 16 can provide the aggressor the opportunity to control the race—and his or her destiny. If the runner can take control of the race here, he or she is granted the privilege of running the famous Newton hills ahead at his/her own pace. Bill Rodgers liked to attack here. As did Uta Pippig, who, when asked about her strategy for the downhill, chided, "How I approach this section of the course is my own little secret."

For wheelchair competitors, this downhill is both strategically important and potentially dangerous. Some push the envelope and attack this section of the course at speeds approaching forty miles per hour. Depending on the weather, crowd control, and the condition of the street, this kind of hell-bent style can be hazardous.

After completing fifteen miles, this hundred-foot drop takes its toll on the runners, who have to call upon different muscles, ones they likely didn't flex during their training runs. The extended, descending strides (and the related contraction of the muscles) adds stress to the quadriceps and lower legs. Track coach Bill Squires speaks to the burden on one's legs in Mile 16: "The hardest thing is to brake. The downhills makes you overrun."

Grete Waitz, who won the New York City Marathon nine times between 1978 and 1988, pointed to the downhills in Boston as the most challenging aspect of the course. Struggling after the quad-crushing descents, she dropped out of the 1987 Boston Marathon with the lead, just a few miles away from the winner's circle. The experience gave her great respect for the course in Boston. "I never train downhill," she said. "No one I know trains downhill—we only train uphill. It can be hard to run downhill. Next year, I'll be ready." She never came back.

Many other elite marathoners, including Alberto Salazar, Dick Beardsley, Greg Meyer, Rob de Castella, and Craig Virgin, echoed Waitz's observation about the course. After pushing themselves in Boston, they were never the same.

The beating these runners were subjected to on the descents is not uncommon. Dr. David Martin of Georgia State University has studied the impact of downhill running on both elite and back-of-the-pack marathoners. In his findings he discovered that downhill running takes so much out of a runner because the dual need for running and braking forces the runner to use more muscles. Even the recovery is affected: "It takes many more weeks to recover from Boston because of the delayed muscle soreness caused by chronic eccentric downhill loading," he explains.

BAA race director Dave McGillivray (who has conquered Boston multiple times and as race director runs the race every year after the event is completed) feels that how well a runner withstands the downhills of Boston all depends on his or her individual style: "If you land like a helicopter, the course can beat the heck out of your quads, knee joints, and feet."

Those who run Boston realize the hidden perils of the downhill. When governing body The Athletics Congress (TAC) disqualified the Boston Marathon as a course where new world or American records could be set, they mostly argued that the dramatic drop in elevation from Hopkinton to Boston gave runners an unfair time advantage. This reasoning raised the eyebrows of many veterans of the race. They respond that it is precisely the downhill running of the Boston Marathon, followed by the daunting hills in Newton, which makes the course uniquely punishing among top marathons. In their view, most runners are unaccustomed to the tricky combination of braking and forward running demanded by the hills, and so the Boston course is actually much *harder* than the pancake courses where world records are normally set. Maybe the TAC should ask Frank Shorter, gold medal winner in the 1972 Olympic Marathon, and one-time critic of the Boston course. Shorter, who once mocked the course's descents, ran Boston in 1978. The course reaped its revenge on him for the insult, sending him home with a twenty-third-place finish.

The hundred-foot descent brings the runner cascading into Newton Lower Falls just fifty-five feet above sea level. (After experiencing such a drop, the runners probably should wave their hands above their heads like the Acapulco cliff divers do as they surface, to let the spectators know they're all right.) At the bottom of the hill, the runners reach the end of the mile and cross the Charles River by way of a small bridge. (The Charles River also begins in Hopkinton and ends in Boston, but it takes a meandering route of eighty miles.) In the last tenth of the mile, the street

The lead group bids goodbye to Wellesley and enters Newton, 1995.
PHOTO COURTESY OF GEORGE MARTELL/THE *BOSTON HERALD*

widens to five lanes, allowing the runners to spread out and give spectators some ideal viewing. The runners are provided with ten feet of flat road to regain their equilibrium after their leap from Wellesley and before they start up the longest uphill on the course.

It is at this brief flat and in the early steps of the ascent that runners can quickly assess their status. This is precisely where runner Wolfgang Ketterle evaluates his condition, flipping the hardware to software and the physical to the cerebral. Ketterle, who has run multiple sub-three-hour marathons, uses the downhill to shift gears and extend his stride. If his body cooperates, he knows that he is positioned for a successful run. Ketterle, a professor of physics at Massachusetts Institute of Technology, and the winner of the 2001 Nobel Prize for Physics for his work related to ultracold atoms, runs this section fast. When he submits surges, it is not against other competitors, but instead to provide himself with data so he can be best informed on how to approach the rest of the race. If his body allows him to stretch out and open up the throttle, he knows he can cross the finish line in stride, leaving nothing on the course but footprints.

Following the brief reprieve of placid running, runners are introduced to the first hill of Newton—what some consider the ugly sister of the Newton Hills. Ready or not, the runners now must begin the ascent through Newton if they want to get to Boston.

Mile 17

The credit belongs to the man who is actually in the arena, whose face is marred by dust and sweat and blood; who strives valiantly . . . who spends himself in a worthy cause; who at the best knows in the end the triumph of high achievement; and who at the worst, if he fails, at least he fails while daring greatly, so that his place shall never be with those cold and timid souls who neither know victory nor defeat.

—THEODORE ROOSEVELT

SHIFTING FROM THE RADICAL DOWNHILL OF MILE 16, THE RUNNER IS now faced with the most trying hill on the course. This segment is so demanding on an already-exhausted runner's legs that it is appropriately nicknamed Hell's Alley. Two-time winner Geoff Smith observed, "This extended uphill [over Route 128], coming off a downhill, is an example of the reverse muscle usage which beats the hell out of the runner's legs."

In the first half of Mile 17, the runners' quadriceps—which were just put through the spin cycle on the last downhill—are put to the test on what is the most extended ascent of the race. It is here that runners must recalibrate their muscles. Olympian Mark Coogan memorably noted that this hill is "the first place where your dreams start to get crushed."

It was running through the fires of Hell's Alley in 2013 that Olympic gold medalist swimmer and sports broadcaster Summer Sanders thought her dream of seeing her mother on the sidelines was about to be crushed. Summer Sanders came to Boston to fulfill a dream, to check an item off her bucket list, and to celebrate her fortieth year of life. As Sanders ran down into Newton Lower Falls, she was starting to tire. Fortunately, she had coordinated with her mother prior to the race to meet on the right side of the road at Newton Lower Falls, prior to the hill over Route 128.

As far back as Summer could remember, she and her mother Barbara had been one. Barbara was born with a competitive gene but, as a girl, had never had an outlet in which to express this desire. In San Francisco, she took up open-water swimming under the Golden Gate Bridge without a wet suit—a dangerous activity that required her to swim fast. Barbara would pass on this strong will to her daughter, who would begin swimming at age three. Summer's dream culminated at the 1992 Summer Olympics in Barcelona, where Summer won two gold medals, a silver medal, and a bronze.

Now Summer needed her mother again. Scanning spectator after spectator, she started to panic that her mom wasn't there, or that she'd somehow missed her. Despite competing at the highest level of sports, it was in Mile 17 that Summer was just another vulnerable runner in need of reassurance—a friendly face. As Summer bottomed out in Newton Falls, she began to climb; suddenly, on the right side, there she was. The very sight of her mother brought back all those memories of support and encouragement she had provided at swim meets. Always there for her daughter, Barbara held up a green sign with the very words she'd uttered to her daughter before every swim meet: SUCK THEIR EYES OUT!

An overcome Summer stopped to hug and kiss her mom. Her mother's support reminded her that she could do it—that she could always do it. Both crying, they let go and parted ways.

Although running a marathon is a particularly solitary pursuit, it often takes a whole family to make it possible. Spouses, children, and parents must sacrifice on behalf of the runner. Joey McIntyre saw running Boston as a privilege; after all, he knew it was his wife and three kids who had made it possible. Their sacrifice filled him with pride, a little guilt, and the weight of obligation to run a race worthy of their efforts.

In Ellison Myers "Tarzan" Brown's case, it wasn't just a family that got him to the starting line—it was an entire tribe. Tarzan Brown was one of the most colorful runners ever to run Boston. Talented and unpredictable, Brown was so impulsive that every time he stood on the starting line, he was capable of either breaking the world record or walking off the course while in the lead.

Brown was a proud member of the Narragansett tribe of Rhode Island and a descendant of Native American royalty. He was named Tarzan by other braves after they saw the way he swung from tree to tree. Born with a natural running gift, he first ran Boston in 1935, wearing a shirt sewn from his mother's dress and shoes so worn that they would unravel on the course, forcing him to complete the race in bare feet. He would finish thirteenth that year, only to return twelve months later and shock the running world by outdueling John "The Elder" Kelley for the championship. His run that year was so exhausting that when he entered into Kenmore Square, he sideswiped a car and came to a halt. It wasn't until his attendant illegally aided him by dousing him with water that he went on to victory—and his attendant to jail. Brown would later say it wasn't the water that got him going but the memory of his mother's dying words: "Run, my boy, and finish."

Tarzan would become a running sensation and a darling of the media, who often referred to him as the "avenging warrior," or—in the parlance of the times—"roaring redskin." Every year, fans of the race would look forward to Brown's run, always wondering what Tarzan might do this time. Included among those fans were the members of his tribe, the Narragansett, who, led by Chief Stanton, would line Mile 17 in "full regalia." Stanton was known to get so excited when he saw Brown run down into Newton Lower Falls that he would run with Brown for up to a mile while dressed in full feathered headgear.

In 1939, Brown would once again claim victory at Boston—the year a race official paid his entry fee. This time the capricious runner created panic in the crowd when he decided to stop while in the lead on Exeter Street with the finish line in sight and competitors in chase. Calmly, Tarzan spun from side to side, taking in the crowd and enjoying the atmosphere, before continuing on to the laurel wreath. It was the unpredictable nature of Tarzan Brown that left fans wondering and coaches scratching their head. Twice running within sight of the leaders, he broke off from the race to go for swims. In 1942, when he came upon his supporting tribe, he left the course to dive into the Charles River, then got in a car and drove home.

Author Tom Derderian said this of Brown: "The economy in these Depression times provided little for most Americans and nothing for Indians. They were a conquered people living on the margin . . . Ellison Myers Brown, born on the margin, saw running as his only way out of poverty." Tarzan Brown would go on to represent the United States in the Olympics, and would master races of all distances across the Northeast. He was the pride of his tribe and a treasure of the race.

<hr />

American poet and novelist Eleanore Marie Sarton (known as May Sarton) once said, "Loneliness is the poverty of self. Solitude is the richness of self." This speaks to the core difference between marathoning and running. While training, the runner enjoys the time to run and separate from the world, while a struggling marathoner feels the pain of detachment. It is a lonely pain. The struggle of a marathon is personal, as if the course holds some type of grudge against the runner.

A marathon invokes the crests and troughs of human emotion. When the gun goes off in Hopkinton, the runner alone is responsible for the day's outcome. No amount of support or motivation from loved ones can help a competitor once he or she is on the course. Their presence may provide a momentary and critical reprieve from the arduous endeavor, but when runner and loved ones part ways, it's just runner against course in a battle of wills.

In Mile 17, both Summer Sanders and Tarzan Brown had to leave loved ones and reenter the arena to begin their climb into Newton. At first, the mile is relatively flat and wide open. On the left is the Baury House. Built in 1755 by shipbuilders, the house was situated on the old Natick Road, almost as if they knew that someday the world's greatest race would pass this way. In recent years, the landmark was remodeled into a professional building and turned to face a road perpendicular to the racecourse. The architect was obviously not a running fan.

At the base of the hill, on the right, sits Gregorian Rugs. Like most successful businesses, Gregorian Rugs recognizes a marketing opportunity when it sees one; it takes advantage of the Boston Marathon to sell rugs while cheering on the runners. Each year during race week, Gregorian puts on a special sale on carpet "runners" for hallways and stairways, and hangs a sign out front depicting a marathoner in order to remind potential customers of the ongoing sale. During the day, thousands of living and breathing reminders pass the store.

Two-tenths into the mile, just past Gregorian Rugs, the five lanes become four and are divided by cement islands. A sign on the right welcomes runners to Newton, the Garden City. Many Newton residents claim that the race should be called the Newton Marathon. By their calculations, Newton hosts a larger portion of the race (six miles) than any of the other seven towns. Within those six miles lie a hospital, two colleges, two country clubs, a town hall, and four hills. Arguably, more races have been won and lost in Newton than in any other town along the route.

Once a part of Cambridge, Newton was known as New Towne in the late 1600s. Upon being separated from Cambridge, it joined the two words and dropped the "e." The town of Newton boasts a population of over 86,000 people spread over 18.2 square miles. In addition to its role in the Boston Marathon, the town is probably best known as the home of the Fig Newton, which was created in 1891 by baker James Henry Mitchell. According to *Foodsite Magazine,* the Fig Newton is the third-highest-selling cookie behind Oreo and Chips Ahoy, with over a billion baked a year.

Former Newton mayor Thomas Concannon sees the race as a cultural event that provides a carnival atmosphere and a kind of reunion for the people of his town. "The Boston Marathon serves as a coming-out party for the people of this town," he said. "After a long winter, the race provides them an opportunity to reacquaint themselves with their neighbors. The event is culturally enriching, allowing the town to benefit in many ways which far outweigh the monetary costs."

Although the three hills ahead on Commonwealth Avenue get most of the attention, many runners feel that the Route 128 overpass is the most difficult challenge on the entire course. Like climbers on Mount Everest, who must ascend to base camp before attacking the peak itself, the runners must climb for almost three-quarters of a mile over the high-way before being in a position to scale the hills up ahead. This gradual but continuous climb often fools runners into using more energy than they planned the day before when surveying the route from a tour bus. Wheel-chair competitors in particular must pay attention to their pace and plan of attack, as wind can be a factor during the exposed run over the bridge.

It is on this underestimated hill that many runners get surprised. Champion Bill Rodgers recognized this fact and took advantage of this part of the course to test his competitors. "It's a great place to make a move if you're feeling good," he says. "It's an exuberant place. You can really go wild there."

But for the average runner, the bridge over this main thoroughfare is not time for surges but for course management. One-third of the way into the mile, the runner passes the ramp for Route 95 South. If they so wish, the runner could run down the ramp and travel as far south as Key West, Florida. One-tenth of a mile above the next ramp can bring travel-ers north to beautiful Bar Harbor, Maine. At 1,925 miles, the interstate is the sixth-longest in the country, cutting through fifteen states.

Grinding up the hill, the runner finally makes it across the open-aired and unprotected Hell's Alley, arriving at the Beacon Street intersec-tion. After reaching the crest of the hill, which is a fifty-five-foot rise in elevation over a half-plus mile, the runners work their way up to another cement island at a set of traffic lights. The road bends left and falls slightly downhill. Runners need to run with care at this spot. It was here in 1949 that a woman driving a car crashed through the intersection, almost elim-inating the lead pack, including Swedish runner Karl Gosta Leandersson, who was forced to leap out of the way, escaping death on his way to the championship.

Following the intersection on the right is Newton-Wellesley Hospi-tal. Each year the hospital is busy caring for wayward runners and serv-ing as their primary source of care, while at the same time testing their catastrophe plan. By law, all hospitals across the country are required to have a disaster plan in place in the event of a catastrophic occurrence. The disaster plan must be rehearsed twice a year.

For Newton-Wellesley Hospital, the chaos of the Boston Marathon approximates closely enough the chaos that would follow an earthquake, a flood, or a nuclear attack, so the Marathon is used as one of the hospital's two annual disaster drills. With runners streaming by outside, doctors, local police, firefighters, nurses, and hospital social workers are busy running their own synchronized race. After September 11th such exercises took on a new urgency and relevance, and indeed, the drill would be put into action after the 2013 bombings at the race.

Founded in 1881 as one of the country's first "cottage hospitals" (so named because patients with common infectious diseases occupied designated cottages), Newton-Wellesley Hospital served as the birthplace of one of the race's most famous Boston Marathon journalists, Jerry Nason.

From the moment Nason was born, it seemed he was destined to contribute to the world's greatest race. Just five days after his birth, he saw his first Boston Marathon when a maternity ward nurse held him on her shoulder while she peered out the window to catch a glimpse of her boyfriend, who was running the race. As a boy, Jerry became a volunteer lemon carrier for the race, and later, a sportswriter for the *Boston Globe*. Nason covered the race for over half a century, making his own contribution to Marathon folklore. Journalists like Nason, Lawrence Sweeney, and Joe Concannon, who also covered the race for decades, provide a historical bond, linking runners in the modern Marathon to past participants, all the way back to 1897.

Some reports claim that more people drop out of the race at this location than at any other point on the course. After traversing Hell's Alley and the pending hills on the horizon, it takes a strong mind and well-trained legs to continue the journey. Over the history of the race, even the most willing of competitors have succumbed to the harshness of the course.

Runners who suffer ailments, illness, or injuries either prior to or during the race only have two choices: to overcome, or to yield to the course. Injuries are simply part of the race. In 1952, Guillermo Rojas of

Guatemala refused to let what he thought were cramps keep him from the finish line. Following the race he discovered that his appendix had burst along the course. In 1982, Bruce Gilkin crossed the finish line and was greeted by his sister, who hugged him and mistakenly head-butted him, breaking his nose. In the same race Guy Gertsch was running at a 2:30 pace in Mile 7 when he started to experience severe pain in his hip and thigh. The pain worsened as he continued to run, causing him to slow in the final miles. When he arrived at the finish line, he collapsed with a shattered thigh bone. After falling to the ground, he dragged himself across the finish line; he finished in 2:47 after running with a broken leg for *nineteen miles*. He would later say, matter-of-factly, "I'm satisfied with what I did under the circumstances."

Injury would again test a runner's spirit and will in 1995, when, six miles into the race, Heather Holmander started to experience radiating pain in her shins. Refusing to stop, she soldiered along to Mile 25, when she thought that she had stepped on a twig and cracked it. But it wasn't a twig—it was her leg. With pain pulsating through her body she finished the race with what would later be diagnosed as a broken fibula. She said later: "I would have crawled across the finish line if I had to. There wasn't any way I wasn't going to finish."

But the one runner in the history of the race who overcame more than any other to run Boston was Donald Heinicke of Baltimore. As a young boy, Heinicke, along with his brother and father, would be afflicted by tuberculosis. Of the three, Donald was the only one to survive. While in the sanatorium recovering from the disease, an accident would cost him four fingers on his right hand. Playing shortstop one day—despite his lack of fingers—he was identified by runner Pat Dengis for his running prowess. Dengis would serve as his mentor and introduce him to the Boston Marathon.

Heinicke would never win, but he was always in the mix, including a second-place finish in 1939, and three third-place finishes. One year he ran Boston while wrapped in bandages just days after a work accident had spilled boiling oil over his arms. Years later he would run after being poisoned by mustard gas at the chemical plant where he worked, singeing his lungs and causing him severe pain with every breath. Prior to the 1942 race, the *Globe* headlines spoke of the HEINICKE JINX LEGACY. Heinicke and his resilience in the face of adversity represents Boston as well as anyone or anything.

The runners move on a declining grade past the hospital. On the left sits the Woodland Country Club, which was built in 1897 to offer recreational activities for vacationers at the posh resort known as the Woodland Park Hotel, a mile down the road. Its beautiful clubhouse, which burned down in both 1970 and 1983, is situated down the driveway about a five-iron's length from the road. The famous golf course architect Donald Ross designed the course. Celebrities such as the Marx Brothers, Babe Ruth, Ted Williams, and Bing Crosby have played the course, along with golf professionals Gene Sarazen, Bobby Jones, and Walter Hagen.

An eighth of a mile past the golf course on the opposite side, the local Green Line train (part of the Boston subway system) drops off passengers at the Woodland stop. Many spectators take the train from the city to watch the race here, making this a congested and supportive area. For runners who are starting to melt, there is a temptation to get out your T-Pass and jump on a train, which stops one mile from the finish line at Kenmore Square, and covers the distance in twenty-six minutes.

The end of the mile turns residential and flat for one last breather before the road turns the corner at Mile 18. There, the turn at the fire station awaits, as do the three epic hills of Commonwealth Avenue.

Mile 18

After climbing a great hill, one only finds that there are many more hills to climb.

—Nelson Mandela

"The long, hard, smooth hills in the distance have proved to be the undoing of many ambitious lads," the *Boston Globe* wrote in 1909, referring to the three hills that lay on Commonwealth Avenue. Before the runners get to those hills, they have a half-mile of flat and relatively straight running. These steps offer limited resistance and arrive at the ideal time for runners, who have been negatively affected by the schizophrenic topography of the course. For a half-mile, runners can use their steps to recuperate and search for yet another wind.

On the right side of the course, runners move past Temple Reyim, founded in 1951 to serve a Conservative Jewish congregation. The word *reyim* is the Hebrew word for "friends." It was here back in 1975, while Bill Rodgers was running to his first marathon championship, that two unlikely men—a Jewish renaissance man and an elderly Japanese runner—came together and formed a lifelong bond.

Rabbi Richard Israel was a beekeeper, writer, and religious leader; in 1975 he wanted to add *marathoner* to his résumé. After running eighteen miles of the Boston Marathon, the rabbi was beginning to wilt. It was one of those defining moments in the race that runners have been confronted with since the very first marathon: to run or not to run?

Facing this crucible, Rabbi Israel decided not to run. Tired and beaten, he downshifted from a struggling gait to a walk. As he prepared to formally surrender, he was suddenly grabbed by another competitor—a sixty-five-year-old runner from the Far East named Tomiji Yamamoto. Looking at Rabbi Israel, he said, "I Japan"; he then ran with the rabbi for the next seven miles—all the way into Kenmore Square and leading him to the finish line. After finishing the race in 1975, the two would become friends for the rest of their lives.

This simple story captures the essence of the Boston Marathon. It's so much more than a laurel wreath and splits and the turn onto Boylston Street. In its purest form, the race has the capacity to break down the hard borders of nations and identities and allow total strangers to realize what they have in common is stronger than what makes them different. From Hopkinton to Boston, each runner is woven together by the thread of collective purpose: They are all there to run the world's greatest race. In a cold world where the line between what separates seems so defined, so final, it's on Patriots' Day that the line begins to fade. In the back of the pack, two runners who would have never otherwise met created a profound bond—despite the fact they were from different countries, belonged to different religions, and spoke different languages—all because they ran the Boston Marathon.

Twelve years before Rabbi Israel and Tomiji Yamamoto met during Mile 18 of the Boston Marathon, a neighbor of the marathon route in Brookline, President John F. Kennedy, articulated the very same hope with his dream for a new frontier, uttering the words: "For, in the final analysis, our most basic common link is that we all inhabit this small planet. We all breathe the same air. We all cherish our children's future. And we are all mortal."

Past the temple, the runners approach the turn from Route 16 onto Route 30 East. On their left before the corner, the runners proceed past the footprint of the famous Woodland Park Hotel. Back in the late 1800s and early 1900s, this hotel was frequented by well-to-do Bostonians who made the trip from the city by horse and carriage. Along with the blue bloods from Boston, President Taft once graced the hotel, as did the Yale football team, which made the hotel its headquarters each year on the weekend of the big game with the Crimson of Harvard. At one time the hotel was owned by a Newton socialite named Joseph Lee, who was also the son of slaves from Charleston, South Carolina. As a young man Lee had witnessed the bombing of Fort Sumter, which signaled the beginning of the Civil War. Along with the hotel, Lee ran a very successful catering business and owned a patent for a bread-crumbing machine.

In 1917, the Woodland Park Hotel was bought by Lasell College, although there was a delay before the college could put its new property to use. In the first year after the purchase, the Newton-Wellesley Hospital commandeered the property during an influenza epidemic. After the sale, the contractor built twenty-seven houses on the site. This location used to be the fourth checkpoint of the race, before they were switched to even intervals in 1983. Prior to the sale of the property to a contractor in 1948, Bill Lanigan stopped his marathon run to admire two girls playing tennis at the college. He proceeded to grab a racket and join the girls in a volley before continuing and finishing the race.

At the intersection of Route 16 and Commonwealth Avenue (Route 30), the course takes a 90-degree turn at the Newton Fire Department. Many runners look to this spot as another landmark on their long list. It's important to temper the excitement that comes from the large crowds as runners make the turn here. In 1907 Canadian Charlie Petch was running stride for stride with Thomas Longboat at the turn onto Commonwealth Avenue. As Petch took the corner, he got caught up in the energy of the crowd and danced his way around the turn. Longboat kept his head down and moved on to the championship, while Petch finished sixth.

Bob Bright, race director of the Chicago Marathon, saw this first of five corners on the course as significant—and dangerous. "For the better part of twenty miles, the race is a moderate descent," he said, "and the newcomer is tempted to open the throttle. Boston traps you. You get sucked into it. Then that firehouse [Newton Fire Department] jumps out and trips you."

The tight corners are a distinct component of the Boston course. They force the runner to factor in strategy and course management—both of

168

which are shaped by previous experience with the route. Two-time New York City Marathon champion German Silva respects the hills on the Boston course, but was more concerned with the five sharp turns that occur on the race route: at the fire station in Newton, at the top of Cleveland Circle, at the bottom of Cleveland Circle, heading onto Hereford Street, and heading onto Boylston Street. "Everybody talks about Heartbreak Hill, but I'm more interested in the corners," he said. "You can take advantage of the corners. If you are prepared [for those], you are prepared for everything."

Runners who arrive at the corner in questionable state can stop at the fire station, which is not only an ideal viewing location but also supports the race by acting as an impromptu first aid station. When the marathon has fallen on warm days, the firehouse has seen long lines of distressed runners in need of assistance.

Along with providing care for participants and spectators throughout the day, fire department personnel are also still responsible for protecting the ordinary citizens of Newton. As in all other towns, they place firefighting equipment on both sides of the race route. Inevitably, the fire engines that sit on the carriage road across the street often turn into a carnival ride for bored kids.

Around the corner, runners cut the tangent with their heads down to ensure the proper placement of their feet. After safely navigating the first of five corners along the route, runners take their first of what will be many steps on Commonwealth Avenue. Past the front doors of the firehouse, runners pick up their heads and come face-to-face with the concrete wall that is the Newton Hills.

Runners make the turn onto Commonwealth Avenue with caution and a wide circle, due to their tiring legs. (Wheelchair competitors approach the corner at speeds of twenty-five miles per hour.) Soon, runners' downhill muscles take a break, and their uphill muscles and rotator cuffs confirm whether or not they spent enough time in the weight room. Wheelchair competitors on the heavy side must wait for the downhills to make their move. For lighter wheelchair competitors, who have a high strength-to-weight ratio, it's time to attack.

For the marathoner, who has by now logged almost eighteen miles, the very thought of confronting these hills sends chills down the spine. Such fright in this neighborhood is not uncommon. It is here in the village of West Newton, up to Nightcap Corner a block away, that the ghost of Patrick Tracey supposedly roams the streets of Newton, looking to avenge the foreclosure of his house back in the mid-1800s. Reports of his specter floating through the streets were widely reported by neighbors, including a sighting of something chasing a fire engine at speeds "no human could travel." The number of sightings prompted the *Boston Globe* to report on the presence in 1896, the year before the first Boston Marathon: "Close upon the border of the Charles River not far from Auburndale, a place mystic, romantic, beautiful and much famed as the country seat of ghosts of all descriptions."

Neighbors were so frightened by the screams of what they believed to be Tracey's ghost that the residents moved out of their homes and vacated the block. These fears would be somewhat validated when three skulls were found in a shallow grave in a vacant lot where screams of fright were often heard, just feet from the Marathon route.

But on race day, it's not ghosts that scare the runners but rather the rising road in front of them. Just after the turn onto Commonwealth Avenue, the runners must attend to hill number one, which *Globe* writer Jerry Nason coined "Carbunkle Hill." The hill rises for approximately a half-mile with a roundabout swing to the left. Here on the right side of the road, Uta Pippig always looks for information on the race leaders: "After turning at the fire station, I look forward to seeing the sign on the side of the road that lists the leaders," she told me. "Every year I look for it. I train with some Kenyan men, so I am interested in how they are doing up ahead."

On the left, runners are boxed in by a grass island that protects a carriage road. This island continues into Mile 22. On the right, at the start of the hill, sits Brae Burn Country Club, founded the same year as the first Boston Marathon, in 1897. The club has hosted numerous golf events, including the United States Open and United States Men's and Women's Amateur, where Walter Hagen, Bobby Jones, and Francis Ouimet all won matches. Brae Burn eventually sold land to developers who built beautiful Georgian estates. These $700,000 to $1,000,000 abodes dot the course on both sides for the next three to four miles.

The first of the three Commonwealth Avenue hills falls in the last steps of the mile, only to jump back up one-tenth later; 1983 champion Greg Meyer sees this elongated uphill stretch as the most difficult of the Commonwealth Avenue hills. "It's steeper and longer than the other two," he says. "Heartbreak Hill is a gradual rise which levels off, whereas the first hill at the turn is a real test to your physical condition at this juncture of the race."

Mile 19

A ship is safe in harbor, but that's not what ships are for.
—William G. T. Shedd

After a slight reprieve at the end of the last mile, Carbunkle Hill again rises for a third of a mile. The slope of the hill is shallow but constant. Runners at all skill levels come up against resistance; the smart ones keep their strides short and their heads down. Each individual competitor has to decide whether to attack on the hills or conserve his or her energy. Wheelchair champion Jean Driscoll—with those "beautiful" strong arms, admired by President Clinton—looks to the hills as an opportunity to knock out her competitors, pushing them past the point of no return. A hundred-plus years ago, 1904 winner Michael Spring determined that the best use of his energies was on the flats and downhills, and thus he walked up any hills on the course. It's amazing to think that in 1904 the champion used walking on the course as a strategy, compared to 2011 champion Geoffrey Mutai of Kenya, who *sprinted* over the entire course, averaging 4:42 miles for the entire race.

The fact that the hills at Boston are situated a full twenty miles into the race separates the race from other marathons. Each runner's approach here will vary, depending on the runner's skill level, experience, and condition at the time that he or she arrives at the base of the slope. Veteran of the race John Ratti, who had run the race thirteen times, and would later become a race official along with his wife Gloria, knew the hills like the hallway in his house. For him the hills were all about approach and survival. As a Purple Heart recipient, this was something he could speak to. "Keep your head down," he advises, "shorten your stride, and pump your arms. Don't think about it, and before you know it, you're at the top of the hill."

It is amid these three hills that the back-of-the-pack runner begins to understand: The Boston Marathon course was designed with the world's greatest runners in mind, not ten-minute milers with items to cross off their bucket lists. In the running world, this stretch of the course is holy land, and should be approached with the reverence and care that that description implies. Bill Rodgers has run all over the world and sees the hills of Commonwealth Avenue not just as unique; to him, this part of the course is the apex of running. "This is the most significant stretch of course in the road-racing world," he argues. "The Fukuoka route [in Japan] has its spots, and other races have nice scenery, but there is no section that identifies the challenge and beauty of marathoning more than this section of the Boston Marathon."

The three hills after the turn at the Newton Fire Department are like the Giza pyramids of running. They stand on the horizon, tall and

The Boston Marathon defeats yet another challenger. PHOTO COURTESY OF THE BOSTON ATHLETIC ASSOCIATION

majestic, demanding a mix of respect, fear, and even wonder. The hills have been described in newspaper accounts over the past century in a variety of ways: teasing, topographically terrorizing, wicked, tortuous. The weak-minded runner advances upon this stretch with shaken knees and tentative strides; champions scale this three-headed monster like a warrior, as Tom Longboat did on his way to his 1907 championship run, despite the mockery of pre-race newspaper accounts that predicted he would go down in the hills of Newton.

Over the 117 years of the Boston Marathon, runners and writers alike have attempted to articulate the challenge of those hills:

- Sportswriter Jerry Nason: "These hills separate the men from the boys."
- Geoff Smith: "The hills are mountains by the time you hit them."
- Jean Driscoll: "The marathon is won and lost on the hills. Those who fear the hills will falter, while those who attack the hills can win."
- Canadian runner Ken Parker: "It's like meeting the queen."
- Runner Robert Dill: "It was tough, those hills. That's where I got my ass kicked."
- Sara Mae Berman: "It's at this point that your physical effort becomes more of a mental effort. You have to *want* to keep going."
- Uta Pippig: "The first time that a runner participates in the Boston Marathon, they can get confused with how many hills there are on Commonwealth Avenue. But after you run the race once, you'll always remember that there are three hills."
- John "The Elder" Kelley, who conquered this course sixty times: "Those hills have special meaning to me. I have great respect for them. They've caused me a lot of problems."

At this point, the runners continue to assess their bodies and adjust their intended splits, rationalizing that the crowded start, headwinds, busy water stops, and weather are responsible for the slower-than-hoped-for times. They don't blame their splits on the sublime racecourse and its corners, climbing uphills, cascading downhills, uneven pavement, traffic islands, littered cups of drunk water, or deafening cries in the Scream Tunnel of Wellesley. But maybe to run Boston one needs this state of mind; the runner must believe what he or she needs to believe, whatever is the most conducive to pushing forward. Running in some state of denial is probably the most rational approach to surviving those hills.

Literature is filled with adventure stories that detail the single journey. The story, its drama, its power, isn't that the person arrived, but *how* he or she arrived. It's the journey itself, whether it's a foolhardy campaign into Russia in winter or the discovery of the Pacific Ocean. It is what happened between launch and conclusion that really tells the story—that dramatic middle. The numbers alone just don't do it. Jesus only traveled half a mile with the cross and Washington's trek over the Delaware River was only a quarter of a mile, while Lewis and Clark trekked 3,700 miles to the Pacific, and *Apollo 13* traveled 200,000 miles *after the oxygen tanks exploded*. The journey is always told in the middle.

It is on Commonwealth Avenue that each runner's story blooms. If the runner arrives in Boston or drops out somewhere along the way, it is usually because of what happened on these hills. Every year, reporters camped out at the hills of Newton try to chronicle what they witness here. Some memorable lines include: "It was on this hill that many a likely winner had met his Waterloo"; "The hills [are] the graveyard of many shattered dreams; and "[the] topographical bludgeon which separates the men from the boys."

❧

Three-time winner Ibrahim Hussein knew that to win Boston, he must win on the hills. To fail on Commonwealth Avenue would mean failure at the finish line. When asked about his strategy beforehand, he candidly answered, "I will sacrifice myself on the hills."

The course for the next seven-tenths of the mile moves down and snakes left and right, sandwiched by beautiful Georgian homes on the runner's right and the extended grass islands on the left. The first hill has been conquered, but there are still two more to go. The course levels off and then declines, as does the runner's pulse. The mile zigzags

through a residential neighborhood and then continues past a set of traffic lights at the Chestnut Street intersection and onward, to the Newton
Cemetery, halfway through the mile on the right. Those interred at these
burial grounds include four congressmen, two governors, Red Sox player
Dom DiMaggio (younger brother to Joe), Morrie Schwartz (chronicled
in the book of great perspective, *Tuesdays with Morrie*), and two Medal
of Honor recipients, including World War II flying ace Robert Murray
Hanson whose citation reads: "For conspicuous gallantry and intrepidity
at the risk of his life and above and beyond the call of duty. Undeterred by
fierce opposition, and fearless in the face of overwhelming odds."

Across the street from the cemetery, a quarter-mile from the town
hall, is Wauwinet Road, which marks the site of the old Wauwinet Dairy
Farm. During the Great Depression, five hundred Jersey cows used to
stop their grazing to cheer on Clarence DeMar as he ran past. At this
point, runners know there can be no grazing; there are two more hills left
to run, and then the "second half" of the race.

Mile 20

If I hadn't been very rich, I might have been a really great man.
—Citizen Kane

After the Newton Cemetery, the runners move down a knoll to the Newton City Hall, built during the Depression. The steeple on top of the hall has a large timepiece on its face, alerting runners to their pace whether fast or slow, on schedule or behind.

For many runners, their preoccupation with time sometimes smothers the very act of running. At the start of the 2013 race, Olympic swimmer Summer Sanders was about to start her watch but stopped, realizing that her fixation with time on this day was misplaced. She recognized that her obsession with time wasn't about running Boston at all—it was about *getting* to Boston by qualifying. But she was already there. Liberated from the burden of time, she would run free, without restraint, determined to exist within the moment. She moved to the side and sought high fives. She smiled. She let the sun shine on her face and the breeze wash over her. She took her place as a member of the running community. As a temporary resident of this community, she discovered what other runners had known before and will know after: The world is good. People are good. It takes a day like the Boston Marathon to reaffirm these truths.

It was this very same spirit of community that made first-time runner David Fortier reconsidered how he viewed the Boston Marathon. For years, he actually went out of his way to avoid the traffic and bedlam of Boston on Patriots' Day, never mind actually attempting to run it. After taking his first steps in Hopkinton on behalf of his buddy, Brad Standley, and the Dana-Farber Cancer Institute in 2013, he couldn't believe that he had been missing out on all this for the past forty-seven years.

Something as large as the Boston Marathon can make you different, better, stronger, and, most importantly, it can make the runner believe— believe that the world is made up of decent people just like them, who care for others. This is why in 1980 runner Ruth Bortz made her way directly to a pay phone after finishing her first marathon, to call her four kids. She told them not to wait until they were forty-eight to run Boston, because once you'd conquered those twenty-six miles, you would realize that you could do anything in life.

John "The Younger" Kelley used to hate the sight of the clock on the Newton City Hall. During the race he made a point of ignoring his watch, fearing that knowing the time would do nothing but demoralize him. As he ran down the hill toward the Newton City Hall, the clock on the steeple would inevitably sneak into his line of sight, invariably show- ing the big hand five minutes farther along than he had hoped.

Ironically, this is the spot where his idol, namesake, and "Runner of the Century" John "The Elder" Kelley is memorialized, in the form of a monument that recognizes his achievements and contributions to the race. Situated on the left side of the course across from the town hall, there is a quaint little walkway leading to a statue sculpted by Rich Muno. The monument portrays two runners holding hands as they run up Heartbreak Hill. One of the figures is a rendering of the young John "The Elder" Kelley as he crossed the finish line to win the 1935 championship; the other depicts an older version of the elder Kelley as he competed in the 1992 race.

Kelley the elder will go down as one of the greatest long-distance run- ners in American history. A veteran of World War II who lost his brother in the battle against Japan, Kelley represented his country at the 1936 Berlin Olympics. He looked to the world's greatest race as a forum for Americans to demonstrate their dominance. Following his win in 1945, it would be twelve years before another American would win Boston. The reign of foreign runners was so supreme that Kelley actually suggested the BAA should consider two separate winners, with a laurel wreath for the top foreign runner and one for the top American runner, admitting "they have too much for us."

In the early years of the race, the very thought of a non-American winning the race was unpatriotic. After a Canadian runner won the race in 1900 and 1901, *Boston Globe* writer Lawrence Sweeney diplomatically would write, "Canadians acquitted themselves nobly, and their performance only served to make American runners the more determined."

From the race's inception in 1897 to the end of World War II, in 1945, American men won thirty-four (of the forty-nine) Boston Marathon championships. But from 1946 to 2013, runners from the United States have only won it nine times.

America came back from World War II and the country went through a transformation. The superior athletes were no longer drawn to running and track and field events. Instead, they found glory running for touchdowns, earning headlines and a cheerleader's smile. The American athlete, and sports fan, no longer emulated the DeMars and Kelleys of the world, but instead the Jim Browns and Bob Cousys. Running may have brought satisfaction to some athletes, but rarely recognition. This paradigm shift allowed athletes from countries that couldn't afford cleats and shoulder pads to run right past Americans and through the tape. Some went on to hero status, while others headed right for the bank.

In the fascinating book *Born to Run: A Hidden Tribe, Superathletes, and the Greatest Race the World Has Never Seen*, author Christopher McDougall describes the attributes that comprise a passionate runner. "Virtues of strength, patience, cooperation, dedication and persistence," he writes. "Most of all, you had to love to run."

This is the schism that separates other great running countries from America. Like soccer players in South America, to be great, to exceed what others think is possible, the sport has to run through your blood. If you are going to win Boston, or play for the Brazilian soccer team, the endeavor has to consume you—no different than eating and breathing.

It was apparent in the years following John "The Elder" Kelley's win in 1945 that there had been a shift in power in the sport. Race administrator Jock Semple was one of the people who recognized the widening abyss, saying in 1956, "[Foreign runners are] better than our guys for some simple reasons. From the country that they come from, people still use their feet and legs. They don't hop into a car to buy a loaf of bread or go to church. Walking isn't strange to them, and running is only exaggerated walking."

❧

The transformation in the long-distance running world was abhorrent to running great and World War I veteran Clarence DeMar. When DeMar won his first Boston in 1911, it roused such a spirit of patriotism that the *Boston Globe* wrote the following day: "Let the American eagle scream! Unloose the fetus that imprisons the sacred codfish and let that denizen of the sea flap his tail in glee."

DeMar saw the radical change in running dominance not as a function of talent but instead as a recasting of *priorities*. DeMar claimed that he ran because he loved to run, and because it gave him the opportunity to prove he was better than someone else; he earned pride and self-worth at the finish line. What he saw later on was runners seeking only the tangible. Athletes in other sports were driving fancy cars and wearing nice clothes; runners wanted the same. This provoked DeMar to admonish the modern-day American runner. "All they care about here is money, money, money," he said.

John "The Elder" Kelley never gave up hope. He believed in the American runner. "We are just as good as they are; if we dedicate ourselves to it, we can do it," he said. In the 1970s, Kelley would prove to be prophetic, as American marathoning made a comeback. The sport was resurrected despite spectators' obsessions with home runs, jump shots, and touchdowns. The pride of American long-distance running returned, led by Frank Shorter's gold medal at the 1972 Munich Olympics and Boston's dominance by Americans Bill Rodgers, Jack Fultz, and Greg Meyer, who won six Boston Marathons between them from 1973 to 1983, with Americans winning eight of eleven during that span.

In *Born to Run,* Christopher McDougall details the resurgence of the American runner, and how the net benefit was a country rediscovering its love for the sport. "They were a tribe of isolated outcasts, running for love and relying on raw instinct and crude equipment," McDougall writes. "[T]he guys in the '70s didn't know enough to worry about pronation or supination. . . . [B]y the early '80s the Greater Boston Track Club had a half-dozen guys who could run a 2:12 marathon. That's six guys in one amateur club, in one city."

Bill Rodgers graced the cover of *Sports Illustrated*—twice. Average Americans were jogging in local parks and on neighborhood streets. Fitness was "in." But then, as quick as it came back, it disappeared again. Clarence DeMar was right when he mourned the "demise" of running back in 1953. He knew that American marathoners were doomed; they were running for a purpose other than the love of the sport. Long-distance running in America was once again dying.

The plague that had infected the sport in the late 1940s had by now metastasized. John "The Elder" Kelley had run for a laurel wreath and a pat on the back. Americans in the 1980s ran as part of the capitalist system, as Christopher McDougall, who traveled to the far reaches of Mexico in order to find pure running for his book, *Born to Run,* writes: "This isn't about why other people got faster; it's about why we got slower . . . American distance running went into a death spiral precisely when cash entered the equation."

No longer were runners doing it because they wanted to be faster than the guy next to them. They were running because they had sat down with their agents and carefully picked races that would allow them to maximize their exposure, protect their legs, and, ultimately, earn the most money possible. This focus and strategy was not built around winning, but instead, by netting endorsements, being audacious in the press's eyes, being articulate or glib, or by looking good on the cover of *Runner's World.* Professional American runners were running with an eye on their hamstrings, as though they were pork bellies being traded on the commodities exchange. And, in a way, they were.

The world, meanwhile, was becoming more connected, borders more porous, and athletes from smaller countries saw an opening. The door was open for athletes from countries with fewer resources but who had more drive and purpose. When Japanese wheelchair champion Wakako Tsuchida was asked whether she thought of pulling off to the side of the road when the physical toll of rolling got to be too much, she firmly retorted, "I [didn't] care if I cut my fingers or anything, I knew I wanted to finish." This is the hell-bent approach that is required to run Boston. Anything less is disrespectful to the thousands of other runners who work all year to get there, and to DeMar and the Kelleys and others who helped to make the race the worldwide event that it is today.

This pride came from the desire to run as a performative act, of declaration and defiance and, in the process, represent something greater than just oneself. When fellow United Kingdom runner Ron Hill saw Canadian runner Jerome Drayton sitting on a curb during the 1970 Boston Marathon, he took it as an insult to the Queen's sovereignty, compelling him to shout, "Get up and walk if you have to. But finish the damn race!" (Drayton would later famously say: "To describe the agony of a marathon to someone who's never run it is like trying to explain color to someone who was born blind.")

In 1943, psychologist Abraham Maslow coined his famous Hierarchy of Needs, which helped to explain the order of people's motivations—all based around personal needs. The tiers of the pyramid begin at the bottom with what is essential for survival, and culminate at the apex of personal fulfillment and realization:

- *Self-actualization*—Pursuit of full potential
- *Self-esteem*—Achievement, respect
- *Belonging*—Family, friends, love
- *Safety*—Security, freedom from fear
- *Physiological*—Food, shelter, warmth

Most people who run the Boston Marathon have achieved the most basic levels of Maslow's tiers, and thus run to fulfill a dream or to realize their potential. Those who have run to obtain the most basic of human needs for themselves and/or their family run with an urgency that propels them forward. Over the history of the race, there have been some heart-wrenching examples of runners who ran the Boston Marathon in desperation, motivated by the more basic levels of Maslow's pyramid.

In 1937, Canadian Walter Young ran to victory because his family was hungry and he hoped the notoriety might earn him employment. Following his win, a reporter asked his wife if the family would celebrate her husband's run; demonstrating how basic the family's needs still were, she retorted, "I'll say there won't be a party—have a heart, mister; it's hard enough to get enough food to live on without throwing a party."

In 1914 a *Boston Globe* writer compared the desire of the marathon runner to the great Athenian runners who ran to save their country, those who run from a "confidence born of desperation." This was never illustrated more acutely than in 1946, when a runner ran for his hungry family and ravaged homeland.

Running for his war-torn country of Greece following the Nazi purge, Stylianos Kyriakides stood on the starting line in Hopkinton carrying a note in his right hand that read, "Do or die." During Germany's occupation of his country, Kyriakides sold every one of his possessions to feed his wife and two children. His country was destroyed; there were no roads or trains or harbors left. "There is nothing—nothing except the soil of Greece and a people determined to survive and be great again," Kyriakides said. When asked if he had the stamina to run the race because of his hunger and the effects of war, he humbly answered, "I think I have the strength for it. If not in my legs, then maybe here in my heart."

When he was the first to break the tape in Boston two and half hours later, he opened up his left hand which held another note that read: "We are victorious." He then raised his hands to the skies as though he were invoking the Greek gods and shouted to them and the people of Boston, "I did my best for Greece."

Globe writer Jerry Nason would call Kyriakides "a modern Pheidippides" after his inspiring run for family and country. At the post-race press conference, the champion didn't speak of his accomplishments but instead pleaded for America to help feed his beloved Greece. While speaking he broke into tears and said, "Once I think of my wife and two kids. You don't believe it, but many times they have only peas—just a few peas to eat!" Every runner and reporter in the room was moved by the runner and his country's plight. Overcome by emotion, second-place finisher John "The Elder" Kelley approached Kyriakides with tears in his own eyes, put his arm around the runner, and said, "It was great that you won. It was great for your country."

Kyriakides returned to Greece a hero that May, carrying supplies, food, and medicine donated by Americans who had heard his story and his plea. In 2004, a statue of the Greek champion was unveiled at Mile 1 in Hopkinton.

This is the essence of marathoning. The piston that drives the champion marathoner forward isn't the legs but the heart. To an extent, American runners have gotten away from the soul of running. "How-to tips" in running magazines, innovative workout routines, and smoothies can't make a champion. Any talent the runner has needs that extra component: a primal need to get to the unbroken tape.

When sports agent Mark Wetmore talked about the key to African runners' dominance of long-distance events, he spoke not of technical advantage but instead, of the sport in its rawest form. "It's a much simpler sport for Kenyans and Ethiopians," he said. "They don't know their VO2 max [which determines aerobic capacity], they don't do treadmill tests. The sport itself is just simpler. It's just running. If you train harder, you run faster. It's not more complicated than that."

In 1963 the Boston Marathon community was treated to a glimpse of the greatness that lay ahead for African runners when Ethiopian heroes Abebe Bikila and Mamo Wolde came to Boston and almost grabbed the laurel wreath before falling off their record pace at Mile 20. Since 1988, African men have won twenty-four of twenty-six Boston Marathons, with Kenyans Robert Kipkoech Cheruiyot winning four times, and Cosmas Ndeti and Ibrahim Hussein each claiming three championships. Since 1997, African women have won fifteen of seventeen Bostons, including Kenyan Catherine Ndereba's four championships and Fatuma Roba of Ethiopia's three titles.

The level of dominance was so overwhelming that *Globe* writer Bob Ryan in 2002 was prompted to ask, in a piece jokingly datelined "Nairobi-on-the-Charles," "When will this Kenyan tyranny end? Whatever happened to the Finns, the Japanese, the Mexicans, and the Ethiopians? And don't even ask about the Americans." Ryan continued, "By our sadly reduced standards, we actually had a good day. But the Bill Rodgers heyday seems as if it took place sometime back near the Civil War. It's hard to get excited when the first American—Keith Dowling—finishes 15th."

Foreign Countries Represented on the Podium of Champions

Men		Women	
Kenya	20	Kenya	10
Canada	16	Ethiopia	5
Japan	8	Germany	4
Finland	7	Russia	4
Ethiopia	4	Portugal	3
South Korea	3	Norway	2
Great Britain	3	Canada	1
Belgium	2	New Zealand	1
Germany	1		
Greece	1		
Sweden	1		
Guatemala	1		
Colombia	1		
Yugoslavia	1		
New Zealand	1		
Australia	1		
Italy	1		
Ireland	1		

The quest for running dominance has shifted through the history of the race, not from town from town or running club to running club, but from continent to continent. From the first marathon in 1897 to the end of World War II in 1945, only one Boston Marathon was won by a runner from outside North America (1932—Paul de Bruyn of Germany). From 1946 to 1974, Europe and Asia accounted for twenty-two of the twenty-eight championships. The United States enjoyed a resurgence from 1973 to 1983, coinciding with Bill Rodgers's *Sports Illustrated* covers and a running resurgence in America. From 1988 to the present day, Africa (exclusively Kenya and Ethiopia, two of the world's poorest countries, with life expectancies under sixty) has taken twenty-four of the twenty-six championships.

We can't know where the winners of the coming decades will hail from, but they'll likely contain the proper mix of talent, drive, desperation, and purpose.

❧

Past the Newton Town Hall and the statue of John "The Elder" Kelley, the runners continue to enjoy some relatively relaxing steps downhill; here, they can catch their wind for the second hill just beyond the Walnut Street intersection. These final moments of flat street allow runners to take a self-inventory and adjust their estimated times of arrival at the finish line, lurking six-plus miles down the road. The fibs that runners told themselves back on the flats of Framingham are meeting the truth on the hills of Newton. This is why coaches and trainers beseech their runners to run with ease in the early miles.

On her way to winning three marathons, Uta Pippig knew that she had to manage the course, and not the other way around. "I always reserve some extra energy for the hills," she says. "I know back in Framingham and Wellesley that they are up ahead, so I plan accordingly. While running them, I stay within my game plan, unless I'm running with someone that I am unfamiliar with. Then I will try to push myself and test my competitor. If they are fast, then they can go ahead. If I'm faster, then I'll go ahead."

For years Commonwealth Avenue has served as a conduit from suburb to city and vice versa. Workers would commute into the city, and the wealthy used to travel to Newton for a day trip or a vacation to the country. In 1895, the Newton Boulevard Syndicate built Commonwealth Avenue; the trolley was added the following year. This mode of transportation was popular among affluent Bostonians who enjoyed taking the five-cent ride out to the country. During the same year, twins Freelan and Francis Stanley introduced their own form of transportation, called the Stanley Steamer, which they used to race up and down the road, defiantly exceeding any speed limits. The steam-powered motorcar set a land-speed record in 1906, reaching the speed of 127.6 miles per hour. The Steamer sold for $600, two times the average annual American salary at the time. Francis would end up dying in a car accident in 1918 in Wenham, Massachusetts, and is buried a half-mile back, in Newton Cemetery.

After Walnut Street, the runners are confronted with the most difficult of the three Commonwealth Avenue hills. In 1933, the second hill was described this way: "[T]he toughest climbing on the course [lay] ahead of them . . . the heart-wrenching hills of Newtonville and Newton Center that kill the runners so."

If there is one mile that encapsulates the physical and mental challenge of the Boston Marathon, it is Mile 20. Just past the Walnut Street intersection and the mile marker, the hill moves up and to the right. The uphill stretches about seven hundred yards. Twenty miles into a race, this feels a lot longer than it actually is. The cumulative toll of the previous miles makes the second hill, quite possibly, the most difficult of the three. The first hill gets attacked with great zest after the turn at the fire station. Running up Heartbreak Hill, the third hill, is the final battle in the war. Runners are so excited to run the iconic obstacle that adrenaline can take them over the summit. The second hill just plain hurts. It is on this hill that many runners turn into walkers, tempting the other runners who have to stay strong enough not to join them. This is why Jerry Nason named this hill "Withering Heights," as it "does all the work—Heartbreak [Hill] gets all the gravy."

Halfway through the mile, the second hill ends. The now-level road snakes back and forth until reaching the Centre Street intersection, where it straightens. At this point the residential neighborhood runs into a small commercial district. On the right at the intersection is the former location

Coaxed on by her friends, Jane Weinbaum entered the 1963 race at the Centre Street intersection in Newton and went on to become the first woman ever to cross the finish line in Boston. COURTESY OF THE TRUSTEES OF THE BOSTON PUBLIC LIBRARY

of the Ski & Tennis Chalet (currently All Season Sports). Tom Foran, two-time third-place finisher in the men's wheelchair competition, used to look for the black sign on the front of the Ski & Tennis Chalet to remind him that he had one more hill to go. It is at this intersection that fans line the course six and seven deep for a glimpse of the runners.

This maelstrom of noise following the difficult second hill can disorient and distract some runners. In 1950, leader Ki-Yong Ham ran past the Centre Street intersection and off the race route on the left side of the barricades. Efforts by police and officials to direct the wayward runner back on the course, before he was nearly disqualified, were futile. Only after local college students from Korea were able to translate the pleas of officials to Ham did he detour back onto Commonwealth Avenue, returning to the course and on to victory.

With Heartbreak Hill up ahead, runners tread water, hoping to stay afloat. Many will not make a conscious decision to continue but instead let the tide bring them forward. It is also an opportunity for elite runners to test their competition. In 1987, two-time champion Geoff Smith decided he would run up next to leader Toshihiko Seko and test him with some gamesmanship. As they ran shoulder to shoulder, Smith looked into Seko's eyes and smiled at him. Seko ignored the look, turned away, and ran on to victory. Smith, the eventual third-place finisher, said later, "I guess I shouldn't have smiled at him."

This is where the race morphs from David Banner into the Incredible Hulk. Many runners are quiet, well-mannered people who participate in the sport because their legs tell them to. But here at the twenty-mile mark, something changes them. This is when the memory of all they've sacrificed bubbles up and manifests itself into a fierce determination. This is where their legs and heart are tested to their natural limits.

Silver medalist John Treacy articulated the difference between the runners' demeanor before the race and at this crucial twenty-mile mark. "There is no animosity between the competitors at the starting line because we all understand the mortality of a marathon," he said. "There is no reason to get the competitive juices flowing at that point. The twenty-mile mark is where you evaluate and assess your competition."

Mile 21

It does not matter how slowly you go as long as you do not stop.
                                                    —Confucius

Back in beautiful Wellesley Center, runners ran past The Cheese Shop (known to locals as "Wasik's," after the family that runs it) and over the "halfway mark" of the Boston Marathon. Though the literal halfway point is much farther back, any veteran of marathoning—and especially the Boston Marathon—knows what champion Rob de Castella knows: "The race is broken down into two halves. The first half of the race is the first twenty miles. The second half of the race is the last six miles."

Mile 21 starts off on flats after moving past the Centre Street intersection. It was here, in 2002, before scaling Heartbreak Hill, that veteran marathoner Tom Frost stopped his run for a moment of silence. It was on that very spot in years past that Tom's daughter Lisa used to stand and cheer for her father. On September 11, 2001, Lisa Frost perished on United Flight 175. On that day in 2002, Lisa ran beside her father.

The runners move past the Newton Tennis and Squash Club on their right. The manager, with a BBC-like British accent, reports that "Only the squash courts are available for the members at that time of the year."

It was here in 1985 that the world record appeared to not only be in jeopardy of falling, but in danger of being ridiculed. But, like the course has done for decades, it compelled its will upon English runner Geoff Smith. Like George Mallory, who in 1924 found that Mount Everest wasn't so much a stage as an adversary, Geoff Smith learned what the course is capable of. When Smith left Hopkinton he had every intention of setting a world record. He completed his first mile in 4:31, and the first three in under fourteen minutes. He passed the half marathon in a blistering 1:02:51. He was not out just to break the record—he was out to destroy it.

Smith acquired his passion for running as a fireman in Liverpool, England. During civil service training, the brigade was routinely asked to run in order to keep their legs in shape for ladder climbing. The privates ran through the Liverpool fog, knowing their commanders awaited them at the finish line, which happened to be situated at a local pub. Geoff figured out that running faster than the others would net him a well-deserved pint while he waited for his slower, less-thirsty comrades. This instilled Geoff's run with purpose, and a star was born. From the soccer fields and fire poles of England to Providence College, and, ultimately, to the streets of Boston, Smith proved himself a runner of remarkable versatility. He has run a sub-4:00 mile, a sub-1:02 half marathon, and a sub-2:10 marathon—an accomplishment matched by very few.

In 1985, Smith was still on pace to break the world record when the course reared its ugly head. For a hundred years, the marathon has had a way of humbling even the greatest runners, and this year was no different. "I thought it was all over," he said, recalling the race years later. "With the pain biting at my hamstrings, I didn't think I could take another step. But the cramp let up somewhat and I was able to run slowly and cautiously to the finish line."

Running in Mile 21 on world-record pace, Smith came to an abrupt halt, feeling as though he'd been shot in the leg. With severe cramping and limited mobility in his hamstrings, the English runner limped forward, looking to the skies for divine intervention. He finished the mile in 6:17. His dream of adding his name to the record books was crushed.

Smith held on to his lead and claimed a ragged victory six miles later, with a time of 2:14:05. Many involved with the race saw this as symbolic. The quality of the field had diminished in recent years as world-class runners migrated to races that rewarded their efforts with prize money. Smith's painful saunter across the line allowed critics to point out that while the winner walked across the finish line, he still beat his nearest competitor (Gary Tuttle, 2:19:11) by a full five minutes.

In retrospect, Smith's 1985 run embodied the essence of the Boston Marathon. There was no prize money, no cars, no hidden purse—just a medal and a laurel wreath. Smith had already won the year before. He could have walked off the course in Newton and still had his name in the circle of champions. But he fought the pain and anguish because his heart told him to. As Geoff Smith walked across the finish line, his run evoked pathos but not pity. He had taken the Boston Marathon's best punch and was still standing. Somewhere high above, the late great champions William Kennedy and Clarence DeMar must have been smiling as Smith broke the tape.

Smith's championship run personified why Olympic gold medalist Frank Shorter asked, after surrendering because of the hills of Newton, "Why couldn't Pheidippides have died at twenty miles?"

But Pheidippides continued on, and thus the run to Boston continues on in Mile 21, past the flats to that make-or-break moment when the runner faces the infamous Heartbreak Hill. After twenty miles, the intimidating hill can make any runner hesitate and question his or her ability to move forward. During her first encounter, American wheelchair athlete Christina Ripp sat at the base of the hill and asked herself, "How am I going to get up there?"

Some run, some walk, some crawl, and some surrender, but without doubt, all who dare to scale the coming "mountain" do so with respect. In American history, hills and summits have long served as the stage for landmark achievements. The very founding of the country was achieved only after 115 colonial fighters made the ultimate sacrifice in the Battle of Bunker Hill during the American Revolution, just miles from where the finish line of the Boston Marathon is situated. In the Spanish-American War, Theodore Roosevelt gets the credit for victory at the Battle of San Juan Hill, but it was Lieutenant Jules Ord who volunteered to lead the Buffalo Soldiers up the hill with a pistol in one hand and a sword in the other, before being shot in the throat after reaching the summit with his men in tow. Roosevelt would subsequently ride his horse up the hill and all the way to the White House.

But the greatest summit occurred on D-Day in June of 1945, on the cliff called Pointe du Hoc in Normandy, France. It was there that the Rangers from the 2nd Battalion—using ladders made of rope—scaled a hundred-foot cliff while battling seventy-mile-per-hour winds. The summit was said to be so unlikely that the Germans left the critical post exposed, allowing the Americans to take control and shut off multiple of the Axis powers' fronts on that day. Of the 225 Rangers who disembarked at the foot of the cliff, only 90 would come home.

Rising up to conquer something above is a powerful image that has long been a symbol for literature and history. It is no different in the running world. Since Boston's first race, runners and writers alike have focused on hills as the major crucible of the race. In the running world, there is no hill more respected and feared than the hill in Mile 21 of the Boston Marathon.

During the race's infancy, *Boston Globe* writer Lawrence Sweeney described the hills in Newton as "heartbreaking hills." As the years went by, and the hills claimed more victims, race correspondent Jerry Nason built on Sweeney's description and formally christened the last and most treacherous of the three hills "Heartbreak Hill." "The big hill . . . has killed off many ambitious marathoners," the *Boston Globe* noted in 1925.

In 2007, after finishing second, two-time New York Marathon champion Jelena Prokopcuka of Latvia mixed up her words, but in doing so got to the core of how she felt about fading on the third hill. She called it "Break-heart Hill."

In all, the hill stretches almost a half-mile. Jerry Nason memorably called it the "winding ribbon of Commonwealth Avenue that rises to the great tall towers of Boston College." Throughout this segment, there are different degrees of steepness, including a fifteen-yard plateau early in the mile at the Grant Street intersection, as if the course were giving the runners a moment to reconsider.

In 1975, Bill Rodgers actually came to a complete stop here—not because of fear, but to tie his sneakers. It was one of five times he stopped on the course that day, still managing to set an American and course record with a time of 2:09:55. Four years later he would win the third of his four Bostons by defeating challenger Toshihiko Seko on the hill. Before the race the Japanese marathoner's coach promised that his runner would destroy Rodgers on the hills. After he lost, Seko said, "If you didn't have Heartbreak Hill, you would have an easy course."

From mile to mile, town to town, the crowd gradually evolves and multiplies—from the well-wishers in Hopkinton into a mob in Newton. On Heartbreak Hill, spectators rally five, six, and seven deep to see men and women wage their own personal battles in front of a supportive, and often inebriated, public. One writer likened the Marathon crowd to "the sadistic mass at the Indianapolis 500, who are more interested in human wreckage than the sporting event itself." Another writer declared, "The fans at this vantage point are sadists, flog artists, and bunion mongers."

In an effort that exemplifies the battle of the Boston Marathon, a 1992 competitor refuses to be denied. PHOTO COURTESY OF THE *BOSTON HERALD*/JIM MAHONEY

The fans arrive in droves here, both to support and to pay witness. It's not every day that you can see the human spirit emerging from the inner core of so many different people. It is here that one by one, the athletes dig in and push, plumbing unknown depths of will rarely done on such a public scale. The masses clap and yell and urge them on, if only for the opportunity to share in the moment and perhaps take home with them the hope of possibility.

While some spectators may take pleasure in the inevitable crashes on Heartbreak Hill, the majority of the fans are invaluable in providing support for the runners. With the fans at the top pulling and the fans behind them pushing, the runners move toward the peak of Heartbreak Hill. For five-tenths of a mile, it's all gritted teeth and clenched fists.

For many the struggle up Heartbreak Hill doesn't seem any harder than the steps on level ground—all of them painful. Each new step presents an obstacle as it arrives and becomes an accomplishment as it passes. The discomfort on Heartbreak Hill is not so much the hill itself as the cumulative exhaustion the runner experiences as he or she continues to swim out farther and farther from the safe harbor of Hopkinton. The runners draw upon their reserves of resilience, persistence, and a refusal to accept any predetermined limits set upon them—traits that the runner uses not only on the road from Hopkinton to Boston, but in their lives as well. The Boston Marathon, at this point, becomes the ultimate metaphor.

Finally, the crest of the hill is within sight. To the spectators, it appears that the runners' arms and legs have done all the work, but in actuality the competitors have relied heavily on one muscle—the heart. At the eight-tenths point of the mile, they arrive at the summit of Heartbreak Hill, sans Sherpa. For months leading up to Boston the runners worry about the risk of failing on this ascent and wasting all that effort. Many runners are so excited as they crest here that they take a moment to rejoice—with whatever adrenaline they have left: Goliath has been slain.

At the top, the crowd welcomes the runners as if they had just been accepted into a special fraternity—and in a way, they have. With the fans in a perpetual state of bedlam, the runners don't know if they should plant a flag in the mountain's peak or collapse right there on the ground. Over on the grass island to the runners' left is the spot where, for years, Lieutenant Feeley of the Newton Police sat in his squad car proclaiming over the loudspeaker, "Congratulations! You have just conquered Heartbreak Hill!"

The scene is a picture of pure elation: The crowd salutes the runners for their effort, and the runners show their appreciation by throwing gloves and hats into the crowd in thanks. The display of adoration is so overwhelming that many of the runners will move to the side of the road to join the party and thank the crowd for their support, even some dutifully accepting a red cup from the drinkers.

When former Boston mayor Ray Flynn arrived at the top of Heartbreak Hill, his running partner Donald Murray said to him, "This will be the closest you'll be to God all day." Flynn, who served as the ambassador to the Vatican, and was blessed to meet two saints along his journeys, responded, "How can't I make it to the peak after that?"

In the last steps of the mile after cresting the monster, the road drops to the right before rising cruelly for one last, brief moment of pain. On the runners' right are the gates of Boston College, founded by Jesuit priests in 1863. By 1897 Boston College was home to 450 male students, who paid less than $100 in annual tuition (plus a $1 library and athletic fee). Now it costs almost 15,000 young men and women $60,706 a head to live and learn at BC. Famous graduates include football star Doug Flutie, Ed McMahon of *The Tonight Show* and *Star Search* fame, and former Speaker of the House Tip O'Neill. The John Burns Library has great holdings of Irish history, and the most heralded faculty member is Raymond McNally (one of the country's foremost experts on Count Dracula).

The ascent to Boston College is an arduous one—for most. As Champion Jack Fultz said, "You don't really attack the hills; you survive them." However, on her way to her first win at Boston, Joan Benoit Samuelson asked in the late miles, "Where is Heartbreak Hill?," not realizing that she had run it with such ease that the hill had seemed irrelevant.

Either way, the downhill into Newton Lower Falls, the rise over Route 128, and the three hills of Commonwealth Avenue are now behind the runner. But amazingly, the toughest miles lie ahead. Runners need to keep their heads down, their feet moving, and their eyes peeled for the CITGO sign.

Mile 22

A cemetery is one of the wealthiest places. There are books unwritten, there are songs to be sung, and there are inventions never invented.
—AENEAS WILLIAMS, NFL PLAYER

IN 1963, THE MOST TALKED-ABOUT MARATHON RUNNER IN SEVEN decades of the sport came to Boston. Abebe Bikila of Ethiopia captured the attention and imagination of the world after winning a gold medal at the 1960 Rome Olympics (the first African to win any medal) while running the twenty-six miles *in bare feet*. Before taking position in Hopkinton that year, he had run in four marathons and won them all, setting records in each.

After the starting gun, Bikila took off to the lead, as predicted, alongside his teammate, Mamo Wolde. The crowds cheered them wildly as Bikila had become a global star who transcended sports. Their lead was wide and apparently insurmountable. Running in third place was Aurele Vandendriessche of Belgium, who was hoping to just maintain his position in the race when he crested Heartbreak Hill and ran into Mile 22. As he ran down the hill he looked up, and to his amazement he could see, for the first time, Bikila and Wolde below. "I thought they were unbeatable," he said. "Now I ran to win."

Little by little Vandendriessche chipped away at the Ethiopians' lead until he finally caught them and passed them two miles down the road— and never looked back. Bikila was so devastated about being passed that he began to walk, and ended up with a disappointing fifth-place finish. A reporter for the *Boston Globe* wrote the next day that Vandendriessche ran with great urgency, looking like an "MTA bus driver late for lunch."

After conquering Heartbreak Hill, some runners, who aren't accli-mated to the course, might run with the false impression that the race is over. Like a space capsule descending, the runners plummet back to Earth in hopes of effortlessly crashing into the sea. Many of these run-ners trained under the premise "If I can run twenty miles, I can run twenty-six." Such speculation is foolhardy, however. "The great mystique of Heartbreak Hill is not getting up it," said the great Irish runner, John Treacy. "It's getting down it."

For over a century, the backside of Heartbreak Hill has been a secret killer, making athletes suffer the consequences for not running with proper respect and remembering Jim Knaub's adage: "There's no such thing as an unimportant mile."

The hills may be done, but the race goes on. After the celebration at the top of Heartbreak Hill, the runners are once again alone. It is in these very steps that the athletes must immediately shift their attention from the excitement of running up Heartbreak Hill to the concern of running down it.

The descent of the first steps of Mile 22 mimics the landslide that the runners survived back in Mile 16 as they ran toward Newton Lower Falls. Again, they need to mobilize leg muscles used in downhill running. This torment on the runners' legs prompted champion Rob de Castella to refer to this section of the race as "an anatomical challenge." Quads are again put to the test as they work to simultaneously propel and brake, while feet must carefully avoid the previous water-stop litter that turns the pave-ment into slippery steps of wet trash. There are still more than five miles to go before the athletes earn the right to revel in their glory.

Plodding forward, the runners rappel down the hill. In a sort of tango, runner and racecourse serve as dance partners, but each is trying to lead and compel their will upon the other. Runners stride, brake, and contract their downhill muscles while the course feels like it's pulling away from each foot strike. It's not uncommon here for runners to face the sight of fellow runners now walking, or even sitting.

With each mile the runner moves in a state of paradox. The satis-faction of crossing over mile marks is actually spoiled by the realization that each new mile only increases the degree of difficulty. It's now that the runner understands those pleas of coaches and veterans who beseeched them to relax and go slow in those early miles. This is why Joey McIntyre's instructor told him to put on his smoking jacket and just chill as he traveled through Hopkinton and Ashland. This is why worrying about running for a personal record is a form of psychological quicksand. This course hasn't subsisted for twelve decades by just letting runners go wild, oblivious to topography and history. The heart of this course pounds every Patriots' Day because it feeds off runners who think they can run without concern.

The runners move past Boston College in a continuous descent of almost a half-mile. At this point, runners must assess their energy reserves to determine whether they can push themselves or whether they should hold on for dear life. To the human eye the course here actually seems inviting—after all, the runner moves with the help of gravity. But at the Boston Marathon the most obvious is actually the most uncertain. Running hard and uninhibited will only hurt things. It's counterintuitive, like the thirsty boater drifting at sea who drinks the salt water—which only makes him thirstier.

This is the seduction of the course, or, as Bill Rodgers calls it, the "topographical trapdoor." After running four hills that are the equal of two miles in total uphill steps, runners may not notice that they have gone through a transformation. Whereas their strides were once intentional, signaled from the brain to the body, their legs now move in an involuntary, almost trance-like state, propelled forward by sheer will and the power of dreams. In Mile 22 the pathway of consent moves, from brain to the legs to heart to the legs.

This change is not just internal, either. Prior to running the hills, the runner ran with shoulders set and legs high. This all changes on the back side of Heartbreak Hill. The runner actually undergoes a physical metamorphosis, with skin pigmentation altered, shoulders drooped, and head now actually dangling downward, bouncing up and down with each step.

This is why the twenty-mile mark (and not the thirteen-mile mark) is considered the second half of the race. It is because the runner traverses the course in two separate states of being. For the first twenty miles, the runner personifies the idealism of the Greek athlete, honoring the gods. In the last six miles, the runner moves as if he were the victim of the gods' wrath. This is why Mile 22 is called the Haunted Mile, or the Superstitious Mile.

It is here in Mile 22 that more runners' dreams have turned to nightmares than any other. Ever since 1903, when Sammy Mellor was forced to surrender the lead and walk down the back side of Heartbreak Hill, both elite and back-of-the-pack runners have feared that they too might fall victim to the eerie mile. Over the history of the race, more leads have been lost on the downhill past Boston College than any other mile on the course. It was this nearly annual tradition of champions' dreams dying a sad death that prompted writer Jerry Nason to call this segment of the course "The Graveyard of Champions."

Many suspect that the spirits housed in the Evergreen Cemetery down the road are to blame for wreaking their demonic whims upon the runners. Whatever the cause, unexpected forces have influenced this section of the course throughout the history of the race. Menacing vehicles, illegal stimulants, and bizarre behavior have all conspired to turn Mile 22 into the Bermuda Triangle of running, a vortex that sucks runners' hopes and yearnings (and energy) into its whirlpool.

The runners' physical and mental exhaustion, the pull of gravity, the blood-alcohol level of the Boston College coeds, and the tricky islands that litter the road all add to the chaos of this mile. What was an open road from sidewalk to sidewalk is now compressed, as the Green Line train tracks force runners to the right side of the road. This course compression only adds to the Haunted Mile's reputation.

For those who know Boston, it is in the Haunted Mile where they can exploit the course and their opponents to their advantage. Clarence DeMar was said to know the course better than any of his competitors. It was during the Haunted Mile where on three separate occasions he struck, taking advantage of the chaos on his way to victory. In 1911, DeMar was running side by side with Festus Madden when Madden was hit by a car, delivering DeMar his first championship.

In 1922, DeMar allowed James Henigan to charge down the hill while he laid back. When DeMar made it to the bottom of the hill, he found the leader on the side of the road, hitting his legs with a yardstick, trying to restart them. One year after beating Henigan, DeMar took the lead at the end of the hills. As the newspaper reported the next day, "It was then that he showed the brain of a workman and showed that he knows himself better than anyone else." DeMar knew that once he ran in front that cars and bikes would fill in behind him, blocking his competitor and allowing him to run to victory. Competitor Frank Zuna was left behind to serpentine his way through the traffic. "He did not exercise the best judgment on the course," the *Globe* reported, "and the congestion of automobiles injured his chances of winning."

Other factors have conspired to make the Haunted Mile worthy of its name. In 1972, leaders Olavi Suomalainen and Jacinto Sabinal were forced to hug each other after they were almost run over by the press bus just after passing Boston College. Six years later, the bus again fell behind and was forced to weave in and out of runners, making them potential residents of the nearby Evergreen Cemetery. In the end, the media bus—with its furious photographers and reporters—failed to arrive at the finish line in time to capture images of the winners. The following day's *Boston Globe* joked, "The officials' bus finished seventh and press bus finished eighth. Their poorest performance in years."

Toward the bottom of the hill, runners are greeted by the pleasing sign welcoming them to Boston. For rookies of the race, this border placard is a welcome sight. Little do they know that the course mockingly cuts through Boston for a moment before regurgitating the runners into Brookline in the coming mile. Former Boston mayor and veteran marathoner Ray Flynn used to compare the sign to a punch in the stomach. "When you see the Boston sign, you feel like you're rounding third and heading for home," he said. "One mile later when the runners are welcomed into Brookline, it can be psychologically demoralizing to have Boston offered and then taken away from you."

At the bottom of the hill, after Boston College, the route passes St. Ignatius Church on the right. It was here that textile worker Doroteo

Flores of Guatemala was running down the hill in 1952 when he looked to the church for support. He had hoped that a win at the world's greatest race might help him to find employment or notoriety and allow him to make a better life for himself and his family. With a prayer in his heart, the Roman Catholic regained his stride and the will to win. "Coming over the hills I asked my God, 'How do I do it?'" he said. "He listened and gave me strength, and I ran with greater sense of purpose." After winning Boston in 1952, Flores's home country named the national stadium in Guatemala City after him.

By the grace of God, or the running gods, the Haunted Mile has always been a mystery. In the very first Boston Marathon, eventual winner John McDermott was running fine down the hill. "McDermott's legs seemed to rise and fall like a phantom Greek," the *Globe* reported. However, just a quarter of a mile later—in front of the cemetery, no less—he was afflicted with cramps, forcing him to come to a stop and scream at his attendant to massage his legs with pleas of "Rub!"

The Boston College Green Line trolley station is located on the left, sending trains down the middle of Commonwealth Avenue toward Boston. Many a runner has boarded the B train after surrendering to the course, including Stylianos Kyriakides, who hitched a ride at Boston College in 1938, and pledged, "Come back again? I think not—never again." Eight years later he did—and won the championship.

Leaving the station, the road now becomes a four-lane throughway divided down the middle by the train tracks. Runners stay to the right of the road. An eighth of a mile farther on, the course moves past the Lake Street intersection and up a slight incline alongside the St. John's Seminary, where in the old days, seminarians would come out to cheer on the runners.

On the right, the runners shield their eyes from the gates of the poltergeist-filled Evergreen Cemetery. The road inclines slightly again and the runners get sandwiched between the student-occupied apartment buildings that line both sides of the street. Ahead, at the end of the mile, the road hugs the Chestnut Hill Reservoir on the right until Chestnut Hill Street, where the runners turn and temporarily leave Commonwealth Avenue.

With the mile coming to an end, the runners' quads are almost wrung dry. Those who approach the course with a plan are wise to make a move here. Three-time winner Cosmas Ndeti always pointed to this stretch of the course as the critical spot during the race, saying, "The race doesn't begin until the thirty-five-kilometer mark." In the 1993 race, he was in sixteenth place at the base of Heartbreak Hill, in third when he crested the peak, and first at the finish line. Two years later, he again waited for this moment to take over, claiming the lead at the thirty-five-kilometer mark and never looking back.

In the final steps of Mile 22, the runner will feel the effect of the hills and need to push past the pain that ends other runners' days early. Such was the case in 1901. Just feet from the mile marker, former champion Ronald MacDonald was confidently running, assured in his mind of victory, when he suffered a bout of discomfort. After running without aid or water to this point of the course, the Canadian called for his attendant, asking for refreshment for the very first time.

In the early years of the race, attendants on bikes were assigned to each runner. Occasionally these attendants focused not on their assigned runner but instead on the wishes of the gamblers who would pay them off if they could affect the outcome of the race.

One method used to affect the outcome—both positively and negatively—was the application of stimulants. In 1923, failing runner Albert Michelson was handed a flask by his attendant, who had been riding a bike alongside him throughout the race. The *Boston Globe* reported that the flask contained peppermint water and a pill of "unknown purpose." Whatever it was, it served its purpose, giving Michelson a second wind and a fourth-place finish.

Race officials were greatly concerned about the use of such stimulants and the influence of attendants on the race. Following the 1905 race, in which many runners suffered aftereffects of their run, Dr. Blake of the BAA was furious. "There were some who were in a bad way, but they can blame their handlers for this," Blake said. "These men were given whisky on the journey, which is a very bad thing. It not only interferes with their running but it acts badly on the heart. The men who did not take alcoholic stimulants fared the better."

Since the very first marathon in Athens in 1896—where runners drank wine at aid stations—runners had been using alcohol and other stimulants to refresh their minds and bodies. In the 1904 Olympics, gold medalist Thomas Hicks (who had placed second in that year's Boston Marathon) was given alcohol as well as drugs to stimulate him to victory. In fact, he was given so much brandy and strychnine (placed in raw eggs) that he started to hallucinate in the final miles, and almost died. After the race Hicks's attendant Charles Lucas boasted, "The marathon race, from a medical standpoint, demonstrated that drugs are of much benefit to athletes along the road."

Hicks would never run a marathon again. The medical field was so concerned about the impact of drugs and alcohol upon the Olympic champion that they recommended banning athletes from using either. The BAA went so far as to require applicants to divulge information about their alcohol consumption throughout the year on their application to run Boston.

Despite the pushback by doctors and race officials, many runners who were backed by the moneymen—mostly the gamblers and oddsmakers—ignored the wishes of the BAA. These differing perspectives were illustrated prior to the race in 1908, when the *Boston Globe* wrote, "The use of drugs is forbidden, and runners resorting to them [are] disqualified." But, being realists, they also wrote, "Stimulants must be figured on, and much depends upon the way they are handed out."

Drugs and alcohol have always been part of the sports world—with both enhanced and diminished results. Gamblers proved they would go to any lengths for money. (In 1890, Boston boxer Johnny Murphy had his food poisoned prior to his bout, rendering him defenseless in the ring.) Marathon runner Robert Fowler was aware of the risk of someone slipping him drugs on the course, and was mad at himself when, running with a significant lead, he accepted an orange from an unknown attendant at the Yonkers Marathon and suddenly collapsed to the ground. He would lie unconscious for five hours. When he awoke, he would blame himself. "I've been in the running game long enough to know better than to accept nourishment from a stranger," he said.

So, in 1901, as Ronald MacDonald ran through the final steps of Mile 22, knowing that "victory would be mine," he didn't account for the intrusion of the wicked. When he asked his attendant for refreshment, he was only concerned about ridding himself of the uneasiness. The attendant, unknown to MacDonald and dressed in army garb, poured the contents of his canteen onto a sponge. The attendant then strangely poured the remaining liquids of the canteen onto the street and disappeared.

MacDonald squeezed the liquid twice into his mouth. Immediately, his stomach and head felt the effects. He pushed forward only to collapse to the ground, his throat burning from the unknown fluid. For hours he would lie unconscious. When he finally awoke, he would explain what the attendant had done. Immediately, Dr. Thompson, a supporter and the runner's physician, ran out to his carriage where the sponge was still sitting. Holding the sponge up to his nose, the doctor discovered that it had been saturated with chloroform. The following day's headlines read MACDONALD COLLAPSES AFTER PLUCKY RACE— UGLY RUMORS AS TO CAUSE.

Some would theorize that the cause of MacDonald's collapse wasn't the solution on the sponge but instead was *Dr. Thompson* and his overuse of stimulants on the runner. Dr. Thompson disputed this account, claiming that someone had intentionally handed MacDonald a sponge with chloroform. "It couldn't well have been an accident," Thompson said, "when there was so much money up on the race."

With his dream of a second laurel wreath stolen, MacDonald would take his doctor's side, claiming that Dr. Thompson had given him two strychnine pills to *counteract* the sponge, thus saving his life. Upon hearing this explanation, Herbert Holton of the BAA called the story "an excuse of a crybaby who was trying to cover up the disgrace of letting down the number of American bettors who had put their trust in him"—a sentence that does a good job of explaining how much influence gamblers once had over the race. MacDonald would continue to defend himself, claiming, "I am the victim of one of the most despicable deeds on record."

Despite Holton's words of virtual approval to those who wagered on the race, the BAA feigned vocal opposition to gambling, dating back to 1911. The *Boston Globe* reported that "The Boston A. A. is to be congratulated on its determination to keep the great Patriots' Day Marathon a sporting event unaccompanied, if possible, by pools or gambling."

This is the peril that runners face in the Haunted Mile. To get to Boston they must pass through Mile 22 and the specter of renegade buses, the motivations of those who wager, and the torment of a downhill bent on compelling its will upon runners with tired legs and wavering conviction.

Mile 23

To live is the rarest thing in the world. Most people exist, that is all.
—Oscar Wilde

At the beginning of Mile 23, the runners continue east down Commonwealth Avenue for two-tenths of a mile, with the Chestnut Hill Reservoir on the right. At the traffic lights of the Chestnut Hill Street intersection, the course forces the runner to turn right. This is one of the five corners along the route where the competitors must be aware of, and navigate, according to their legs' capacity. Past the corner, the road brings the runner down into the insanity of Cleveland Circle. Before this landmark, the runner must descend an eighty-foot gauntlet with the added challenge of train tracks, embedded into the pavement in the middle of the road. These tracks are slippery if wet and perilous where raised. On the right side, the course is boxed in by a public pool and skating rink.

Although this descent can be worrisome, if approached properly, runners can take this opportunity to relax, let go, and actually add to their pace. It was here that three-time champion Uta Pippig liked to take advantage of a course that too often takes advantage of the runner. "I look forward to the right turn which moves you down to Cleveland Circle," she said. "If you let yourself go just a little bit, and don't push too hard, you can really fly."

Three-quarters of the way down the hill on the left sits the former location of the Bill Rodgers Running Center. Back in 1981 Toshihiko Seko used this landmark to throw a surge on his competitors. Spotting his old adversary's store, he pushed past Craig Virgin all the way to victory. Later, he found great irony in the fact that en route to breaking Rodgers's course record, he had made his critical move in front of Rodgers's store. After the race, the always-gracious Seko actually apologized to Rodgers for breaking his record.

Elite runners wisely use the challenge of the topography to test their opponents. In 1981, Craig Virgin couldn't answer the bell after Seko surged up to him and then past him. For any runner in the lead, the pressure is magnified by the fact that he or she is the only athlete on the course that has to worry about both the finish line in front and the entire field of people behind.

In 1968, Amby Burfoot ran through Cleveland Circle with the lead and a side cramp; he assumed that he would soon be reeled in by his pursuers, figuring his pace had greatly slowed. Fearful that the entire marathon field was closing in on him, he set his eyes forward, never once looking over his shoulder. Burfoot spent the greatest five miles of his life in a state of panic, waiting to be passed. Finally, just yards from the finish line, he turned and, to his great relief, saw that no one was there, allowing him to enjoy the moment and break the tape.

Even though no one passed Burfoot on that day, the very thought of having a runner move up on his shoulder drove him into a state of paranoia. If they had challenged him, he would have had to decide whether to defend his lead or to allow the bold competitor to take control. When Sara Mae Berman was passed by Nina Kuscsik in the 1971 race near Cleveland Circle, it was the first time in the race she had surrendered the lead. Only after she'd had a private conversation with herself did she say, "I'm not going to let anyone beat me." Later she recalled: "Seeing her run by was like a kick in the pants. I knew that there was another level that I could push myself to, and I did it." Berman regained the lead and won the race.

Four-tenths into the mile, runners reach the bottom of the hill and have to be cognizant of yet another traffic island—this one directly in the middle of the road. Past the island, the runners turn left onto Beacon Street through the middle of Cleveland Circle. It is here that runners are confronted with a smorgasbord of train tracks (five sets of them), alcohol-impaired college students, loose pavement, and a leg-testing turn. It all makes the Circle an ideal location for the spectators—and a nightmare for the runners.

The sensory overload of the Circle can be overwhelming to the weary runners, who must descend, navigate, and turn, all at the same time. It is not unusual for competitors to become disoriented by the mayhem in this multi-branch intersection, as Jack Fultz was in 1976. Running with the lead, Fultz turned prematurely onto the wrong side of the road; fortunately, a fan yelled at him that he was on the wrong side of Beacon Street. Jack made a 90-degree turn, worked his way over the train tracks to the eastbound side, and headed off to victory.

The chaos is only magnified for the wheelchair competitors, who fly down the hill at speeds close to thirty-five miles per hour only to be faced with a turn and tracks. Racers are advised to start braking early so that they can safely travel the bend and cross over the sometimes-slippery tracks. But it's difficult to convince world-class competitors in the middle of a world-class event to slow down for safety's sake. Thus, the Circle has claimed its share of victims, including the leader in the 1980 race, George Murray, who caught his wheel as he attempted to cross the tracks. It cost him the championship, as it did for Jean Driscoll in 1997, who was in the midst of her run to become the most decorated champion in Boston Marathon history. With Boston in the distance, Jean and Australian Louise Sauvage were locked in one of their classic head-to-head duels. As the two raced down the hill into Cleveland Circle, Driscoll caught a wheel on an exposed track, sending her to the ground with a flat tire and propelling Sauvage to the podium.

One year later the two competitors would wage yet another battle. As they approached the fateful tracks together, Louise suggested to her contemporary, "Take it easy here." After safely crossing over the tracks, Sauvage then offered, "Let's go!" Over the next miles, Driscoll built up a significant lead, only to have Sauvage come from behind and heroically beat her at the tape. Both racers recorded the same time, 1:41:19. One year later, in 2000, Jean finally won her record-setting eighth championship before retiring.

The Cleveland Circle area is comprised mostly of commercial enterprises, with apartments situated above bars and businesses. College students frequent the two famous drinking establishments in the Circle, Mary Ann's and Cityside. Cityside is located on the left side of the Circle, with rooftop seating giving patrons a fantastic view and employees a lot of headaches; the manager of the bar describes the profits from Marathon Day as "blood money." But as politicians from the eight towns along the course might say about their town, the Cityside has a moral obligation to quench the thirst of those parched spectators.

The six-deep crowds and mayhem of Cleveland Circle provide fans with a great venue from which to watch the race, and for businesses to increase receipts. In 1981 the police union, unhappy over recent firings, identified this site as the ideal place to stage a protest. When members of the police force were made aware of the union's plans, they immediately instructed their leaders to retract their threat, claiming that the boycott "would do for our cause what Albert DeSalvo [The Boston Strangler] did for the door-to-door salesman."

On the right side of the route after the turn, Mary Ann's hops with shoulder-to-shoulder coeds from Boston College, hoisting cold beers. The manager of Mary Ann's (previously known as The Jungle) described the scene at his establishment as a "madhouse" filled with fun and energy.

Many spectators move in and out of the establishments throughout the day as they enjoy the atmosphere of the race. One such fan in 1979 took this a step further. Caught up in the excitement of the moment, a well-meaning spectator left the side of the road and fell in next to leader Joan Benoit Samuelson as she passed through the Circle. In one hand he had a beer, in the other a Red Sox cap. As he ran alongside her, he offered her the following choice: "Either wear the hat or chug the beer." The Maine native chose the hat, which she wore in the closing miles of her first victory.

Past the Circle, the course moves to the right side of Beacon Street and into the town of Brookline, the seventh municipality of the route. The race borrows the town on Patriots' Day for 2.25 miles of the race. Not incorporated until 1705, the village known as the "Hamlet of the Muddy River" had to petition the city of Boston in order to win its own identity. After much dispute, the villagers' request was granted, and the new town's boundaries were made to follow the natural line drawn by the Smelt Brook. The waterway (and border) ran through a 350-acre farm owned by the infamous Judge Samuel Sewall, who had inherited the property from his wife. Sewall was the judge who sentenced the Salem witches to death during the infamous trials of 1692.

Moving east on Beacon Street, runners—especially those in the back of the pack—will feel the temperatures dropping significantly by the time they arrive onto this thoroughfare into Boston. After surviving Cleveland Circle, the runners now move east directly toward the Atlantic Ocean, exposing the competitors to the chilly sea breeze that rushes down the street from Boston. On the left, the road is split down the middle by the Green Line tracks. These tracks carry the C train at a very deliberate pace. Runners who throw in the towel here and jump on the train will soon realize that they probably would have arrived in Boston faster by running. A local writer once quipped, "A person tied to the Green Line tracks was found dead; he starved to death."

The route works its way straight up Beacon Street with a slight incline. This area is a mix of apartment buildings and businesses. Continuing down Beacon Street, many runners realize just how much their pace has slowed when they notice that they are no longer gaining much on competitors who are walking. For runners who have something left, this stretch is a prime opportunity. Kathy Switzer found this scenario ideal. "When you are finishing strong, you can pick off as many as a hundred people in a very short distance," she said. "The people who are struggling seem like they are going backwards, while you feel like the course is coming to you."

Up an incline and down the other side, the runners move toward the end of the mile near the Washington Street intersection, where the crowds continue to pull them forward. Uta Pippig found the crowds here to be very well informed: "Running down Beacon Street is pretty cool," she said. "The people are so knowledgeable about the race and the sport. Many of them have radios and are aware of who is leading, and are ready for the leaders as they pass."

Running into Cleveland Circle in 1910, Fred Cameron's attendants yelled to him, "Four miles to go!" Hearing he was that close, he responded,

"Is that all? Why, I'm just getting warmed up." The runners are now just a short distance from Coolidge Corner, near Boston's gate, and about three-plus miles from the finish. It was here that a runner of great promise would fall to the ground.

In 2002, Cynthia Lucero was running Boston as a celebration. She had received her doctorate the week before, and her family was at the finish line to rejoice in her accomplishment. She had written her thesis on the healing powers of running a marathon. In 1908, the *Boston Globe* warned runners that "water is almost fatal to a runner's chances, and only the inexperienced ask for it during the run." But two decades later in 1927, it was reported that Clarence DeMar drank "gallons" of water before what would be his fifth Boston victory. Lucero was prepared to run but had over-hydrated for her first Boston Marathon. Running through Cleveland Circle, the volume of water that she had drunk started to have the reverse effect, virtually drowning her brain cells. With her parents and the finish line just miles away, Cynthia tragically dropped to the ground and died.

Cynthia was the second runner at Boston to die from the effects of the race. In 1996, Swedish runner Humphrey Siesage died of a massive heart attack while crossing the finish line. In the end, the tragedies of their deaths are not lost in some medical studies' statistics but are personal stories of loss to their families and the Boston Marathon community. Cynthia would live on, as her organs were donated to seven women in need. Her run that year reminds everyone of the magnitude of the challenge. For over a century, runners have ventured to Hopkinton, accepting the associated risk. Dr. Marvin Adner, medical director for the Marathon, reminds people: "The last thing you should do to be healthy is run a marathon."

Like climbing Mount Everest, the danger comes with a wonderful reward and sometimes tragic consequences. The risk of running twenty-six miles has been debated for decades. In a 1912 newspaper article in the *Winnipeg Tribune*, titled MARATHON RACES ARE BARBARIC, a reporter notes, "The lesson seems to be that the distance is too great to [be] run by a human being at high pressure." Two years earlier, the same paper had printed a similar article with the headline RACE OVER MARATHON ROUTE NOTHING SHORT OF MANKILLER.

As far back as the 1898 Boston Marathon, doctors have been concerned with the impact that such a challenge could potentially have on runners. Following the second year's race, reporters noted that "runners were examined for the effects of the hard run upon their hearts, lungs and blood. In addition to a sport the race served in the cause of medical science." Every year until the race got too big, doctors would examine every runner's heart, weight, and feet prior to the race to ensure they were worthy of the challenge.

Medical exams before and after the race couldn't account for the long-term impact long-distance running can have on athletes' bodies. Incredibly, four of the first ten winners of the Boston Marathon were dead within just years of their victory. John McDermott, the winner of the inaugural race, ran that day with lung disease and never recovered. This threat inherent in marathoning prompted *Boston Globe* reporter Lawrence Sweeney to pen a piece that questioned the whole purpose of the event, titled WHY RUN A MARATHON?

A study conducted by cardiologists Dr. James O'Keefe and Dr. Carl Lavie suggested that running both fast and far is not only counterproductive but categorically dangerous. "Running too fast, too far and for too many years may speed one's progress toward the finish line of life," they wrote. Their research showed that running more than twenty-five miles a week and/or over eight miles per hour actually neutralized the benefit of exercise.

In the 1920s, a popular Boston runner named Bill Prouty used to run the Marathon every year, but instead of taking the train to the starting line, he would run from Boston to Hopkinton and *then back* in the same six hours. Prouty would die at age forty-two—while running. Though most runners live a healthy and full life, sadly, there are those whose physiology makes running a perilous, if not fatal, activity.

Runners by nature want to push, to challenge, to do more than just be average or sit on the sidelines. It was Clarence DeMar who was told by his doctor never to run another step; he ignored his doctor's warnings and went on to win six more Bostons. DeMar's story was so inspiring that a high school student, Wendell Powers of Medford, went for a run after the 1924 Boston Marathon, trying to emulate his hero, only to drop dead in front of his house. This is why only 1 percent of the world has ever run a marathon—it's difficult and sometimes even dangerous.

The last third of the mile finishes down Beacon Street at a slight incline. Up ahead lies Coolidge Corner, bringing the runners within sight of the Boston skyline—where the finish and glory awaits.

Mile 24

How far that little candle throws his beams! So shines a good deed in a weary world.
—WILLIAM SHAKESPEARE, *THE MERCHANT OF VENICE*

WITH THE SHADOWS OF BOSTON'S SKYSCRAPERS DRAWING NEARER, THE runners move through Cleveland Circle and down Beacon Street. Riding up and down small inclines and declines that rise and fall like waves, the runners move toward Coolidge Corner. Uta Pippig starts to get excited here, because "[f]or the first time in the race, you can feel the closeness of the finish line."

The course takes the runner down to the Washington Street intersection and continues to bend, with businesses and apartment buildings on the right and the snail-like Green Line train on the left. Three-quarters of the way through the mile, the runners pass through Coolidge Corner.

The Corner takes its name from a local store owner, David Sullivan Coolidge. His general store—Coolidge & Bros.—was located on the corner of Harvard and Beacon Streets, a major throughway from the city to the country. In 1888 the street was widened to two hundred feet at the Corner to accommodate an electric train, at the time the longest continuous electric train route in the world.

The aristocrats of Brookline, who could afford to arrange their own transportation, had long been opponents of the train. One blue blood called it an "unpleasant mechanism of unproven worth. [A] vulgar common carrier." One wonders whether those aristocrats of Coolidge Corner would have turned up their noses at their latter-day neighbor, John Fitzgerald Kennedy, who years later would keep

America from nuclear war with Russia and lead the charge to put a man on the moon.

Condominiums in this location can cost upwards of $3 million, while shop owners can pay dearly for the honor of leasing space in this busy corner of commerce. Despite the prices, Coolidge Corner is a melting pot. Visitors here are exposed to a great diversity of religions, cultures, and lifestyles. This is reflected in the variety of delicatessens, ethnic specialty shops, and independent films being shown at the historic Coolidge Corner Theatre, a nonprofit celebrating its eightieth year in 2013.

After the runners work their way by the Corner at the intersection of Harvard and Beacon, the course moves downhill toward the end of the mile. In the early years of the race, the affluent inhabitants of the Coolidge Corner brownstones used to sit in their windows and acknowledge the runners as they did in 1902, when Sammy Mellor ran toward the tape. "Brookline's aristocracy leaned out of windows and waved lace handkerchiefs in the April breeze," the paper reported, "as the white shadow wended his way, acknowledging the salutation with a smile and nod."

Not to be outdone by the upper class, fifteen years later the laborers working on these urban estates used to take time from their honest day's work to cheer their favorite runner—William "Bricklayer Bill" Kennedy. Kennedy, an actual bricklayer, won the 1917 race, and was a consistent top-ten finisher during the 1920s. In the midst of his championship run, Kennedy was overcome by emotion as he ran through Coolidge Corner and was saluted by his brothers-in-trade, who took a quick break from their toil in order to clap their bricks together in an appropriate salute.

Falling just over two miles from the finish line, the crowds and chaotic atmosphere of Coolidge Corner have made this point an important benchmark in the race—as well as an obstacle to survive. At times, runners have been forced to run single file through the onslaught of well-wishers. As far back as 1907, the Coolidge Corner crowd was termed "a mob" by the *Globe,* which wrote: "From Coolidge Corner to Massachusetts Ave., the runners and attendants had to fight their way along practically, for they are mobbed. The police do everything in their power to keep the crowds back, yet each year the conditions become worse."

Running in white shorts and a top with the lead into Coolidge Corners, Sammy Mellor is surrounded by bike attendants and overambitious spectators.
© RUNNING PAST

Greg Meyer compared the zeal of the populace in Mile 24 to that of a hungry reptile. As he ran toward his championship in 1983, the crowds from each side of the street seemed to meet in the middle of the road. When he approached them, he recalled, "They seemed to open up in front of me like a snake eating." As he passed through, he realized he could no longer see the competitors behind him because "the crowd reunited like a snake swallowing."

For many runners this wild environment can be frustrating. It was here where lead runner Clarence DeMar fell victim to the craziness in 1920, when a car drove over his foot at Coolidge Corner, ripping open his shoe. Others feed off the passion of the masses, as Gayle Barron did during her run to the wreath in 1978. "Back when I won the race," she said, "the Marathon was a personal event between the runners and the fans. I ran the last miles in 1978 on a route with just enough space for one runner to squeeze through. Every step had a fan, on each side, just inches from my ear, yelling encouragement."

While the fans of Coolidge Corner may inadvertently pose a danger, Bill Rodgers faced a very literal danger in 1980: Just days before the race Rodgers was the target of a death threat. In the weeks prior to the Marathon, Bill Rodgers had publicly castigated President Jimmy Carter for his decision to boycott the 1980 Olympics in Moscow, a protest against Russia's invasion of Afghanistan. Rodgers, who had been a conscientious objector during the Vietnam War, announced that he would advertise his position by wearing a black armband during his run in the 1980 Boston Marathon, drawing the ire of many who felt that he was tainting the race by using it as his personal political forum.

While most voiced their displeasure through normal channels, one "patriot" called the Bill Rodgers Running Center days before the race, vowing that Rodgers would never run through Coolidge Corner alive. The threat was taken seriously, but there was only so much the police could do when more than a million people were waiting to see Rodgers run along a twenty-six-mile course.

Rodgers decided not to wear the black armband; he ran the race, won, and survived. It's possible the threat was just an idle one, or that the crowd discouraged the would-be assassin. But he did have a tough time staying focused, with the yelling of the boo-birds and the fists shaking in his face, knowing about the threat on his life.

On Patriots' Day, the world doesn't halt on its axis, but instead orbits around the Boston Marathon. The Olympic showdown between the United States and Soviets found a way to inject itself into the race. The Marathon reflects the world and its times, and sometimes the rest of the world intrudes and claims the Marathon as its podium. This was never more true than in 2013, when the worst of the outside world compelled itself upon the race.

Over the history of the race the Boston Marathon has never existed in a bubble; the race has somehow found a way to coexist with the world around it. Since 1897, every April, headlines across the globe brought news of America's Marathon. To many across the world, Boston was known not as the Athens of America, or the City upon the Hill, or the Hub of the Universe, but instead, simply as the "Marathon City." The Boston Marathon and all its fixings, including the warm smiles of fans, the beautiful landscape, and the open front (and bathroom) doors of Hopkinton, made the race a wonderful ambassador of America and its people.

But the Boston Marathon belongs to a world of free will, and sometimes that outside world works its way into the race. In 1957, a man who murdered his ex-girlfriend was so frustrated by the traffic of the Marathon as he attempted to escape that he placed the gun on the passenger seat and turned himself in to a policeman responsible for crowd control. "I'm the guy you're looking for," he said. "I've just killed somebody, [and] I want to give myself up."

In the same block twenty-three years earlier, while the runners ran through Coolidge Corner, a group of adults were escorted in pairs by armed guards along the sidewalk. Careful not to step out of line, these spectators came to the Boston Marathon to get away. For weeks they had been confined within the walls of sequester.

This "remarkably average group of male Americans" was actually a group of jurors sitting on the case of the century. In February of 1934, three men—Murton Millen, Irving Millen, and Abraham Faber—were accused of a machine-gun bank robbery, in the process killing two policemen in the town of Needham, next to Wellesley. The manhunt would be one of Boston's largest; only the searches for the Boston Strangler in the 1960s, and the terrorists responsible for the 2013 Marathon bombing, would match the hunt in intensity.

Following a shootout in a New York City hotel lobby, the bank robbers were captured. Their trial would be the longest capital case in state history up to that point, lasting eight weeks. In the midst of the trial, the judge saw the Boston Marathon as the perfect outlet to allow the jurors furlough, as long as they stayed clear from conversation and newspapers. The jury would watch Canadian Dave Komonen run to victory in 1934, and would leave the race only after Clarence DeMar passed them. The case received so much national attention that even President's Roosevelt's son would attend the trial. The jurors traveled from the courthouse as virtual celebrities; the *Globe* reported, "On every hand could be heard the cry, 'There's the Millens-Faber jury.' Pretty girls waved madly but the jurymen, placid and sedate, conducted themselves with great propriety."

Finally, after 158 witness and 128 exhibits, it would take the jury six hours to return with a guilty verdict for first-degree murder. The thousands assembled outside the courthouse cheered wildly. That crowd was reported to include a formidable lynching party. (Later appeals by the defendants' attorneys argued that the jury had no choice but to return a guilty verdict, as the chants of the outside crowd could be heard in the courtroom.)

Following their verdict, the three defendants were sentenced to death, and would be killed in the electric chair in the Charlestown neighborhood of Boston in June of 1935. In the end the jurors were sent home with the thanks of the court. The case would cost the state $52,416—more than 10 percent of the entire income of the state that year. Each juror was paid $5 a day, or $322 in total for the case—although that doesn't account for their memorable visit to the Boston Marathon.

The mile moves past Coolidge Corner and works down the hill toward Boston. When Larry Brignolia ran down this hill in 1898 with the lead, he slipped on a rock and twisted his ankle. As he attempted to get up, medics held him down for five minutes to make sure he was capable of continuing the race, costing Brignolia the world record and almost the championship. It was in this same mile in 2010 that Robert Kiprono Cheruiyot ran an astonishing 4:36 (as a comparison, John McDermott's splits in 1897 were 6:41).

The runners pass the mile marker, looking for that famous CITGO sign to rear its head above the horizon.

Mile 25

I dream my painting and then paint my dream.
                                        —Vincent van Gogh

After Coolidge Corner the runners are still escorted by the C train, which runs along their left. Behind the train sits the Holiday Inn. One year hotel workers threatened to blockade the race route to protest what they felt were deficient benefits. When Tommy Leonard of the Eliot Lounge heard of the planned demonstration, he memorably remarked, "Stopping the Marathon is like shooting the Easter Bunny."

Still descending, the runners spill into the city limits of Boston. Halfway through the mile, the train goes underground, and the runners are left to find the finish line without it. On the left side of the submerging train sits the local Irish pub, O'Leary's. The owner, Aengus O'Leary, is used to his steady customers throwing down a cold one and zipping out to see the leaders run by. He's also accustomed to having runners stop by the bar for some late carbo-loading. One year two Irish priests running the race pulled up a couple of stools and fueled up for the last mile, compliments of a properly poured Guinness. As to their condition, O'Leary had one thing to say: "They were thirsty."

～

Boston was founded in 1630 and named after St. Botolph, a town in Lincolnshire, England. It had previously been known by the name of *Shawmut,* the Native American word for "living waters." The city was originally dominated by three hills, with water on three sides. The hills were eventually scaled down and used as landfill to create the Back Bay and Copley Square out of the Charles River marsh.

Boston has played a central role in American history, through the events of the Boston Massacre, the Boston Tea Party, and the Battle of Bunker Hill, among others. In the first half of the nineteenth century, Boston was a center of the abolition movement, and many runaway slaves headed to Boston for refuge. The first all-black regiment, the 54th Massachusetts Volunteer Infantry, came from Boston and fought valiantly during the Civil War.

Boston has always been known for its prominent citizens and affluent families, including the Franklins, Samuel Adams, the Cabots, the Lodges, and the Saltonstalls, all of whom figured in the molding of this international city. (The Adamses, from nearby Quincy, and the Kennedys from Brookline also produced their fair share of statesmen.) Luckily for them, they didn't live long enough to have to commute through the construction of "The Big Dig"—the Central Artery/Tunnel Project—the most expensive road project in American history, costing over $20 billion and taking more than fifteen years to complete.

Today Boston is one of the world's greatest college towns and the largest city in New England, with a population of almost 600,000 people spread across an area of ninety acres. The professional sports teams have won eight championships over the last twelve years, leading to some labeling Boston "Title-town."

The twenty-year mayor of Boston, Thomas Menino, looks forward each year to the running of the Boston Marathon: "It's incredible to me how, year after year, the Boston Marathon brings people together like that. The crowds aren't rooting for anyone in particular—they're rooting for everyone." He adds, "No tradition quite captures the spirit of Boston like the Boston Marathon . . . as runners from all over the world run through the city's streets, spectators from all over rally together to welcome them and spur them on. It's incredible to me how, year after year, the Boston Marathon brings people together like that."

❧ ❧

Running across the intersection of Park Street, the runners enter the Audubon Circle where, on the left, the Church of the Cross bears a sign that reads GOD IS OUR REFUGE AND STRENGTH. Runners likely believe anything would help at this point. In days gone by, the Circle used to be where Boston's affluent would race their horse-drawn sleighs over the winter snow for sport or leisure. The *Boston Globe* wrote in December of 1902, after the first storm of the year: "No matter where one happened to be, the jingle of silver-toned bells was to be heard."

Moving through the Circle, runners look up and are confronted by the sometimes unexpected and never welcome obstacle called "Citgo Hill." This unpleasant bump in the course takes its name from the large neon sign advertising Citgo Fuel that shines high in Kenmore Square up ahead. The CITGO sign has dominated Kenmore Square since 1965. Shut down during the energy crisis in the early 1970s, it was soon relit and eventually listed as a historical landmark.

Two-time winner Geoff Smith covered this final hill in contrasting states during his consecutive championships. "In 1984, I didn't even know it was there," he said. "I felt great at the time, and just breezed over it. In 1985, when I struggled to make it to the finish line with cramps, I was shocked to find this hill in the middle of Mile 25. I wondered if it was always there, or if it was new." Three-time winner Sara Mae Berman echoed these thoughts. "Citgo Hill feels like Mount Washington," she said. "When you get to the base of the hill and look up, your body tells you that it doesn't want to go."

This one last incline rises for a grueling two hundred yards, giving the fresher runners an opportunity to gain ground and the worn-out runners an excuse to go limp. The rise over the Massachusetts Turnpike comes at a bad time on the course, and has a surprisingly negative effect on the athletes. At this point, most runners are in the process of physically shutting down. Peripheral vision narrows to about two yards on either side, and the runners' hearing may be greatly impaired.

Despite the fact that the finish line is drawing closer, the minds of anxious or exhausted runners will start to wander, as if to distance themselves from the body. This disorientation is almost like an out-of-body experience, not uncommon among marathoners in the last miles. Even elite runners sometimes find themselves running on automatic pilot while their minds vacate the premises.

In 1976, Jack Fultz suffered through this condition. With temperatures exceeding 90 degrees, he felt giddy as he soldiered on down Beacon
Street. First he started to giggle when he realized that he had a shot at
achieving his greatest dream. Next, he found himself watching himself
from above, like a sports commentator analyzing his run. Finally, Fultz
caught himself rehearsing answers for the post-race press conference. He
later explained, "If I was going to win it"—which he did—"I didn't want
to be full of clichés and one-liners. I wanted to sound intelligent."

Both elite and amateur runners might find themselves traveling above
themselves, their heads hanging low and their eyes fixed on the ground,
blindly following the footprints laid down by Clarence DeMar, William
Kennedy, John McDermott, Roberta Gibb Bingay, and hundreds of thousands of others who sought glory—both public and private—on the streets
of Boston.

It was here in 1996—during the hundredth Boston Marathon—that
one of the greatest of female runners launched into the record books (her
third straight victory) while experiencing the ultimate in discomfort. Running through Mile 25, thirty-year-old Uta Pippig of Germany chose to
stage one of the most courageous comeback victories in Boston Marathon
history. Battling cramps and multiple internal ailments (including those
common to women, and an impatient stomach that was desperate to purge),
Pippig was chasing Tegla Loroupe from Kenya as they approached Citgo
Hill. As she closed in on the front-runner, Pippig ran to the side of the road
and grabbed a water bottle. She returned to the middle of the route, ripped
the top of the container off with her teeth, slugged the water, spiked the
bottle down on the ground, and then proceeded to pass Loroupe for good
on her way to her third straight Boston Marathon victory.

Pippig recalls:

> Four different times during the race, the pain was so bad that I contem-
> plated dropping out of the race altogether. Somehow I kept going and
> pushed myself. As I approached Citgo Hill, I saw Tegla up ahead and I
> said to myself, "Come on, Uta—this is your chance!" I just started fight-
> ing, and imagined I could fly. Somehow I caught her. I don't know how I

*did it. I replay that part of the race in my mind, and I still can't explain
how I did it. I guess I won't figure it out until I run the race again and
pass that spot. In retrospect I would say [that] this was my greatest victory, with respect to overcoming mental and physical adversity.*

Uta Pippig's courageous run and beautiful smile endeared her to the
people of Boston. Fans of the race and citizens of the city only ask for
sincerity. The public saw her triumph as one of the greatest victories in
the history of the race. It was impossible not to be enamored with her as a
runner and as a person. When she ran through the streets of Boston, the
ten-deep crowd on the sidewalk chanted, "Uta, Uta, Uta!" In gratitude for
the fans' support, she threw kisses to the crowd. Following her second win,
Boston writer Dan Shaughnessy wondered: "Could she be just a little
more gracious, courageous, intelligent, and charming? Is that possible?"

Over the history of the race Boston has grown fond of runners who
have traveled to its city and shown courage and heart. Consequently, certain runners have been adopted as one of their own by the masses who
line the eight towns along the racecourse. Despite the fact that Uta Pippig
was born behind the wall in East Germany, she is a New Englander to the
millions who line the route to Boston.

Local runners such as DeMar, Kelley "The Elder," Kelley "The
Younger," Rodgers, Bingay, Benoit Samuelson, and the Hoyts have been
loved by Boston for their running, but also because they are one of them.
Runners like Uta Pippig have given of themselves to the race, and thus
the city has opened its arms to embrace them.

In 1926, Boston was introduced to Johnny Miles of Nova Scotia.
When he arrived at BAA headquarters to sign up for the first marathon
of his life, he asked, "By the way, you won't be terribly disappointed if I
win the race?" Race official Ton Kanaly would laugh, noting, "The kid has
a sense of humor."

The unknown runner wouldn't remain so for long. Despite the fact
that the twenty-year-old had never run in a race over ten miles before,
he would shock the greatest field ever assembled in front of an estimated
one million fans. The headline the following day in the *Boston Globe* read

LEAPED FROM OBSCURITY INTO RANKS OF CHAMPIONS AT A BOUND. His spunk and underdog spirit made him an immediate fan favorite.

Following his victory, the city fell in love with Miles and wouldn't let him go home for a week. Finally, Nova Scotia needed their hero home, compelling him to board a train at North Station, where fans mobbed him all the way to the steps of a train. Under his arm he held a newspaper from his hometown in Nova Scotia, with a front-page headline that read BOSTON GOES WILD OVER JOHNNY MILES.

Miles returned home to Nova Scotia where he was carried to the town hall on the shoulders of his people. In the same Marathon that made Miles famous in Boston, former winner William Kennedy would finish eighth. Kennedy was also adopted by the people of Boston, engendering feelings of great warmth in those who watched him run.

William Kennedy, known lovingly as the "Bricklayer," came from Chicago and New York, depending on where he could find work. He couldn't afford train fare, so he would hobo from train to train, sometimes taking days to arrive. Unable to afford a hotel room before or after the race, he would sleep wherever he could lay his head—sometimes on the floors of friends' homes, or at pool halls, or at BAA headquarters. But unlike Miles, Kennedy would often stay in Boston before and after the race, finding work as a bricklayer.

Before running in 1916, Kennedy worked on a home in the Back Bay during the day and then would train at night in the uniform of the common man: trousers, sweater, and cap. After winning Boston in 1917, he arrived at work the next morning at 5:30 a.m. and proceeded to lay over 1,500 bricks. The blue-collar hero further captured the hearts of Boston, inspiring America in the midst of the hardship and dourness of World War I. One of his fellow bricklayers was quoted as saying, about Kennedy, "For aside from his running ability he had already gained their friendship and esteem by his companionship qualities and ever-ready smile and words of encouragement."

While Boston adopted runners of great sincerity, some runners adopted the city of Boston after getting to know the city and its charm. Following his third straight win in 1995, Kenyan Cosmas Ndeti proved

Morrison

Jas Henigan

Leading Boston aa marathon

Led for 16 miles

James Henigan, the 1931 winner, is surrounded by the entourage that always encircles the leader. PHOTO COURTESY OF THE *BOSTON HERALD*

the love shown him was mutual when he returned home and named his newborn son after the city he had fallen in love with—Gideon Boston.

With just over a mile to go, the runners scale Citgo Hill, the CITGO sign smiling at the competitors at eleven o'clock. On the right is Boston's most storied landmark—Fenway Park, home of the beloved Boston Red Sox. For eight decades, between 1918 and 2004, it was the home of futility, where men like Bucky Dent, Tony Perez, and Mariano Rivera crushed the hopes and dreams of the Boston faithful. Being a fan of the Sox was like being a victim in an abusive relationship. Despite the pain they endured, the fans would blindly utter at the end of each season, "Wait till next year." But since 2004, the Red Sox have not only brought joy to Boston, with three World Series championships, they've also been able to bring unity and healing to the city following the tragic Patriots' Day of 2013.

In their first game following the bombing, Boston turned to the Red Sox as a source of communal recovery. Prior to the game, captain of the team David Ortiz addressed those in attendance and overcome by emotion proclaimed: "This is our fucking city and no one is going to dictate our freedom—stay strong!" Later in the game Daniel Nava would hit a profound home run to win the game. Announcer Don Orsillo would proclaim to all watching at home, "Boston this is for you!" while Nava circled the bases with tears in his eyes as those in attendance cheered wildly to release and heal.

Six months later following their championship, millions of fans came to the city to cheer the Red Sox at a celebratory parade. When the caravan carrying the players made its way down Boylston Street, the parade stopped and players exited the duck boats that carried them across the route. With them was the World Series trophy, which they placed on the finish line. The trophy was draped in the "617 [the city's area code] Boston Strong" uniform that had hung in their dugout since the marathon. Then tenor Ronan Tynan toasted the city with a rousing version of God Bless America, in which he was joined by thousands in an emotional tribute to that day back in April.

The runner now moves toward Kenmore Square, where Red Sox fans have emptied out after their traditional morning game, held the morning of the Marathon since 1903. For the runner, passing Fenway may provide further inspiration, for what seemed implausible now seems possible. Those 37,400 Red Sox fans now line the sidewalks of Kenmore Square, helping to propel the runners those final steps.

Mile 26

Twenty years from now you will be more disappointed by the things that you didn't do than by the ones you did do, so throw off the bowlines, sail away from safe harbor, catch the trade winds in your sails. Explore, dream, discover.

—MARK TWAIN

AT THE END OF THE BRIDGE AT CITGO HILL, THE RUNNERS PASS INTO the last full mile of the race. Those who have survived to this point begin to curse King Edward VII of England, who ordered the race to be lengthened (from 24.5 miles to 26 miles, 385 yards) so that the 1908 Olympic Marathon would start at Windsor Castle and end in front of the royal box at the Olympic stadium in London. The King could not have foreseen the ramifications of his decision. For decades runners have suffered the consequences of his selfish proclamation.

Like a battered boxer forced to go extra rounds, the runners now have to traverse the last mile-plus with the burden of bankrupt legs and weakened resolve. The downhill into Kenmore Square is the last real chance for the sadistic course to wreak havoc on the field. Runners who wrote checks on the hills of Newton find them getting cashed in this last mile.

When the course finally leads the runners into Kenmore Square at the end of Beacon Street, the athletes arrive back on Commonwealth Avenue, the same street that housed the hills. The route continues, on a level grade, through the square—just a mile from the finish line. Years ago, when beef stew was served to everyone at the finish line (to a far smaller field), the runners probably began to salivate here, as they could almost

Lelisa Desisa makes the turn from Commonwealth Avenue onto Hereford Street with the lead that he would maintain to the 2013 championship.

smell the finish. In truth, by this point in the race, most runners are more interested in finishing than eating.

Kenmore Square has long been compared to Times Square in New York City because of the intersecting streets (Beacon, Commonwealth, and Brookline) and the odd angles they make. Like Times Square, the location is ideal for billboard advertisements. The Square is best known for its proximity to Fenway Park and the many bars and pubs that serve as a virtual "water stop" for thirsty Red Sox fans on game days.

Kenmore Square is also a bustling gathering spot for the thousands of downtown college students from Boston University and the colleges of Simmons, Emmanuel, and Wheelock. It was once known as Governor Square, and was the center of Boston's hotel district: Hotels such as the Somerset, Braemore, Sheraton, Buckminster, and Kenmore all stood here, but they gave way to condominiums, nightclubs, and Boston University dormitories. In recent years, hotels have returned to the Square, including the five-star Commonwealth Hotel, which is sold out every Marathon weekend.

The square takes its modern name from the Green Line train stop set in the middle. Thronged with students lugging schoolbooks, girls with purple hair, and commuters hustling to the T, Kenmore Square is a distinctive section of the Marathon, and the city.

World-class marathoner Craig Virgin found the fans and location at Kenmore Square taxing. "The crowd can suffocate you here and make you become claustrophobic," he said. With thousands of Red Sox fans lining the sidewalks, the noise and mayhem of the Square is palpable. This pandemonium was never more pronounced than in 1935, when John "The Elder" Kelley ran through Kenmore Square on the way to his first wreath. Kelley, who had gobbled chocolate glucose pills along the route, had been struggling with his stomach ever since Coolidge Corner. As he made his way over Citgo Hill, he was five hundred yards in the lead over Pat Dengis when his intestinal pains brought him to an abrupt halt, forcing the press car to slam on its brakes to avoid hitting the suddenly stationary runner.

With the hometown favorite bent over at the waist in pain, the crowd urged him on. Kelley unfolded himself and ran two steps before stopping again, sending the crowd into a frenzy. Behind him, Pat Dengis was closing the gap: Kelley had to move or lose. According to the following day's *Boston Globe,* a desperate Kelley applied the "Roman Cure," sticking his fingers down his throat to relieve himself. The trick worked, and Kelley ran on to the first of two championships. He had "overdosed on glucose pills," he later admitted.

Like Kelley, most runners plunge into Kenmore Square in some form of mental or physical free fall. By this stage the legs may no longer have the ability to brake; many runners let gravity throw their bodies down the hill, praying they regain their balance without crashing. Glycogen is a distant memory, and the low fuel light is shining. When Greg Meyer was running through the Square with the lead in 1983, a friend of his jumped out of the crowd and yelled while pointing, "You've got to fucking go that a way." Halfway through the square, the runners pass by a sign with the most pleasant message known to a marathoner: 1 MILE TO GO.

John "The Elder" Kelley had fond memories of this milestone from his wins in 1935 and 1945: "A mile from the finish, they have painted a wonderful sign, and when you know you have it won, you know if you can keep it up for another mile it's all over, the chills go up and down your spine and tears are in your eyes and you know you've got the Boston victory, the one you wanted most of all."

Passing the 1 MILE TO GO sign doesn't always ensure victory for the lead runner, however. In 1931, as local favorite Jim Henigan ran through Mile 25, his oldest son saw him and reported to other family members who were gathered in Kenmore Square, "Pa's in front, but gosh, he's going awfully slow." After Henigan slowed to a walk, a fan, alarmed by the runner's poor appearance, showered Henigan with cold water from a milk bottle. The press vehicle, which usually sped ahead of the runners to the finish line, decided to hover around the leader in the hope of capturing his inevitable collapse on film. Henigan, who had dropped out of his first seven races, eventually made his way to the finish line to break the tape and ruin the hopes of the photographers.

On the left side of Commonwealth Avenue, in the Square, is a bar called Cornwall's Pub that bears a sign reading ROSIE RUIZ STARTED HERE. While Ruiz started in Kenmore Square, many runners struggle not to be finished there. In 1936, an exhausted Tarzan Brown was trying to carry on and hold on to his lead. As he attempted to navigate the cars and fans, he swerved left and right, drunken-like, and was almost hit by a passing vehicle. Finally, Brown came to a complete halt, prompting his illegal attendant—who happened to be his coach—to douse his weary runner with water, reviving him and sending him off to victory. The coach was arrested for this, spending time in jail, while Brown enjoyed the fruits of his championship.

Ten years later, Mayor Maurice Tobin again violated the "no attendant" rule, but no one was going to arrest him. His runner of choice was Fred McGlone. McGlone was a local harrier who had captured the attention of the city official. During the race, the mayor illegally jumped out of his car and provided water to McGlone. When Tobin got back into his car, he slammed the door on his hand, severing his fingers with a one-inch laceration. Approaching the finish line, McGlone would repeatedly collapse to the ground only to courageously rise each time. On his last fall a policeman couldn't take it anymore, and helped McGlone to his feet. The runner would cross the finish line bleeding from both legs and with no recollection of the last three miles. In the clubhouse he would recover enough to be told that he'd been disqualified because he was aided by the policeman.

Over the history of the race, politicians and politics have played a role in the race—either through running, officiating, or exploiting. Mayor Ray Flynn (1983–92) ran Boston five times, running fourteen marathons in all. In 1951, future governor Mike Dukakis ran as a teenager from Brookline High School. Secretary of Agriculture John Block ran in 1981, having his number switched right before the race for security reasons. In 1912, President Teddy Roosevelt had hoped to attend the race, but couldn't find the time. Jimmy Carter would connect with the winners by phone to congratulate them, while President Clinton would actually invite the champions to Washington to share a run with him.

Politics has often been injected into the Boston Marathon because it's a local, national, and international event, with runners who often become symbols or representatives of a place or an ideology. In 1932, German runner Paul de Bruyn ran Boston with reservations, not sure how he would be treated just fourteen years removed from World War I. The German sailor represented "Das Faterland" (as the *Globe* put it) twice in the Olympics. However, de Bruyn would never go home; he stayed in the United States, serving in the American navy, where he was injured during World War II.

Japanese runner and Hiroshima survivor Shigeki Tanaka had similar worries when he came and conquered Boston in 1951 (in split-toe running shoes), just six years after World War II. Fortunately, he was accepted and cheered on by a supportive Boston crowd. During the Korean War (1950–53), Korean runners were politely uninvited from participating in the Open race, while in the middle of the Cold War, in 1958, a runner from Yugoslavia, Franjo Mihalic, won Boston, earning the headline THE MARATHON'S FIRST IRON CURTAIN ENTRY HAD SLAMMED THE GATE.

For a hundred-plus years the Boston Marathon has been a forum for people to express their opinions, views, and ideology. In 1982, pacifists and protestors of the arms race passed out literature which demonstrated the effects of a nuclear bomb set off at the finish line. The finish line in their drawings was labeled GROUND ZERO, with concentric circles drawn around it to show the impact of such a catastrophe.

The race moves through Kenmore Square, past the Commonwealth Hotel on the right, up to the intersection of Charlesgate West. It was here in 1961 that John "The Younger" Kelley continued his stretch of frustrating runs when three-time winner Eino Oksanen passed him for the lead with less than a mile to go. (Over his career, Kelley finished second five times, and in the top ten no fewer than ten times. He won in 1957, becoming the only runner from the Boston Athletic Association ever to win the Boston Marathon.) Kelley was a favorite with the fans and the press, although his "close but no cigar" finishes frustrated the often-temperamental Boston media. After another one of Kelley's second-place finishes, the press ripped the Connecticut schoolteacher. Colin Heard of the *Boston Herald* wrote, "How stupid can a schoolteacher be?" John Gihooley, also of the *Herald,* wrote, "If our schoolteachers are like that, it's no wonder our school system is in trouble."

After making it through Kenmore Square, the runners are greeted by the hysterical crowd in the Back Bay. Some line the streets, some hang out of apartment windows, and still others dangle from the rooftops of the connected condominiums. The athletes, who back at the starting line looked like kids on Christmas morning, now look like deserters from the Foreign Legion. The screams of "One more mile!" are finally—mercifully—accurate.

The runners move under the ramp to Storrow Drive, and then past Charlesgate East, where a statue of the Norse explorer Leif Eriksson greets them. Like the doughboy in Hopkinton, he also faces away from the finish line.

After the statue, the runners fork left down a descent and travel under a bridge that carries Massachusetts Avenue. On the right at the Mass Ave. intersection sits the Harvard Club, where members used to cheer from a temporary grandstand set up in front of the brick home of Harvard alumni and faculty. Now they watch the race from inside on a big-screen television, with the bar and grill open for the day.

Next door to the Harvard Club is where the Eliot Hotel, the old home of the legendary (and now extinct) Eliot Lounge was located. This watering hole, which served as a virtual clubhouse for runners, became famous in 1975 when a victorious Bill Rodgers told a national audience while being interviewed, "I'm going to the Eliot Lounge." It was behind the bar that Tom Leonard talked running with patrons and made Rodgers' favorite Blue Whale drink. In 1996, sadly, the lounge was closed. Crossing in front of the Eliot Hotel, the runners move over Massachusetts Avenue on their way toward the big right turn off Commonwealth Avenue.

It was at Mass Ave. that 1897 winner John McDermott came to a halt when he ran into traffic. With less than a mile to go in the inaugural race, McDermott found himself running in front of a funeral procession and two trolleys, bringing all of them to a stop on his way to the finish line at the Irvington Oval. When McDermott entered the oval, the crowd was still wild with excitement from Boston College upsetting the favored Fordham in the hundred-yard dash at the annual BAA track-and-field handicap event. As McDermott circled the oval, he was said to finish with the speed and strength of a half-miler.

The race now takes the runner to the right turn onto Hereford Street, eight-tenths into the mile. In 2008, women's champion Dire Tune almost missed this turn while running side by side with Russian Alevtina Biktimirova. Fortunately for her, she was able to turn back on the course and eventually win the race by two seconds.

From 1897 to 1964, the competitors used to run past Hereford down Commonwealth Avenue and take a right turn onto Exeter Street. After the turn onto Exeter, the runners proceeded straight up the street, passing over Newbury Street and then through Boylston Street to the finish line, which was sandwiched by the BAA clubhouse and the Lenox Hotel. It was on Exeter Street in 1925 that Chuck Mellor wearing newspaper under his shirt to protect against the cold spat out his wad of tobacco, which he had been chewing throughout the race, so he wouldn't have a protruding cheek as he was photographed crossing the finishing line. It was also where John "The Elder" Kelley blessed himself and then dropped his aunt's handkerchief—which he had been carrying the entire race for good luck—before crossing the finish line in 1935.

Hereford Street moves up toward Boylston on a gradual incline as the course continues to punish the runner, even in the final steps. Over Newbury Street—where on the other 364 days of the year the sidewalks are filled with college kids and the bourgeois of Boston, with their shopping bags—the runners need to grind out the final steps. Of course, they can't help but peek ahead where Boylston Street sits.

The race now rises toward its crescendo. Throughout the day, the waiting fans have been updated on the race as they struggle to hold on to their viewing positions. These crowds are stacked sometimes thirty deep in the last mile, and are known for their intensity and fervor. During the 1935 race, the excitement and jostling of the crowd overwhelmed

Champion John "Elder" Kelley crosses the finish line in 1935. Note that officials never put the tape up and that Kelley dropped his aunt's handkerchief just yards before crossing the line. COURTESY OF THE TRUSTEES OF THE BOSTON PUBLIC LIBRARY

Victor MacAuley, Clarence DeMar, and Chuck Mellor (l to r) run stride for stride in 1925. PHOTO COURTESY OF THE *BOSTON HERALD*

a seventy-five-year-old spectator named Edward Redman. He collapsed with a heart attack, badly cutting his chin in the process. The Wellesley native was taken to a nearby hospital where he was nursed back to health.

A hazardous crowd inevitably becomes a problem for the runners. Especially in the early days, sidewalks lined with spectators can suddenly turn into streets crowded with mobs. In 1901, runners lost vital minutes off their times after they were forced to snake through the Exeter Street crowd. In 1905, eventual winner Fred Lorz had to leap over a bike in the closing yards and then repeat the feat at the finish line. While leaping for the line, he caught his foot and crashed through the tape onto Exeter Street.

Efforts to control the chaos over the years have sometimes only added to it. In the tenth year of the race, police almost ran over the leader, Tom Longboat, in their zeal to control the crowd. In 1905, Superintendent Pierce added patrolmen and mounted police to aid with crowd control. Their significant presence was welcomed by the *Globe*, who reported the following day that "they left the scene with every spectator feeling they were human and capable."

After crossing the intersection, the road takes an unexpected and nasty little climb. Rising toward Boylston Street, the runner gets understandably giddy with excitement. Just around that corner—after one left turn at the top—and soon their dream will become a reality.

385 Yards of Treachery[*]

Even in our sleep, pain which cannot forget
falls drop by drop upon the heart,
until in our own despair,
against our will
comes wisdom
through the awful grace of God.
—Aeschylus, from *Agamemnon,* as quoted by Robert Kennedy, reporting the death of Dr. Martin Luther King Jr., April 4th, 1968.

From the very first marathon, the journey has been associated with both tragedy and joy. When the Greek courier Pheidippides arrived in Athens, history's first long-distance runner dropped dead—right after he delivered the message of Greece's victory over Persia. Inspired by his courageous run, people have followed in his footsteps in search of—honor, fulfillment, satisfaction, wealth, glory, and camaraderie.

To the pragmatic, the Boston Marathon is just a road race. It starts and finishes. It travels over pavement and, in the end, if the participants fulfill the goal of traversing these roads within the requirements, they are presented with a medal. But that's not why people run Boston. The medal is simply a symbol; the race is simply a metaphor.

---

[*] *The basic premise of* 26.2 Miles to Boston *is to move the reader along the route in the most fluid and linear fashion possible, essentially mimicking the race. However, due to the tragic events of 2013, I found it inappropriate to weave together stories of glory and malevolence on the same pages. Consequently, I separate the final steps of the Boston Marathon into two distinct sections.*

People run Boston for reasons far beyond running. The race possesses the ability to literally change lives. People don't run it because it is there, but because of *what* is there. It's within those borders between start and finish that enlightenment can be found. It is here at the Boston Marathon that a person discovers who he or she is—and can be.

❧

In the autumn of 2001, writer Timothy Wollaston of Wellesley was awarded the Massachusetts Film Office's Screenwriting Award for his screenplay called *Marathon Monday*. The screenplay is a drama set at the annual running of the Boston Marathon. At its climax, there is a terrorist at the finish line, trying to set off a bomb. Sadly, twelve years later, life imitated art. In the most horrifying way imaginable.

Since the day that John Graham and Henry Holton rode their bikes out to Ashland in 1897, marathoners have traveled east in search of glory and accomplishment. In their training and along the course, the runners work for one reason: to run those last 385 yards.

At the top of Hereford Street the runners arrive. Working in concert, their hearts and feet have brought them to the corner of Boylston Street. The runners may take a beat before proceeding, as if peeking around the edge to make sure the finish is really there. For months they have dreamt of running the last 385, and now it is upon them. On Boylston Street each runner gets his or her moment.

It's here that the runner realizes those final steps of glory. But it is also here on Boylston Street, and during the twenty-six miles behind, that there have been moments of pain, tragedy—even death. It is on the streets of the Boston Marathon that runners Humphrey Siesage in 1995 and Cynthia Lucero in 2002 tragically perished. It was in the skies on his way to the Marathon in 2000 that Richard Kornisher, flying a plane with a banner attached, crashed to his death. And it was across the train tracks that Marathon fan Bartholomew Ryan was leaving the 1935 race to see his wife and children when he was struck and killed by the inbound Boston and Albany train. It was in Medford that high school student Wendell Powers was so excited after watching the great Clarence DeMar that he tied up his sneakers and went for a run, only to die when he finished. It was at the finish line in 1984 that Tony Nota, the official timer and race administrator for forty-seven years, dropped dead of a heart attack while overseeing the race that he'd cared for like a child.

Over the century-plus history of the race, there have been car accidents and unbridled horses; threatening buses and deadly heat indexes; overaggressive fans and lethal manhole covers. In his book, *When Bad Things Happen to Good People*, Rabbi Harold Kushner writes about the randomness of life and how it is impacted by God's gift of free will that was bestowed not just upon his people, but also upon the Earth itself.

❦

Following the September 11 attacks, the Massachusetts State Police released a report that stated the Boston Marathon was a "possible prime terrorist target." As a world-class city administering a world-class event, Boston became susceptible to the random whims of those who wish to harm others. Efforts to prevent such acts are extensive, but as Secretary of Public Safety Ed Flynn warned, "We will do our best to provide security. But we can't start canceling all these traditional events in the face of nonspecific threats. We just have to realize that right now, we do not live in a risk-free world."

Because they are public, crowded, and often televised, sports events have always provided a forum for groups to protest a perceived injustice, or to bring attention to a cause through violence. In 1920, British soldiers used a Gaelic football match at Croke Park in Dublin to send rebels a message by firing a machine gun into the crowd, killing fourteen fans and player Michael Hogan. In 1972, Jim McKay told the world that members of a radical faction of the Palestine Liberation Organization had kidnapped and killed eleven Israeli athletes at the Olympics in Munich, solemnly reporting to the television audience: "They're all gone." In 1996, two were killed by a bomb at the Summer Olympics in Atlanta; in 2008, a bomb at the Sri Lanka Marathon killed fifteen.

Boston itself has not been immune to the horror of tragedy. The city's worst tragedy—and one of the largest building fires in history—occurred in November of 1942 when the Cocoanut Grove nightclub was consumed by fire. Of the 1,000 patrons there that night, 492 would perish. Efforts by servicemen, first responders, and seventy-five cab drivers saved those who could be saved, demonstrating the soul of the city that would be tested again seventy-one years later.

⟞⟝

April 15, 2013, was a beautiful day. The sky was blue and the sun was shining. There was a crispness to the air which runners love. At Hopkinton 20,000-plus runners took their turns lining up to head east on Route 135. The competitors and fans reveled in the special beauty of the event, knowing that no matter their point of origin, they were now collectively part of an extraordinary community.

Prior to the start that day, the runners and fans had bowed their heads for a twenty-six-second moment of silence to honor the school victims from the Sandy Hook Elementary School massacre that had occurred four months earlier in neighboring Connecticut. In addition to the moment of silence, the last mile of the race was dedicated to the victims. Family members were invited to the race, and were situated in the VIP bleachers at the finish line.

Following the moment of reflection, the starter sent runners down the road, paying tribute to those who had perished, to those who had run before them, and to an event that celebrates life, spirit, and community. Through the eight towns, the runners ran in the steps of DeMar and Benoit Samuelson and Rodgers and Eugene Roberts.

At the finish line, the race was won, yet again, by runners from Africa. First place was taken by twenty-three-year-old Lelisa Desisa of Ethiopia, running in only his second marathon. There was a hint of a possible revival for American running, as six competitors from the United States earned top-fifteen finishes, more than any other country.

As the day moved on, the sun rose and then started to fall. Morning gave way to mid-afternoon. In Boston, thousands had already run Boylston Street in honor of the Sandy Hook victims, in honor of those who had run before, in honor of those who had committed so much to allow them to realize their moment. One by one, each crossed the finish line, arms raised and hearts full. Dr. David King, who had saved lives as a trauma surgeon in Afghanistan; Summer Sanders, whose mother had cheered her on to Olympic Gold, and now Boston glory; and local Joey McIntyre, who as a teenager would watch the race with friends and wonder about running it some day. On the sidewalks, thousands of fans cheered, yelled, smiled. Some friends, some family, many more perfect strangers.

Fans on the sidewalks of Boylston Street cheered not who or what, but why. Most did not care about times and speeds. Some fans would decide to move on, some would go home, some would decide to stand in one spot instead of another. Such is the randomness of life.

On the course, Dave Fortier ran the final steps to Boylston that day, his first Boston. When he turned onto Boylston Street, he stopped to hug his wife and girls who had given him so much. Turning to his left, he looked at the fans that cheered for him and treasured their kindness. They were happy. And he smiled.

Then a force knocked him off his axis, turning his attention to the right, toward the Boston Public Library—the same library that houses within its walls poems of love, stories of tolerance, accounts of great courage, depictions of life's glory. The momentum of the force then propelled him all the way around. He had come full circle. He looked back to that very same sidewalk—but the people were all gone.

Moments earlier, in front of the library to Fortier's right, holding an American flag and wearing a cowboy hat, Carlos Arredondo had been cheering on the field of runners, his scarred heart pounding, waiting for those who were running on behalf of his family. Carlos had already lost so much: two sons, both now only a memory. On this day they were brought to life—if only for a moment—by those who ran for them. He stood and cheered. Then a fireball rose from the ground, and those who stood there "melted" into it.

Carlos saw but didn't wonder. He didn't process. And he didn't seek cover; in fact, he ran toward those in need. He had lost so much and would refuse to allow others to do so. He leapt over fencing, into the abyss, and found Jeffrey Bauman lying on the sidewalk torn and bloodied. In an instant, Carlos applied a tourniquet to the thigh of the fading Bauman, got him into a wheelchair, and rushed him to help averting certain death.

Carlos, and all the first responders that day, helped make Boston's saddest day also one of Boston's greatest days. It is because of the actions of these men and women that historians can write of valor, courage, love.

At the medical tent past the finish line, Dave Fortier was still on his feet, unaware that a piece of metal had shot across his foot, ripping his sneaker and exposing his bone. Nurses were alarmed when they saw the puddle of blood, and rushed to attend to him. Looking back, he told them, "They are coming!"

And they came, victim after victim; 3 would die, 264 were hurt, many losing limbs. In a cab on the other side of Boston, runner David King was celebrating his personal record with his family when he turned on his phone. The first text message communicated notes of congratulations. And then questions. "Are you all right?" "Did you get out of there?"

Immediately King, a trauma surgeon at Massachusetts General Hospital, turned around and drove back into Boston. Walking through the doors of Mass General that afternoon, he was sent back in time. He had been stationed in Afghanistan and knew trauma, knew war, knew malevolence. He had once performed surgery for forty straight hours, because that's what he had to do.

Dr. King would later explain, "Marathons and moments of need cause people to realize that they have depths of capacity they never knew existed. You know when you are in the moment that you can do so much more. You can just keep digging and reaching and it will come out of you—because it is there; you just have to want to find it."

Within ninety seconds of entering the hospital, King was preparing for surgery. Ten hours later he would sit in a conference room with the sun closer to rising than setting. Staring at X-rays and consulting with his team, he realized that he hadn't eaten or drank since Hopkinton that morning.

The city had been frozen in time. Clocks hadn't moved—seared at 2:49 p.m., the moment of the first explosion. Out on the course, almost five thousand runners were brought to a halt, confused, cold, and tired. *What had happened to their Boston?*

Exhausted from her run and standing in her room at the Lenox Hotel, seven floors above the street, Summer Sanders was knocked sideways from the blast. Looking out her window, she broke into tears as she witnessed the carnage. Knocks on the door and yells from the hallway told them they were not to leave, and to refrain from cell-phone use. Minutes later they were told to evacuate. *What had happened to her Boston?*

On Huntington Avenue, Joey McIntyre walked in shock. This was his Boston—his city. He loved this place. How could he reconcile the irreconcilable? He just walked for miles until he came upon Mission Church, where his parents were married, where he and his eight brothers and sisters had gone to Mass. He pulled on the doors to do all that he could do—pray. But the doors were locked. He kept walking until he showed up at his sister's front door. Inside, he called his wife and cried. *What had happened to his Boston?*

In the song, "The Thorn upon the Rose," Irish singer Mary Black sings of the paradox of joy and pain that comes with the gift of love. The song connects the beauty of the rose with the pain of the thorn. The last line of the song speaks to the risk of caring about something but the reward that awaits: "I'd rather feel the thorn than to never see the rose."

How can an event of such happiness and innocence morph into one of such sadness? How can the spirit of Johnny "The Elder" Kelley, the love of the Hoyts, and the bliss of Marathon Day give way to such a malicious act? How can the same arena provide a stage for both joy and tragedy, happiness and pain, smiles and tears? In the last 385 yards of the course that day, both the best and worst of mankind were on display.

This is the essence of the Boston Marathon and, of course, the essence of life. You commit your entire being and in turn expose yourself to the possibility of all the joy and all the pain that comes with such a commitment. It's a paradox; you have to take the chance that either could come.

This is Boston. This is the Boston Marathon, and the world that orbits around it.

Three crosses bearing the names of those who died at the finish line in 2013 stand tall at the Boston Marathon Memorial. © FMUA

385 Yards of Triumph

So be sure when you step, step with great care and great tact. And remember that life's a great balancing act and you will succeed. Yes! You will indeed (98 and 3/4 guaranteed). Kid, you'll move mountains.
—Dr. Seuss, *Oh, the Places You'll Go!*

Up Hereford and a left turn onto Boylston, and the runner has arrived: 385 yards—1,155 feet—13,860 inches—that's all that's left. It is here on Boylston Street that the runners take their final steps over the greatest finishing stretch in the marathoning world. This is the place where dreams are realized and runners are rewarded with what eight-time champion Jean Driscoll describes as a goose bump–raising experience that causes all the stress of the journey to disappear. "It's a euphoric feeling whenever anyone achieves a goal," she says, "whether it's winning, beating a time, or just finishing the race."

Like Caesar returning to Rome, every runner that enters the arena of Boylston Street is greeted by the fans with the same fervor and sincerity, no matter their finishing time. It was on Boylston Street that Boston's adopted daughter, three-time champion Uta Pippig, expressed her gratitude to the fans that had helped her get there. "Some people feel that I'm too emotional, but that's me," she said. "I feel a special connection with the people who line the streets to cheer, and I want to show these people who are sharing in the moment that I appreciate them and the race."

The start in Hopkinton seems weeks ago; with each step, it becomes a distant memory. To just get to these last 385 yards, the runner has faced the cold, the heat, sometimes the rain, sometimes even snow, the traffic,

Will Cloney, director of the BAA, is determined not to let a college prankster cross the 1959 finish line. COURTESY OF THE TRUSTEES OF THE BOSTON PUBLIC LIBRARY

the spilled beers, the cloud of exhaust fumes, and, of course, the fatigue—all for the euphoric feeling of crossing a simple line.

But it wasn't just these twenty-six-plus miles; it was also all of those runs in the morning, at lunch, in the dark, past the chasing dogs, through the soaking spray of puddle-splashing trucks, around cars pulled into the crosswalk, away from drivers and their obnoxious high beams—all to cross a simple line.

But of course, the finish is not just a simple line. It's a mental and physical barrier that, when conquered, offers exaltation; it will pay dividends to the runners for years to come. During training runs, or physical therapy sessions, or nights of restless sleep, runners drift off to visions of running down Boylston Street—to convince themselves that it's all worth it. The commitment and the agony would be worth it, had to be worth it, they *needed* it to be worth it—every step, every bead of sweat, and every twinge of pain.

They now know it was indeed worth it . . . to be here, at this moment, running the final steps of the Boston Marathon down Boylston Street.

Prior to being named Boylston Street, the thoroughfare was called Frog Lane, and then Common Street. The street name was changed to honor philanthropist Ward Boylston back in the 1800s. Ward was previously known by the last name of Hallowell, but changed it to Boylston after his uncle, Dr. Zabdiel Boylston, pledged a share of his estate if he would take his name. Dr. Boylston, who was related to the famous Adams family of Quincy, Massachusetts, was a renowned doctor who became the first American physician to operate in this country. His radical methods of inoculating those afflicted by smallpox made him an outcast in the medical world, subjecting him and his family to violent rebuke, including a bomb attack, which they survived.

After the testing corner, twenty-six miles into the race, the runners can now look straight down Boylston Street and see the photographers' bridge that hangs above the finish line. The very sight can cause runners to drop their guard and ease their effort. But there are still steps to take. Although they can see the summit, they can't plant their flag and claim victory. Not yet. Strangely, the closer the runner gets to the finish, the farther away the race's end seems to stretch.

Gérard Côté wins one of his four Boston Marathons as he crosses the finish line in 1944. COURTESY OF THE TRUSTEES OF THE BOSTON PUBLIC LIBRARY

In 1941 the crowd in the final steps created such a wall of noise that winner Leslie Pawson was chased to the finish line by a spooked horse pulling an ice-cream cart. This is where Tarzan Brown was so moved by the fans that he stopped in sight of the finish line, with the lead, and spun 360 degrees to take in the crowd and the special moment. It's the greatest 385 yards—only two-tenths of a mile—in the running world. It is running down the stairs on Christmas morning; walking down the aisle at your wedding; the sprint out the school door on the last day of classes.

The competitors move down Boylston Street past the Prudential Building on their right, and its fountain, where 1971 winner Alvaro Mejia frolicked after adding his name to the history books. From 1965, when the Prudential Building was built, to 1985, when the controversy of prize money dominated conversation, the finish line was located in front of the city's then-largest building. In 1986, the finish was moved down Boylston Street to outside of the public library, where it remains today.

Contained within the Prudential complex is the Hynes Auditorium, named after John Hynes, mayor of the city from 1950 to 1960. Mayor Hynes, like many government officials, recognized the power of the Boston Marathon; he saw it as an ideal forum to brand and promote not just his city, but himself. Consequently, many of Boston's mayors have used their executive powers to claim the duty of placing the laurel wreath on the annual winner. To maximize their exposure, mayors would place the wreath on the runner immediately as they crossed the finish line, ensuring that they, too, would appear in the finish-line photos. However, in 1951, Shigeki Tanaka of Japan was so excited, he kept running past the finish line, forcing Mayor Hynes, in topcoat and hat, to chase him down the street. Four years later Hynes would actually miscalculate when positioning the wreath, pushing it into the eye of Finnish winner Antti Viskari, subjecting himself to the media's ridicule.

The runners continue down Boylston Street, guided by the Old South Church steeple that stands behind the finish line and its ringing bells. They glide past bars and restaurants that sit on the corners of the perpendicular streets of Gloucester and Fairfield. Up ahead on the right, just before the intersection of Exeter Street, the course moves past that

Boston Marathon landmark, the Lenox Hotel. The Lenox has long been associated with the Boston Marathon because of its proximity to the finish line. When the race used to finish outside of the BAA clubhouse, the hotel's side door on Exeter Street was often prominently displayed in newspaper photos of the winners breaking the tape. The hotel has 214 rooms, and throws a party on the rooftop for their top clients on race day.

In 1986 the start and finish of the race were rearranged to accommodate the new sponsor and savior of the race, John Hancock Financial Services. Consequently, the starting line was moved back to the east side of the Hopkinton town green, while the finish was moved down Boylston Street, from the Prudential Center to the front doors of the Boston Public Library. The Boston Public Library opened in 1854 as the first publicly supported library in the world, the first to lend out books, and the first to open branch sites throughout the city.

Architect Charles Follen McKim based his design on the plans of a building in Paris, Henri Labrouste's Bibliothèque Sainte-Geneviève, but the library was customized to fit in with the neighboring buildings: the Romanesque Trinity Church and the Italian Gothic Old South Church. In 1965, the library added the Johnson Building, where the BAA clubhouse once stood earlier in the twentieth century. The library receives more than two million visitors a year, and holds over six million books, three million government documents, and ten million patents.

These final steps, and the finish line, are sacred, and the crowd understands them as such. So much so that when an MIT prankster jumped from the crowd in 1950, hoping to break the tape before leader Ki-Yong Ham, milkman and 1942 winner Joe Smith jumped from the crowd and tackled the student ten yards deep in the crowd, clearing the path for the South Korean runner.

On Boylston Street, when a leader is running by him- or herself, the connection with the crowd is intimate. When the leader is running shoulder to shoulder with a competitor, it's incredible—there's nothing like it: twenty-six-plus miles reduced to one exhilarating sprint.

For the lead runners, the street is wide open, making the last yards an ideal stage for the dramas that occur when rivals reach the home stretch together. After twenty-six miles of racing, yards, feet, or even inches can determine their fate. It almost seems unfair that a runner could persevere against all the internal and external obstacles, only to lose the victory in the final steps.

. In the history of the Boston Marathon, there were fifteen races in which the first and second runners were separated by five seconds or less at the finish line (see below). This included the acknowledged greatest race in Boston history between Alberto Salazar and Dick Beardsley in 1982 (who fought off motorcycles, punching fans, and potholes), as well as four straight women's finishes, separated by *three* seconds or less, from 2008 to 2012.

Close Finishes

2000—Men: Elijah Lagat of Kenya wins race against Gezahegne Abera of Ethiopia, both with recorded time of 2:09:47.

2009—Women: Salina Kosgei of Kenya over Dire Tune of Ethiopia, by one second.

1988—Men: Ibrahim Hussein of Kenya over Juma Ikangaa of Kenya, by one second.

2012—Women: Sharon Cherop of Kenya over Jemima Jelagat Sumgong of Kenya, by two seconds.

2011—Women—Caroline Kilel of Kenya over Desiree Davila of United States, by two seconds.

2008—Women: Dire Tune of Ethiopia over Alevtina Biktimirova of Russia, by two seconds.

1982—Men: Alberto Salazar of United States over Dick Beardsley of United States, by two seconds.

1978—Men: Bill Rodgers of United States over Jeff Wells of United States, by two seconds.

2010—Women: Teyba Erkesso of Ethiopia over Tatyana Pushkareva of Russia, by three seconds.

1998—Men: Moses Tanui of Kenya over Joseph Chebet of Kenya, by three seconds.

2002—Men: Rodgers Rop of Kenya over Christopher Cheboiboch of Kenya, by three seconds.

2011—Men: Geoffrey Mutai of Kenya over Moses Mosop of Kenya, by four seconds.

1994—Men: Cosmas Ndeti of Kenya over Andres Espinosa of Mexico, by four seconds.

2013—Men: Leslie Desisa of Ethiopia over Micah Kogo of Kenya, by five seconds.

1971—Men: Alvaro Mejia of Colombia over Patrick McMahon of Ireland, by five seconds.

As Dr. George Sheehan says about all Boston competitors: "Everyone who finishes the Boston Marathon has their own great moment in sports. Each one of us, on this day, has achieved greatness." No matter where in the pack a runner finishes, in those final steps, he or she realizes that if *this* is possible, then all is possible. Through eight towns, over hills known as "Heartbreak" and "Withering," and through miles called "Haunted" and "Hell's Alley," they ran. Now they can clear any obstacle and accept any challenge in all the races of life. It's not even about running; it's about resilience, and a spirit that refuses to say no when all else tells you different.

Nobody knows what motivates a runner to push past the limits that stops others. Is it the heart or the mind or the body? Is it the prize money or the pride of accomplishment? Is the glory for the runner, or family, or country? Is it a rare spirit possessed by those in search of greatness? For those who want to, as Dr. David King said, "search for more within themselves"?

So they run the final steps, the finish line within their grasp. They are in a dream, running the last yards of the Boston Marathon. It is one of those rare moments in life when dreams and reality become one. As they approach the finish line, wearing a smile of pride or tears of joy, runners know that they now possess a spirit that will forever allow them to reach to the skies and exist among the stars.

This is Boston, and you have just run it.

Congratulations!

Rejoice, We Conquer

It's not the years in your life that count. It's the life in your years.
—Abraham Lincoln

When John McDermott entered the Irvington Oval for the final steps of the inaugural Boston Marathon, the crowd was said to have risen to their feet, cheering wildly for the runner on his last lap. As McDermott approached the tape, the crowd went strangely quiet. It was almost as if they were witnessing something so special, so extraordinary, that there was no precedent for how to respond. Then, in a collective release, they showered the runner with such a raw ovation of admiration that some were compelled to rush the track, place McDermott on their shoulders, and carry him around the track for a spirited victory lap.

"The race was a big success," a BAA official said the next day. "There is assurance that this event will be an annual fixture." And it has been ever since.

Every April, for one hundred and seventeen years, runners have toed the line in Hopkinton in hopes that they too might enter through the gates of Boston to the cheers of the crowd and join the ranks of John McDermott and all the others who have passed before them. In 1907, *Globe* writer Lawrence Sweeney wrote about those special few that have answered the call to run Boston: "The competitor possessed the sturdier legs, more lion-like heart, and [was] endowed with the spirit which carried Pheidippides into the marketplace at Athen."

Like the competitors themselves, the race has persevered—through two world wars, a terrorist attack, bankruptcy, the transformation from an amateur contest into a professional one, rogue dogs, rambunctious police

Ellison "Tarzan" Brown proudly wears his laurel wreath in 1939 after winning one of his two Boston Marathons. COURTESY OF THE TRUSTEES OF THE BOSTON PUBLIC LIBRARY

on motorcycles, spooked horses, manic media buses, chauvinistic officials, scorching heat, and slippery sleet. For more than a century, runners have worked their way through Hopkinton, Ashland, Framingham, Natick, Wellesley, Newton, Boston, Brookline, and back into Boston in order to fulfill a dream held by runners the world over.

Across the finish line the runner steps through a portal, going from challenger to conqueror. It is on the other side of the finish line—the line that separates those who do from those who don't—that they are permanently changed. They know, like women's champion Sara Mae Berman, that their run is eternal: "The wonderful thing about athletic achievement is that it is finite," she said. "There is no ambiguity. You did it, and no one can ever take that away from you."

To toe the line of Boston is an honor. To cross the finish line is a blessing. While the prize money (now $150,000 for first place) draws some athletes to the race, the laurel wreath's value goes far beyond the tangible. For over a century, the elite have run Boston for the opportunity to be crowned in the woven leaves of the *kotinos* (wild olive) tree, from just outside of Marathon, Greece, strengthening the link between the Boston Marathon and Pheidippides' run.

Following John "The Elder" Kelley's win in 1945, just a week after President Franklin D. Roosevelt's death, fellow runners tried to persuade the two-time champion to send his wreath to First Lady Eleanor Roosevelt. Kelley, although sympathetic to the loss of the nation's leader, would not part with the cherished memento. "I think the wreath has more significance to me than it would for Mrs. Roosevelt," he said.

The power of the wreath has caused some nefarious behavior through the years. In 1909 Henri Renaud had his wreath and trophy stolen by a traveling circus; in 1939 Tarzan Brown's wreath was stolen from his bag in the Boston University locker room while he showered. In 1980, Rosie Ruiz returned to New York with the wreath, but not victory.

Five-time wheelchair champion Jim Knaub looks at the wreath and related trophies in a different light. "Admiring my trophies or daydreaming of past accomplishments is an act of looking backwards," he says. "For me, I have to continue to move forward. I'm afraid if I look back, I might stop moving forward. It's like running a race: Just concern yourself with what's ahead—anything behind you doesn't matter." After each victory, Knaub immediately left the winners' circle and gave his laurel wreath to a young child in the crowd.

For the average marathoner, the medal is the confirmation of his or her own personal victory. The ribbon with its attached pendant provides the runner with validation for the blood, sweat, and tears that have been shed in order to participate in this event. Each year after receiving his medal, Pat Williams ponders how a fifty-cent medal could be worth a million dollars. But it's clearly worth even more—it's about what it represents to each runner.

The winner in 2013, Lelisa Desisa of Ethiopia, donated his medal back to the city of Boston, still suffering from the aftereffects of that year's bombing. "Sport holds the power to unify and connect people all over the world," Desisa said. "Sport should never be used as a battleground."

In 1972 Sylvia Weiner ran the marathon in a time of 3:47, calling upon her survival instincts to meet the challenge. Weiner had spent her youth trapped in the terror of a Nazi concentration camp. After crossing the finish line that day, she cried, "I always wanted to live. I always had the will for it. Now I have victory."

In the earlier years of the Marathon, following the Ceremony of Champions, after the runners crossed the finish line, protocol suggested that the winners and other runners be assessed by physicians. Then the champion would be rushed off to meet with the media—although it didn't always go as planned. In 1907, winner Thomas Longboat, instead of cooling down after twenty-six miles, proceeded to run *additional laps* on the BAA track until officials convinced him to walk, fearing he might drop dead of a heart attack. Half a century later, in 1963, BAA officials attempted to whisk the winner, Aurele Vandendriessche of Belgium, away from the crowd to give him a post-race physical. He pushed the officials away, discarded his blanket, and proceeded to mingle with the crowd like a president disobeying his Secret Service agents.

The same couldn't be said for John McDermott, winner of the inaugural race. He spent the hours following the race in the BAA locker room, in pain and discomfort. "Yes, I feel pretty tired in my legs," he said. "My body is all right, but my feet are pretty sore, of course. My toes are blistered, and the skin has peeled off the bottom of my feet. . . . This will be my last long race. I hate to quit now, because I will be called a quitter and a coward, but look at my feet. Do you blame me for wanting to stop it?" No one knew at the time that McDermott had run in 1897 with a lung ailment that would ultimately prove fatal.

The very thought of running another marathon soon after completing one is considered unthinkable by any runner. It's in the locker room, or wrapped in a Mylar blanket (looking like a "baked potato," writer Leigh Montville once quipped), or in the medical tent that exhausted runners might question the sanity of what they just did. Like a woman who has just given birth, swearing off having any more children, they pledge to never run again.

But they will. Because Boston is like a drug. Its reward possesses powers that can't be found on a bus to work, or a chair in the living room, or standing in the crowd of a sporting event. They will run again; they always do. But not until they forget. As Olympic marathon champion Frank Shorter once said, "You can't think of your next marathon until you've forgotten your last one."

Back when runners were required to submit to a physical before the race, runners had their temperature taken. In 1902, winner Sammy Mellor was being assessed when he mistakenly bit the thermometer. Initially he laughed, not knowing that there was poisonous mercury inside the gadget. He would end up suffering for hours through bouts of vomiting until he had fully purged the mercury from his body.

In the early days, Dr. John Blake was the overseer of all medical-related issues for the Boston Marathon. He was a physician at Massachusetts General Hospital who refined his talents as a doctor caring for soldiers in battle during the Civil War. Over a century later, Dr. David King would go to Afghanistan as part of the American trauma team, only to return to Boston to work at Massachusetts General where, in 2013, in a fit of twisted irony, he would have to use his experience on the battlefield to save Marathon runners.

Runners used to gather after the race and seek closure in the locker room of the BAA, or in the garage of the Prudential Center. While they talked about the race and reflected on their run, they would be provided with their much-anticipated bowl of beef stew. It wasn't until 1980 that doctors suggested that the beef stew be replaced with yogurt and PowerBars. Saddened to see yet another Boston Marathon tradition die, race director Will Cloney responded defiantly to the change, saying, "We've been serving runners beef stew for more than five decades, and it hasn't killed anyone yet."

Like traditions, there are certain constants that thread themselves into the fabric of the race: The course has remained relatively the same for twelve decades; the spirit of the fans who line the sidewalks of the eight towns continues to capture the essence of community; and the challenge is still a challenge. While these constants have remained, so have the questions from the media following the race: "What does winning Boston mean?"; "How were the hills?"; "Did you feel special today?"

While the answers to these questions differ, they are essentially the same, varying based on the physical condition of the runner. Some speak as if they are running on air, while others speak of survival.

"How Do You Feel?": Quotes from Winners

- 1904 winner Michael Spring, after beating forty-one other competitors: "I am sort of surprised at winning the race—I always thought there was a yellow streak in me."

- 1935 winner John "The Elder" Kelley, after winning his first Boston: "This is fleeting fame. No one knows it better than I do. I will live the same, feel the same, and think the same. But boy, it sure is a swell feeling to be the Marathon winner."

- 1948 winner Gérard Côté, after his fourth win, handling the press like only he could: "Gentlemen, gentlemen! One beer! One cigar! Then we can talk about the race."

- 1957 winner John "The Younger" Kelley was always curious about why he ran and where it took him in life. "I had to prove something to myself. I never figured out what the hell it was, but I did it."

- 1968 winner Amby Burfoot recounted his race as the perfect run. "From the moment the gun sounded, I ran with an ease that I had never experienced. I felt like I was running beyond my means while at the same time staying within myself. I can only explain my run as one of supreme effortlessness."

- 1975 Women's Champion Liane Winter of West Germany graciously accepted the accolades of the press, but finally said, through her translator, "Thank you. Could you get me a beer? I would really like a beer."

- 1976 winner Jack Fultz spoke after running through one of the hottest races in the history of the event (where 40 percent of the starters dropped out). The overheated champion was hurried into the press conference without an opportunity to cool down or stretch out. There he was thrown into a barber's chair and peppered with questions for over an hour. When he finally got up, he could barely keep his feet. During the press conference he said, "My run was so relaxed and comfortable that I was concerned that I wasn't pushing myself enough. But when I finally came upon a clock, I was on the exact pace that I had hoped."

- 1976 Women's Champion Kim Merritt was so exhausted after her run in torrid temperatures in the famous Run for the Hoses that she said after the race, "I don't know if I'll do it over again." She was later taken to the hospital for observation.

- 1978 Women's Champion Gayle Barron saw her run as one in which the stars had aligned—almost as if she was destined to win a race for which she'd had very low expectations. "I had run a number of marathons previous to 1978. In each of those races, I always would be afflicted with some type of ailment, whether it be blisters, cramps, or something worse. This year everything worked perfectly. I ran like I had never run before. Each mile was quicker than I had ever run, but I felt like I was in a light jog. I remember being on the winner's podium and being shocked. I could have kept going. I felt perfect. The day was perfect."

- 1978 Men's Champion Bill Rodgers didn't share Gayle Barron's opinion that the day had been perfect, as he'd had to fend off Jeff Wells—which he did, by two seconds. "My legs were gone. The last six miles were real bad. In the end I was falling apart. I have never had to gut it out at the end like that."

- 1984 winner Geoff Smith was cognizant of the lasting legacy he had established by winning Boston. "I'm going to be remembered."

- 1996 winner Uta Pippig competed like no Marathon runner had before, other than Eugene Roberts. Overwhelmed by physical and emotional stress, she came from behind to win a championship for the ages: "Psychologically, you can do more things than what you believe."

- 2005 champion Hailu Negussie of Ethiopia articulated the feelings of every runner: "Day and night, I was dreaming of winning the Boston Marathon. And I did what I was dreaming of."

In 1988, Scott Nan spent Marathon Monday on an operating table undergoing hours of surgery to remove a brain tumor. One year later, he stood on the starting line of Hopkinton. After crossing the finish line, he made his way over to Massachusetts General to present the nurses who had cared for him with an arrangement of roses. "After I ran Boston," he said, "it was the greatest feeling in the world."

For more than a hundred years, images from the Boston Marathon have been ingrained in the souls of those who came to challenge, conquer, or cheer. The memories endure: Clarence DeMar's proud chest, breaking

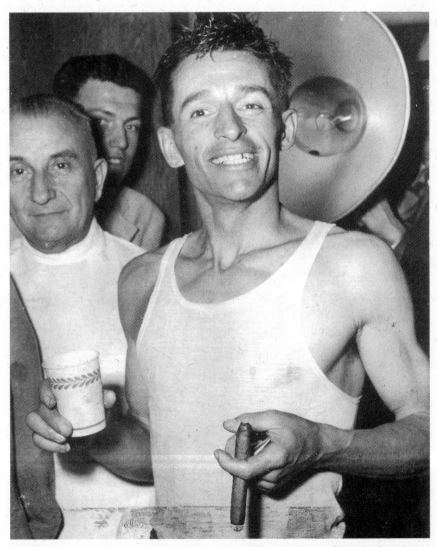

Four-time winner Gérard Côté indulges in the fruits of victory after winning the 1948 Boston Marathon.

the tape; Uta Pippig's radiant Boylston Street smile; Bill Rodgers's gloved hands; John "The Elder" Kelley's immortal stride; the sight of a small boy on his father's shoulders.

For competitors and spectators alike, it's a love affair. It is a link to the past. Like the New England seasons, it changes while remaining constant. It represents tradition and—despite the horror of 2013—innocence. It is the one day of the year that the people of Boston come from every corner of the world to share a bond.

The decision to run Boston can come out of impulse or deliberation. But from the time one decides to do it until the moment they cross the finish line, runners are introduced to the depths of who they are, what they have undertaken, and why they are there. Afterwards, they can look in the mirror and know that they have the resolve to confront life's challenges. Runners run because they have questions. After crossing the finish line, they have their answers.

Fulfillment comes in many shapes and colors. Running the Boston Marathon means now that all is possible. It is between Hopkinton to Boston that one runs with great sincerity. It is on Boylston Street that every member of the Boston Marathon community can find the power of the city, the power of the Boston Marathon, because after running Boston, they are now Boston Strong!

Epilogue

The flower that blooms in adversity is the most rare and beautiful of all.

—Mulan

Six weeks after being injured during the Marathon Day bombing, Sydney Corcoran walked into her senior prom in her white dress, escorted by her friend, Tyler Veiga. But in actuality, all of Boston was her date that night.

Sydney's resilience was symbolic of the city and the community of which she is a part. Sydney and the city got back on its feet, looking just as proud and beautiful as ever. Boston had fulfilled John Winthrop's dream of being "The City upon the Hill," a place where people hold the core values of decency, and live them by caring for others and being there when needed.

Following the bombings, President Obama came to Boston to lend his support. He hurt like the city was hurting. He'd once lived in Boston, and had gone to school across the Charles River, at Harvard. He knew how special the city was, and spoke to this at a service to help the country to heal and move forward:

Even when our heart aches, we summon the strength that maybe we didn't even know we had, and we carry on; we finish the race. We finish the race, and we do that because of who we are, and we do that because we know that somewhere around the bend, a stranger has a cup of water. Around the bend, somebody's there to boost our spirits. On that toughest mile, just when we think that we've hit a wall, someone will be there to cheer us on and pick us up if we fall. We know that.

Joey McIntyre walked the streets of his hometown with a medal around his neck and the ringing of the explosions still in his ears. He wondered how this could happen to the city he loved—to the Boston Marathon community of which he was now a member. One month later he stood on the stage at the Boston Garden for the One Fund concert with his brothers from the New Kids on the Block, and other entertainers, including James Taylor and Aerosmith. He wore his marathon medal around his neck. With the emotion of the bombing still raw he looked out at the crowd—his community—and said: "Didn't matter where you were that day—it happened to all of us. We are one city . . . Love conquers all. Love crushes hate. Love crushes hate!"

In all, the One Fund has raised over $60 million for the victims, from thousands of donations—some as big as $1 million, from race sponsor John Hancock Financial, and some as small, but no less significant, as coins collected in classrooms. Over 185,000 people from every state in the country and from fifty countries around the world have made donations, and thus played a role in the recovery of Boston and its people.

It's the spirit of giving that exists within this community that compelled first responders to go toward the smoke. That roused doctors and nurses to stay on their feet to keep people on their feet. That prompted runners to run straight from the finish line to the hospital to give blood. That moved strangers to offer rides to stranded marathoners, back to their homes or hotel rooms. That urged neighbors to open their doors and welcome new friends. That motivated store owners to bring water and aid to those in need.

In 1931, the *Boston Globe* reported after the race: "The old course could tell stories of shattered hopes, of triumphs lost when the goal seemed at hand, and of men who fought off seemingly insurmountable handicaps and managed to reach the finish line." This is the spirit that has enveloped the Boston Marathon for decade after decade, and the people who run it, watch it, work it, and love it.

In June of 1945, people filled the streets of Boston to celebrate V-J Day (Victory in Japan). It was from Boylston Street to Scollay Square that Bostonians cried and kissed and hugged. It was a moment of unadulterated release that allowed the people who sacrificed so much to eradicate the conflict that had consumed them and the world around them, to be free of such constraints. Up above them fighter planes dipped their wings in victory, while in the waters of Boston Harbor, battleships sounded their horns.

The Boston Marathon in 2014 will be more than a celebration. It will be a rebirth; it will be a tangible message that, as Joey McIntyre said, love crushes hate.

All along the racecourse, volunteers have been busy planting daffodil bulbs with the hope that they will bloom in the spring and be in full flower when the marathoners run to Boston. It is the hope that this garden of love will serve as a tangible symbol of rebirth and life. For over a century, the Boston Marathon has been a harbinger of spring. This year it will be more than this; it will be a communal celebration of all that is good about the Boston Marathon.

In 1930, Admiral Byrd was paraded through the streets of Boston after his famous expedition to Antarctica. The *Globe* would write: "Never before had any visitor been accorded such an outpouring of tape, confetti . . . it was like a great snowstorm." Like they did back in 1930, the city will once again welcome heroes through its gates. It will be in 2014 that first responders and victims and fans and runners will come back to Boylston Street. There will be tears and reconciliation and satisfaction. "At the finish line I am going to look around and see the crowd and how strong we all are," said victim Lee Ann Yanni. "It is going to be a magical moment."

Dr. David King will run again in a race that he envisions as "twenty-six miles of catharsis." Victim Kaitlynn Cates will also run. "I'm not gonna let something that happened define who I am," she says. "To cross the finish line will be absolutely incredible. I can't even imagine what it will feel like. But I'm sure it will feel kind of like winning."

The outpouring for the race and the runners will be unprecedented. The competitors will run the streets and the roads and the hills and the corners of the eight towns in triumph.

It will be on the starting line in Hopkinton and the sidewalks of the eight towns and *especially* at the finish line that the race will bring the community full circle. Where there was pain, there will be life. Where there was a moment of hate, there will be eternal love. Where Boylston Street was empty, it will be full. For 117 years, the Boston Marathon has endured. Boston will forever be the City upon the Hill, where people come every April to pay witness to the world's greatest race.

Appendix

Men's Open Champions

1897	John J. McDermott, New York City, NY	2:55:10
1898	Ronald J. MacDonald, Cambridge, MA	2:42:00
1899	Lawrence J. Brignolia, Cambridge, MA	2:54:38
1900	James Caffery, Hamilton, Ontario	2:39:44
1901	James Caffery, Hamilton, Ontario	2:29:23
1902	Sammy Mellor, Yonkers, NY	2:43:12
1903	John C. Lorden, Cambridge, MA	2:41:29
1904	Michael Spring, New York City, NY	2:38:04
1905	Fred Lorz, New York City, NY	2:38:25
1906	Timothy Ford, Cambridge, MA	2:45:45
1907	Tom Longboat, Hamilton, Ontario	2:24:24
1908	Thomas Morrissey, New York City, NY	2:25:43
1909	Henri Renaud, Nashua, NH	2:53:36
1910	Fred Cameron, Amherst, Nova Scotia	2:28:52
1911	Clarence DeMar, Melrose, MA	2:24:39
1912	Mike Ryan, New York City, NY	2:21:18
1913	Fritz Carlson, Minneapolis, MN	2:25:14
1914	James Duffy, Hamilton, Ontario	2:25:01
1915	Edouard Fabre, Montreal, Quebec	2:31:41
1916	Arthur Roth, Roxbury, MA	2:27:16
1917	William Kennedy, Port Chester, NY	2:28:37
1918	Armed Services relay, Camp Devens, Ayer, MA	2:29:53
1919	Carl Linder, Quincy, MA	2:29:13
1920	Peter Trivoulidas, Greece	2:29:31
1921	Frank Zuna, Newark, NJ	2:18:57
1922	Clarence DeMar, Melrose, MA	2:18:10
1923	Clarence DeMar, Melrose, MA	2:23:37
1924	Clarence DeMar, Melrose, MA	2:29:40
1925	Charles Mellor, Chicago, IL	2:33:00

1926	John Miles, Sydney Mines, Nova Scotia	2:25:40
1927	Clarence DeMar, Melrose, MA	2:40:22
1928	Clarence DeMar, Melrose, MA	2:37:07
1929	John Miles, Sydney Mines, Nova Scotia	2:33:08
1930	Clarence DeMar, Melrose, MA	2:34:48
1931	James Henigan, Medford, MA	2:46:45
1932	Paul de Bruyn, Germany	2:33:36
1933	Leslie Pawson, Pawtucket, RI	2:31:01
1934	Dave Komonen, Ontario, Canada	2:32:53
1935	John "The Elder" Kelley, Arlington, MA	2:32:07
1936	Ellison Myers "Tarzan" Brown, Alton, RI	2:33:40
1937	Walter Young, Verdun, Quebec	2:33:20
1938	Leslie Pawson, Pawtucket, RI	2:35:34
1939	Ellison Myers "Tarzan" Brown, Alton, RI	2:28:51
1940	Gérard Côté, Sainte-Hyacinthe, Quebec	2:28:28
1941	Leslie Pawson, Pawtucket, RI	2:30:38
1942	Bernard Joseph Smith, Medford, MA	2:26:51
1943	Gérard Côté, Sainte-Hyacinthe, Quebec	2:28:25
1944	Gérard Côté, Sainte-Hyacinthe, Quebec	2:31:50
1945	John "The Elder" Kelley, Arlington, MA	2:30:40
1946	Stylianos Kyriakides, Greece	2:29:27
1947	Suh Yun-Bok, South Korea	2:25:39
1948	Gérard Côté, Sainte-Hyacinthe, Quebec	2:31:02
1949	Karl Gosta Leandersson, Sweden	2:31:50
1950	Ki-Yong Ham, South Korea	2:32:39
1951	Shigeki Tanaka, Hiroshima, Japan	2:24:45
1952	Doroteo Flores, Guatemala	2:31:53
1953	Keizo Yamada, Japan	2:18:51
1954	Veikko Karvonen, Finland	2:20:39
1955	Hideo Hamamura, Japan	2:18:22
1956	Antti Viskari, Finland	2:14:14
1957	John "The Younger" Kelley, Groton, CT	2:20:05
1958	Franjo Mihalic, Yugoslavia	2:25:54
1959	Eino Oksanen, Helsinki, Finland	2:22:42

1960	Paavo Kotila, Finland	2:20:54
1961	Eino Oksanen, Helsinki, Finland	2:23:39
1962	Eino Oksanen, Helsinki, Finland	2:23:48
1963	Aurele Vandendriessche, Belgium	2:18:58
1964	Aurele Vandendriessche, Belgium	2:19:59
1965	Morio Shigematsu, Japan	2:16:33
1966	Kenji Kimihara, Japan	2:17:11
1967	David McKenzie, New Zealand	2:15:45
1968	Ambrose (Amby) Burfoot, Groton, CT	2:22:17
1969	Yoshiaki Unetani, Japan	2:13:49
1970	Ron Hill, Cheshire, England	2:10:30
1971	Alvaro Mejia, Colombia	2:18:45
1972	Olavi Suomalainen, Otaniemi, Finland	2:15:39
1973	Jon Anderson, Eugene, OR	2:16:03
1974	Neil Cusack, Ireland	2:13:39
1975	Bill Rodgers, Melrose, MA	2:09:55
1976	Jack Fultz, Arlington, VA	2:20:19
1977	Jerome Drayton, Toronto, Canada	2:14:46
1978	Bill Rodgers, Melrose, MA	2:10:13
1979	Bill Rodgers, Melrose, MA	2:09:27
1980	Bill Rodgers, Melrose, MA	2:12:11
1981	Toshihiko Seko, Japan	2:09:26
1982	Alberto Salazar, Wayland, MA	2:08:52
1983	Gregory Meyer, Wellesley, MA	2:09:00
1984	Geoff Smith, Liverpool, England	2:10:34
1985	Geoff Smith, Liverpool, England	2:14:05
1986	Rob de Castella, Canberra, Australia	2:07:51
1987	Toshihiko Seko, Japan	2:11:50
1988	Ibrahim Hussein, Kenya	2:08:43
1989	Abebe Mekonnen, Ethiopia	2:09:06
1990	Gelindo Bordin, Milan, Italy	2:08:19
1991	Ibrahim Hussein, Kenya	2:11:06
1992	Ibrahim Hussein, Kenya	2:08:14
1993	Cosmas Ndeti, Kenya	2:09:33

1994	Cosmas Ndeti, Kenya	2:07:15
1995	Cosmas Ndeti, Kenya	2:09:22
1996	Moses Tanui, Kenya	2:09:26
1997	Lameck Aguta, Kenya	2:10:34
1998	Moses Tanui, Kenya	2:07:34
1999	Lameck Aguta, Kenya	2:09:47
2000	Elijah Lagat, Kenya	2:09:47
2001	Lee Bong-Ju, South Korea	2:09:43
2002	Rodgers Rop, Kenya	2:09:02
2003	Robert Kipkoech Cheruiyot, Kenya	2:10:11
2004	Timothy Cherigat, Kenya	2:10:37
2005	Hailu Negussie, Ethiopia	2:11:44
2006	Robert Kipkoech Cheruiyot, Kenya	2:07:14
2007	Robert Kipkoech Cheruiyot, Kenya	2:14:13
2008	Robert Kipkoech Cheruiyot, Kenya	2:07:45
2009	Deriba Merga, Ethiopia	2:08:42
2010	Robert Kiprono Cheruiyot, Kenya	2:05:52
2011	Geoffrey Mutai, Kenya	2:03:02
2012	Wesley Korir, Kenya	2:12:40
2013	Lelisa Desisa, Ethiopia	2:10:22

Women's Open Champions

1966	Roberta Gibb Bingay, Winchester, MA	3:21:40 *
1967	Roberta Gibb Bingay, San Diego, CA	3:27:17 *
1968	Roberta Gibb Bingay, San Diego, CA	3:30:00 *
1969	Sara Mae Berman, Cambridge, MA	3:22:46 *
1970	Sara Mae Berman, Cambridge, MA	3:05:07 *
1971	Sara Mae Berman, Cambridge, MA	3:08:30 *
1972	Nina Kuscsik, South Huntington, NY	3:10:26
1973	Jacqueline Hansen, Granada Hills, CA	3:05:59
1974	Michiko Gorman, Los Angeles, CA	2:47:11
1975	Liane Winter, Wolfsburg, West Germany	2:42:24
1976	Kim Merritt, Kenosha, WI	2:47:10
1977	Michiko Gorman, Los Angeles, CA	2:48:33

1978	Gayle Barron, Atlanta, GA	2:44:52
1979	Joan Benoit, Samuelson, Cape Elizabeth, ME	2:35:15
1980	Jacqueline Gareau, Montreal, Quebec	2:34:28
1981	Allison Roe, Takatuna, New Zealand	2:26:46
1982	Charlotte Teske, Darmstadt, West Germany	2:29:33
1983	Joan Benoit, Samuelson, Watertown, MA	2:22:43
1984	Lorraine Moller, Putaruru, New Zealand	2:29:28
1985	Lisa Larsen Weidenbach, Battle Creek, MI	2:34:06
1986	Ingrid Kristiansen, Oslo, Norway	2:24:55
1987	Rosa Mota, Porto, Portugal	2:25:21
1988	Rosa Mota, Porto, Portugal	2:24:30
1989	Ingrid Kristiansen, Oslo, Norway	2:24:33
1990	Rosa Mota, Porto, Portugal	2:25:24
1991	Wanda Panfil, Poland	2:24:18
1992	Olga Markova, Russia	2:23:43
1993	Olga Markova, Russia	2:25:27
1994	Uta Pippig, West Berlin, Germany	2:21:45
1995	Uta Pippig, West Berlin, Germany	2:25:11
1996	Uta Pippig, West Berlin, Germany	2:27:12
1997	Fatuma Roba, Ethiopia	2:26:23
1998	Fatuma Roba, Ethiopia	2:23:21
1999	Fatuma Roba, Ethiopia	2:23:25
2000	Catherine Ndereba, Kenya	2:26:11
2001	Catherine Ndereba, Kenya	2:23:53
2002	Margaret Okayo, Kenya	2:20:43
2003	Svetlana Zakharova, Russia	2:25:19
2004	Catherine Ndereba, Kenya	2:24:27
2005	Catherine Ndereba, Kenya	2:25:12
2006	Rita Jeptoo, Kenya	2:23:38
2007	Lidiya Grigoryeva, Russia	2:29:18
2008	Dire Tune, Ethiopia	2:26:11
2009	Salina Kosgei, Kenya	2:32:16
2010	Teyba Erkesso, Ethiopia	2:26:11
2011	Caroline Kilel, Kenya	2:22:36

| 2012 | Sharon Cherop, Kenya | 2:31:50 |
| 2013 | Rita Jeptoo, Kenya | 2:26:25 |

* *unofficial*

Men's Wheelchair Champions

1975	Robert Hall, Belmont, MA	2:58:00
1976	No contestants	
1977	Robert Hall, Belmont, MA	2:40:10
1978	George Murray, Tampa, FL	2:26:57
1979	Kenneth Archer, Akron, OH	2:38:59
1980	Curt Brinkman, Orem, UT	1:55:00
1981	Jim Martinson, Puyallup, WA	2:00:41
1982	Jim Knaub, Long Beach, CA	1:51:31
1983	Jim Knaub, Long Beach, CA	1:47:10
1984	Andre Viger, Quebec, Canada	2:05:20
1985	George Murray, Tampa, FL	1:45:34
1986	Andre Viger, Quebec, Canada	1:43:25
1987	Andre Viger, Quebec, Canada	1:55:42
1988	Mustapha Badid, St. Denis, France	1:43:19
1989	Philippe Couprie, Pontoise, France	1:36:04
1990	Mustapha Badid, St. Denis, France	1:29:53
1991	Jim Knaub, Long Beach, CA	1:30:44
1992	Jim Knaub, Long Beach, CA	1:26:28
1993	Jim Knaub, Long Beach, CA	1:22:17
1994	Heinz Frei, Switzerland	1:21:23
1995	Franz Nietlispach, Switzerland	1:25:59
1996	Heinz Frei, Switzerland	1:30:14
1997	Franz Nietlispach, Switzerland	1:28:14
1998	Franz Nietlispach, Switzerland	1:21:52
1999	Franz Nietlispach, Switzerland	1:21:36
2000	Franz Nietlispach, Switzerland	1:33:32
2001	Ernst van Dyk, South Africa	1:25:12
2002	Ernst van Dyk, South Africa	1:23:19
2003	Ernst van Dyk, South Africa	1:28:32

2004	Ernst van Dyk, South Africa	1:18:27
2005	Ernst van Dyk, South Africa	1:24:11
2006	Ernst van Dyk, South Africa	1:25:29
2007	Masazumi Soejima, Japan	1:29:16
2008	Ernst van Dyk, South Africa	1:26:49
2009	Ernst van Dyk, South Africa	1:33:29
2010	Ernst van Dyk, South Africa	1:26:53
2011	Masazumi Soejima, Japan	1:18:50
2012	Joshua Cassidy, Canada	1:18:25
2013	Hiroyuki Yamamoto, Japan	1:25:33

Women's Wheelchair Champions

1977	Sharon Rahn, Champaign, IL	3:48:51
1978	Susan Shapiro, Berkeley, CA	3:52:35
1979	Sheryl Blair, Sacramento, CA	3:27:56
1980	Sharon Limpert, Minneapolis, MN	2:49:04
1981	Candace Cable, Las Vegas, NV	2:38:41
1982	Candace Cable-Brookes, Las Vegas, NV	2:12:43
1983	Sherry Ramsey, Arvada, CO	2:27:07
1984	Sherry Ramsey, Arvada, CO	2:56:51
1985	Candace Cable-Brookes, Long Beach, CA	2:05:26
1986	Candace Cable-Brookes, Long Beach, CA	2:09:28
1987	Candace Cable-Brookes, Long Beach, CA	2:19:55
1988	Candace Cable-Brookes, Long Beach, CA	2:10:44
1989	Connie Hansen, Denmark	1:50:06
1990	Jean Driscoll, Champaign, IL	1:43:17
1991	Jean Driscoll, Champaign, IL	1:42:42
1992	Jean Driscoll, Champaign, IL	1:36:52
1993	Jean Driscoll, Champaign, IL	1:34:50
1994	Jean Driscoll, Champaign, IL	1:34:22
1995	Jean Driscoll, Champaign, IL	1:40:42
1996	Jean Driscoll, Champaign, IL	1:52:56
1997	Louise Sauvage, Australia	1:54:28
1998	Louise Sauvage, Australia	1:41:19

1999	Louise Sauvage, Australia	1:42:23
2000	Jean Driscoll, Champaign, IL	2:00:52
2001	Louise Sauvage, Australia	1:53:54
2002	Edith Hunkeler, Switzerland	1:45:57
2003	Christina Ripp, United States	1:54:47
2004	Cheri Blauwet, United States	1:39:53
2005	Cheri Blauwet, United States	1:47:45
2006	Edith Hunkeler, Switzerland	1:43:42
2007	Wakako Tsuchida, Japan	1:53:30
2008	Wakako Tsuchida, Japan	1:48:32
2009	Wakako Tsuchida, Japan	1:54:37
2010	Wakako Tsuchida, Japan	1:43:32
2011	Wakako Tsuchida, Japan	1:34:06
2012	Shirley Riley, United States	1:37:36
2013	Tatyana McFadden, United States	1:45:25